THE ELUSIVE MADAME G

A life of Christine Granville

by Ron Nowicki

Also by Ron Nowicki
Warsaw, the cabaret years

Ron Nowicki asserts the moral right to be identified as the author of this work.
©2013
ISBN-13: 978-1494936976
ISBN-10: 1494936976

All rights reserved under International and Pan American Copyright Conventions. By payment of the required fees you have been granted the non-exclusive, non-transferable right to access and read the text of this ebook on-screen. No part of this may be reproduced, transmitted, downloaded, decompiled, reverse engineered, or stored in or introduced into any information storage and retrieval system, in any form or by any means, whether electronic or mechanical, now known or hereinafter invented, without the express written permission of the author.

This book was published in association with Bletchley Park Research.
www.bletchleyparkresearch.com

Cover photo: Christine Granville seated in Andrew Kennedy's BMW 324 Roadster somewhere in West Germany. This photo first appeared in *The Observer Magazine* 20 October 1972.

For the habitues of Big Table 5 at The National Archives

Diana Truszkowski Hall, Eugenia Maresch

John Gallehawk and David List

Polish Pronunciation

The Polish alphabet contains the same characters as the English with two exceptions. In Polish there is no letter 'v'. The 'w' takes that sound except at the end of a word when it has a soft sound as in 'Krakoof' (Krakow). The second difference is in the presence of two 'l's' in the Polish alphabet. The first pronounced as in English. The second is written with a forward diagonal stroke and is pronounced as the English 'w'.

c is pronounced as 'ts'

c when accented is pronounced as ch

cz is pronounced as in the English *ch* sound in 'cheese'

b, d, g and z all take a soft sound when appearing at the end of a word

dz is pronounced as a hard English 'j'

j is pronounced like the 'y' in 'yes'

rz - the closest English sound equivalent is the second syllable of 'pleasure.'

s when accented is pronounced as is 'sure'

sz as the *sh* in 'shout'

Contents

Polish pronunciation ii

Introduction v

List of Plates xviii

Part I. 1908 - 1939

Chapter 1. A Country Idyll 1

Chapter 2. Secrets and Lies 19

Chapter 3. 'Notes on Madame G' 32

Part II. 1940

Chapter 4. An Obstreperous Pupil 51

Chapter 5. To Poland and the Musketeers 68

Chapter 6. The Woman in the Tyrolean Hat 83

Chapter 7. Lost among the Magyars 98

Chapter 8. The Fall of Paris and a Narrow Escape 107

Chapter 9. Last Mission to Poland 122

Chapter 10. Breakout from Budapest 135

Part III. 1941 - 1943

Chapter 11. The Flight Into Egypt 148

Chapter 12. Honourable People 159

Chapter 13. Breaking Hearts at the Gezira Club 169

Part IV. 1944

Chapter 14. Mixed Doubles 194

Chapter 15. Plots and Rumours of Plots 214

Chapter 16. Death and the Darkness of Night 231

Chapter 17. Resistance in France 249

Chapter 18. Christine to the Rescue 266

Chapter 19. The End of a Perilous Journey 278

Part V. 1945 - 1952

Chapter 20. Surplus to Establishment 291

Chapter 21. Missed Opportunities 303

Chapter 22. End Game 316

Post-Mortem 330

Notes 341

Acknowledgments 352

Bibliography 354

Index 361

Introduction

Christine Granville, daughter of the Polish gentry and former SOE* operative, was one of the most enigmatic characters to have served on British intelligence operations during the second world war. Her courageous actions, especially in France in 1944, have long been part of the Special Operations Executive legend, enhanced by undocumented tales of courage appended to her list of known achievements by well-meaning admirers. But to distinguish between what she actually accomplished and what is apocryphal one has to wade through a tangle of half-truths, rumours and hyperbole that had its origins in the euphoria and worldwide sense of relief that followed the conclusion of the war in 1945.

Christine first came to public attention through an article published in the *London Gazette* in 1947, reporting that she had received the Order of the British Empire for rescuing three British officers from a German firing squad. *The Daily Telegraph and Morning Post* followed with an article (written by their 'special correspondent') reporting that, acting alone, she established an escape route from Germany to Budapest for British POW. The article went on to report that she later worked in northern Italy though the unnamed

---

*SOE (1940 -1945) was born out of the many committee meetings held in Whitehall, beginning in 1938, between ministers and military officers to plan a response to the looming threat posed to Europe by Germany. After the failure of their first effort, Section D, they presented Winston Churchill with an improved model in the summer of 1940. He authorised its organisation and is often, and erroneously, given credit for the creation of Special Operations Executive. No one man can be said to have been its founder. Neville Chamberlain drafted SOE's original charter at Churchill's request and gave the organisation its name.

correspondent neglected to report that the planned mission never got off the ground, so to speak (she was to parachute into Poland). The correspondent added a *soupcon* of excitement to the piece by revealing that Christine avoided speaking publicly about her European adventures for risk of alerting foreign 'Powers' who might harm her. This was the first in a series of articles about Christine to amplify her activities on behalf of British intelligence. SOE files, when finally made available to the public, revealed that it was actually her colleague and lover Andrew Kennedy**who was foremost in establishing escape routes from occupied territory. Even the British consul in Budapest had a hand in it.

On the same day (May 23) the *News Chronicle* carried an article by one Victor Azam excitedly reporting that Christine had 'wrought havoc' in central Europe. Azam graciously 'shook the hand' that blew bridges, derailed trains and had laid down dynamite charges. None of this is true but as news of secret service activities was sequestered and would remain so for decades, his report could not be challenged. But his judgment could be, for he reported that Christine was only five-feet tall when she was in fact eight inches taller.

More dis-information was supplied by former SOE agent and author Billy Moss[1] who wrote a three-part series about Christine for the *Picture Post* with melodramatic headlines such as 'Fast Cars Across Europe' and 'Bullets and Bluff with the *Maquis*'. The Christine legend grew from these pieces, helped along by her reticence and the impossibility of checking such stories with government sources. Thereafter, she remained out of the public eye until her brutal murder in 1952, a crime widely reported in the British press as well as

---

**Andrew Kennedy (*ne* Andrzej Kowerski) Mechanised Brigade, awarded Virtuti Militari by the Polish government. Recruited by SOE with the rank of lieutenant, General List (of Infantry). Awarded MBE (Mil) by the British government.

in some international newspapers. Since then writers searching for newsworthy material have continued to discover and re-discover Christine but their articles, spaced months and even years apart, rarely contained anything new until very recently.

British government policy of secrecy regarding SIS (Secret Intelligence Service) and SOE activities resulted in a veritable catalogue of poorly researched pieces about Christine. The near-destruction of SOE files after the war made fact-checking even more difficult. Passages in the memoirs of several SOE operatives, similarly ill-informed, also contain inaccurate details about her life. This assortment of recollections has raised a number of unanswered questions about what actions could be properly attributed to her. One British author wrote, 'she was born de Gisycka' and 'her husband fought in the Warsaw Uprising.' Both statements are wildly inaccurate. It has also been asserted that she helped the British 8th Army to take Syria in 1941*** but the 8th Army's War Diary, available at The National Archive (TNA), makes no mention of her contribution. Since her death in 1952 many such tales and exaggerations have found their way into Christine's story and have proved difficult to dislodge. In 2013 a religious service was held to mark the refurbishment of Christine's London grave. The anonymous author of the printed program wrote that she had played 'a pivotal role in WW2' and 'had made a significant contribution to the Allied war effort.' Unfortunately, the facts of her career do not support these statements.

The former FANY Margaret Pawley**** alluded to these exaggerations in this passage: 'Christine's considerable acts of bravery in the field have passed into legend; there have been many accounts, some of them contradictory, and the sequence is not always easy

---

****The Women Who Lived For Danger*, by Marcus Binney (London: Hoddard & Stoughton 2002).

to determine.' At least some of the confusing accounts to which Pawley alluded had as their source Andrew Kennedy's recollections and those of a small group of SOE officers. After Christine's death they attempted to shield her reputation from the sensationalist press by refusing all cooperation with journalists scenting a lurid tale. What Andrew and his friends sought to conceal were tales of affairs and flirtations though these never interfered with the commission of her duties. Andrew obviously preferred that Christine be remembered for her courage rather than for her *amours*. For her heroism she had been justly awarded the George Medal and the War Medal in addition to her OBE, and from the French government, the *Croix de guerre*. But journalists and others who knew less about her helped to obscure any real appraisal of her record as an SOE operative.

John Roper, an SOE agent who had known Christine for some years, revealed in a letter to me why the decision was made to refuse cooperation with reporters and potential biographers, 'Christine's death led to a stampede of journalists and writers of various sorts. ... five of us - without whose help nobody could piece together a serious account of her life - agreed we would only cooperate with one writer acceptable to us all and give no help to anyone else.'+ Roper seems to have been scrupulously honest in his recollections of Christine. But others either distorted the record of her actions as an SOE operative or else preferred not to mention incidents which might have tarnished her reputation.

Not long after Christine's death Andrew, Roper and three other former agents met to form the Panel to Preserve the Memory of Christine Granville, an informal group whose

---

****In Obedience to Instructions: FANY [First Aid Nursing Yeomanry] with the SOE in the Mediterranean* (London: Barnsley, Leo Cooper 1999).

only purpose was to withhold information from would-be biographers and sensation-seeking journalists. They then went about their private business, maintaining their silence for nearly two decades. In 1973 Vladimir Ledochowski, a Polish officer and briefly one of Christine's lovers, contacted Andrew in an attempt to secure his cooperation in writing her biography. At the time he was unaware of the Panel and naively suggested the formation of the Club of the Saved, consisting of men who had been rescued by Christine from certain death. Andrew appeared to give his assent but concealed any mention of the fact that he and the Panel members had already found someone to do exactly that.++

Andrew was determined not to allow anyone else to write Christine's story, certainly not one of her former lovers. Billy Moss, riding the success of a book describing how he and Patrick Leigh Fermor had kidnapped a German general, confided in Vladimir that he too was interested in writing a biography but never followed through. With the competition vanquished Andrew proceeded to give Madeleine Masson, the chosen biographer, his version of Christine's life and thus established himself as the architect of her legend.

Throughout the war and for several years afterwards he was her lover, comrade-in-arms and her only confidante. In his role of zealous gatekeeper of the secrets he more than anyone else is responsible for much of what is known about her. At her death Christine left no will, only a letter naming Andrew as executor of her meagre estate. After her funeral and the conviction of the assailant Dennis George Muldowney, he removed some personal effects from her hotel room but left behind an unopened trunk. He never revealed the contents of any letters or papers he might have found in the room and remained faithful to her

+Letter to the author (29 Aug 2002).

memory as he had been faithful to her in life (with just one known lapse of self-discipline). This was to be the first of two occasions in which documents, letters and family photographs belonging to Christine vanished. A second batch of letters written to her brother's family was apparently destroyed by authorities in Warsaw after the war. Thus, few of her personal thoughts and opinions about a particular subject or person remain.

Andrew Kennedy continued to exert his influence over his dead lover's biography until the early 1970s when he met Mrs Masson. After they presumably agreed an agenda she tape-recorded a series of interviews with him over a three-month period. Once these sessions had been completed and the tapes transcribed, he took them away. As far as is known no one else has ever heard those recordings nor does anyone know if they still survive. What motivated Andrew to throw such a protective shield around Christine after her death was not simply a desire to possess her memory but a deep and abiding affection. He had been in love with her ever since they had begun working together in Budapest in 1940. He idolised and idealised her, and his devotion was such that he tolerated her infidelities though they must have hurt deeply (he didn't seem to mind that she was still married to her second husband throughout their own affair).

The difficulty in writing about Christine, in knowing the truth about her, is that there are often several contradictory accounts of some of the actions in which she featured in addition to conflicting tales about her personal life. Most of these are of minor import though a few are significant, such as her role in allegedly alerting Churchill to German

++*Christine, a search for Christine Granville*, by Madeleine Masson (Hamish Hamilton 1975, reprinted and revised as *Christine, SOE Agent & Churchill's Favourite Spy* (London: Virago 2005)

plans for the invasion of the Soviet Union. It was in fact an independent resistance group in Poland that discovered preparations for Operation Barbarossa yet she accepted full credit for that intelligence *coup* and neglected to mention the efforts of her colleagues.

Though Christine is often described as a staunch Polish patriot few writers have paused to examine her divided loyalties towards her country. For all her vaunted patriotism her eagerness to eavesdrop on her fellow Poles in Cairo and report her findings to SOE seems to accurately illustrate her desire to please her British handlers. In that regard a civil servant, responding succinctly to my request for verification that she was indeed 'spying' on Polish intelligence officers, replied only that 'some of her papers will probably never be released.' The possibility that information about her activities is being withheld by some unidentified government ministry has only enhanced her reputation as a spy.

In telling their story the Panel described by John Roper muddied the waters by adding unsubstantiated details to their friend's CV. Writers who followed in their wake accepted as fact what had so far been written about Christine without bothering to investigate. She contributed to the confusion by refusing to either confirm or deny the many rumours surrounding her personal life and career that were rife in certain quarters of Cairo and London. Her friend Lady Livia Deakin offered this 'left-handed' compliment, 'She [Christine] was not a liar, not ever, but she just had to cover her tracks.' Thus, we have been left with an image of Christine Granville that is slightly out of focus.

Baptised Krystyna Maria Janina Skarbek, she was born into the volatile world of what was then known as Russian Poland on the 1st of May 1908. Yet for nearly sixty years 1915, the year etched on her gravestone in a London cemetery, was generally accepted as her date of birth. That date first appeared on a bogus travel visa created by the British consul in Budapest in order to facilitate her escape from Hungary. Krystyna Skarbek became Christine Granville on that occasion (1941) along with a much-enhanced age as part of her disguise. She maintained those fictions for the remainder of her life.

More confusion was added by the revelation that even before the war she had occasionally inserted 1909 as her birth year on several documents including her application for an entry visa into Britain (1939). On that occasion she gave her age as thirty. The discovery of her birth certificate in the village of Beczkowice towards the end of the twentieth century finally confirmed that she had been born in 1908. It was revealed then that she had evidently been baptised twice, once at birth and again five years later.

There are few first-hand accounts of Christine's childhood and adolescence, leading to speculation about her life in pre-war Poland and about the manner in which she had been recruited by the British. Documents discovered in a more accessible Poland after the trades' union Solidarity came to power in the late 1980s confirm that she was raised on her parents' modest estate Trzepnica in southwestern Poland, and that she attended two Catholic boarding schools. An academic report from one of those schools was discovered by the Polish biographer Jan Larecki. After completing her education she returned to the family home and remained there for several years until the disastrous financial events of the late 1920s compelled her parents to sell their rural properties and move to Warsaw.

To add to the aura of vagueness that seemed to emanate from Christine there is a paucity of anecdotal or documented evidence of her movements in the mid-1930s, a time when the Nazi party had come to power in Germany and when Europe was facing the real threat of war. It may seem a minor point to some but there still remains the question of how she progressed from her status as pampered daughter of the landed gentry to the more exciting and secretive world of British intelligence. The commonly accepted view until now has been that either George Taylor, corporate executive turned director of espionage, or Sir Robert Vansittart recruited her. In 1939 he was Chief Diplomatic advisor to His Majesty's Government. It seems unlikely that a man of his rank would be moving furtively about London seeking recruits for Section D, precursor to SOE.

Since the remaining SOE files were made available to the public in the mid-1990s evidence has emerged pointing to the former *Manchester Guardian* correspondent FA Voigt as the person most likely to have introduced Christine to the British secret service. Voigt, a covert agent himself, reported from Berlin in the late 1920s and was known to have visited Poland several times during his stay in central Europe. Christine would have been living in Warsaw at the same time. In his primary role as the *Guardian's* foreign correspondent Voigt was well-acquainted with British politicians one of whom was Vansittart. At her first interview with Section D in 1939, Christine revealed that she had known Voigt 'for about five years', that is to say 1934. Her movements from then until 1938 are obscure and apparently uneventful. She must have left Poland shortly before that in order to make her appearance in the disputed territory of Teschen (Cieszyn in Polish) in October. In that portentous year she also met and married the author-diplomat Jerzy Gizycki who had already made his debut as a covert agent.

Those who knew Christine for any length of time (no one except Andrew Kennedy could be said to have known her well) were generally agreed that she was a very private person in spite of the youthful antics of her school days. Aside from Andrew, Christine had no close friends, certainly not among women. Men were her preferred choice of companions and those few who were close to her were brave, larger-than-life characters. Besides the courageous Andrew there was Gizycki, diplomat, adventurer, SOE agent and author, and Francis Cammaerts, former headmaster, one-time conscientious objector and leader of Jockey Circuit in France. Others were military officers or SOE colleagues with one notable, and fatal, exception.

Christine's first recorded intelligence operation was completed in 1940 when she penetrated the Polish-Slovak border and made her way to Warsaw, narrowly escaping arrest by German police. The frequency of her clandestine visits to Poland is another matter often disputed. Only two return journeys out of four known attempts are documented. Other claims of visits, ranging from six to fifteen times, are the result of speculation and reveal a lack of research on the part of the writer. The Musketeers and the *Armia Krajowa (AK* or Home Army*)* had carefully planned a route for couriers running from Budapest northeast across Hungary to Kosice, over the mountains of the Polish-Slovak border to the Zakopane ski resort and then down to Warsaw. That route described a zig-zag and was lengthy, arduous and fraught with danger. As Christine served in Hungary for only twelve months, and her movements there are accounted for, frequent excursions into occupied Poland seem highly unlikely.

Since the gradual, and grudging, opening of SOE files to the public by the government of the day, a process begun in 1994, we can now track Christine's movements as she travelled from Warsaw to London to Budapest, back to Poland and the Middle

East before finally returning to London where her life reached its dramatic conclusion. These files also provide insight into the conflicts that frequently erupted within SOE, between SOE and SIS, and between the British and Polish intelligence services with Christine at times caught in the middle.

Though she was quite willing to deceive Polish intelligence bureaux on behalf of SOE she herself was the subject of British surveillance. Captain Richard Truszkowski was appreciative of information she had gleaned from Polish officers in 1943 but in the next breath he asked SOE colleagues for any intelligence they in turn might have on her. While she was risking her life in France a month after D-Day, another SOE officer wrote to his superiors to complain that she was again consorting with Poles as if those associations were forbidden to her. He then added '[but] anything that comes to hand from her in a Polish connection will of course be passed on to you.'

SOE files also reveal the extent to which she sometimes acted independently and impetuously, much to the chagrin of her superior officers. The story of her cooperation with the Musketeers has not been thoroughly described to an English-speaking audience even though they were a primary source for information from inside occupied Poland for 1940 and 1941. However, they gradually became a major source of irritation to both SIS and SOE. But before their demise they provided just the sort of environment in which the free-spirited Christine could thrive. She had provided what the Musketeers had lacked, a necessary and legitimate link between Warsaw and Budapest for the exchange of vital information. Their reach later extended into the heart of Germany and even to Istanbul. This system was maintained in the face of official opposition from both the British and the

Polish governments until 1942 when the *Armia Krajowa* (AK) gave the green light for the assassination of the Musketeers' leader who had by then become a liability. There are contradictory accounts of who murdered him, whether it was the AK or German police in Warsaw with whom he had established a close relationship bordering on collaboration.

Christine had her critics as well as supporters. The HS4 series at The National Archives, part of the remaining SOE record, contains a number of disparaging remarks made about her by SOE officers (as well as derogatory remarks made about the Poles and Jews). Such criticism often followed on the heels of the sometimes imprudent unauthorised actions she took. Previously published accounts of her personal life have also contained inaccuracies. The primary reason for this lies in the almost total lack of research done in Poland by those who have previously sought to tell her story. The very first biography of Christine was begun in the early 1970s, a time when admittedly doing research in communist-dominated Poland would have been difficult. The author relied primarily upon the anecdotes and recollections of Andrew Kennedy and his circle of friends. Those who wrote about her after the collapse of the Soviet Union would have had much better access to Polish archives but did not take advantage of Poland's new openness. Only the filmmaker Slawka Wazacz has devoted any serious effort to research in those archives in an attempt to unravel the knot of rumours about Christine's early life and present them to an audience beyond Poland. She incorporated these results into her documentary film 'No Ordinary Countess', first screened in Poland in 2004 and later in London venues.

Much of what we know about Christine has only come to the light in the first decade of this century sixty years after her death. Many if not all the details of her activities as an

SOE operative have now been made public and some of those alleged accomplishments are now being critically appraised. Statements in Polish land registries seem to have settled the question of the extent of the Skarbek estates and there can be no question about her date of birth despite her youthful attempts to disguise her true age. The details of her mother's arrest and death and inaccurate accounts of her adventures that have been circulating uncontested for decades are finally being emended.

As a result of research carried out in post-Soviet Poland, genealogists struggling through the maze of their nation's 1000-year-old history have now cast doubt on the provenance of Count Jerzy Skarbek's title and therefore on the claims of Christine's *devotees* who refer to her as countess. She herself rarely used the title. Christine's cousin Jan Skarbek commented to Mrs Masson that the family name was much over-rated and that there should not be too much emphasis placed on its influence in Poland.

Regardless of how much we know about Christine she will undoubtedly remain an unsullied heroine to some but a riddle to others. Though many if not all her activities as an SOE operative have now been brought out into the open, segments of her life still remain obscured in shadow. Perhaps the full story of her life will never be told but it appears that she might have arranged it just so.

Ron Nowicki
September 2013
London

List of Plates

facing page 82
1. Christine's Polish ID card.
2. FA 'Freddy' Voigt, journalist and covert SIS agent.
3. Gustaf Getlich, Christine's first husband.
4. Andrew Kennedy
5. Captain Richard Truszkowski, SOE
6. Christine in the Haute-Savoie.

facing page 158
7. Christine and Lady Deakin at the Gezira Club, Cairo.
8. Lieutenant Colonel Francis Cammaerts, SOE
9. Andrew Kennedy, Christine and unidentified officer.
10. Christine and Muriel Bankes in post-war Paris.
11. Kate O'Malley and Lord Tweedsmuir.
12. Lt (Count) Vladimir Ledochowski

facing page 290
13. Andrew Kennedy in Germany
14. Dennis George Muldowney
15. The Shellbourne Hotel
16. Christine's grave.

Who shall I be for men,

many generations later,

when after the noise of languages

the award goes to Silence.

> from *The Thistle, The Nettle*
> - Czeslaw Milosz
> (Translated from the Polish by
> the author with Robert Haas)

xx

Part I. 1908 - 1930

Chapter 1. A Country Idyll

Christine Granville was born in an occupied country in a city whose cobbled streets were still being patrolled by Russian troops more than a hundred years after the final partition of Poland in 1795.1 Her birth in 1908 followed decades of riots, strikes and armed clashes led by Polish rebels demanding an end to tsarist rule from Moscow. Unable to dislodge their oppressors they retreated from the streets to re-deploy and prepare for the next round of fighting, unaware that Europe was about to explode and would leave in its wake the independence that Poland had so desperately sought for more than a century.

Christine's birth in such turbulent times may have presaged the course her life would eventually take though her childhood in the Polish countryside seemed idyllic and unaffected by personal trauma or by political chaos. Even the tumult and destruction of the first world war passed her by.

Her parents' marriage however was not as blissful. Count Jerzy Skarbek and Stefania Goldfeder were an ill-matched couple brought together by the manipulations of their respective families. The marriage between the penurious count and the well-educated Stefania came at a critical time for one of Poland's most prestigious families and at an opportune moment for Adolf Goldfeder's daughter. She was the only girl in a family of bankers that had begun to accumulate its wealth in the late nineteenth century. They owed their good fortune to Goldfeder (d 1896) who was said to have parlayed the proceeds from a winning lottery ticket into the foundations of a successful business. He had previously owned a modest *kantor,* a counting-house or book-keeping firm, in Warsaw and developed it into one of the country's most prestigious banks by clever application of his lottery profits. The Skarbeks by contrast were a family of minor aristocrats with a long and distinguished history of military service to their country. But like many families of the Polish aristocracy, centuries of war and occupation had devastated their fortunes and, approaching the twentieth century, their very survival was threatened for lack of heirs and a dwindling supply of money. Desperate measures had to be taken to maintain ancient family lines and so society just had to look the other way when the sons of titled families took Jewish brides. Provided of course that they came to the altar bearing large dowries.

It cannot be said with absolute certainty which family made the first overture to the other but in 1898 Stefania was introduced into the exclusive company of the landed gentry (*szlachta*) through marriage to the young Count Skarbek. Adolf Goldfeder's widow and family matriarch Roza no doubt played a major role in this social triumph. The match was sealed by presenting Skarbek with a dowry of some 340,000 rubles plus a country property. In such a predominantly Christian country arranging a marriage between a Catholic and a Jew was no simple matter, especially when the scion of one of Poland's most storied families was involved.

After the terms of the marriage between the count and Stefania had been agreed, and money changed hands, Skarbek 'donated' an undisclosed sum to the Bishop of Warsaw to secure his blessing for the wedding to proceed. But there were other conditions to be met, primarily Stefania's conversion to Catholicism. The wedding ceremony eventually took place in the secluded chapel of a women's cloister reserved for those of noble heritage (*kanoniczki*), out of sight of the good burghers of Warsaw.[2]

Christine's father had the most to gain from this arrangement for he had neither money nor property. As a young man he had led a dissolute life and had exhausted whatever allowance he had by the time the couple's engagement was confirmed. Among the aristocracy he was disparagingly known as a *kopertowy hrabia*, an 'envelope count', one who assumes a title of nobility without permission. That could only be granted by the tsar himself. Nevertheless, in return for her generous dowry Stefania gained entry into an exclusive segment of society with the rank of countess. She wore her new status with pride even though her husband's title was of dubious provenance.[3]

Christine was born nearly ten years after her parents' marriage, eight years after the birth of her brother Andrzej. The established facts of his life are few. After the first world war he wed a German woman, Irena von Arndt, who later dropped the 'von' and substituted the more sociably acceptable 'de.' He allegedly participated in the calamitous Warsaw Uprising of 1944 but there is no evidence to substantiate this claim. The Home Army (*Armia Krajowa* or AK) roster of some 250000 combatants survives but does not include his name. His adult life was a troubled one - a year in a concentration camp, arrested after the war by the communist government and painful death from suspected tuberculosis.

After Andrzej's birth the count reverted to the reckless behaviour of his bachelor days. He absented himself from the family home for weeks at a time leaving Stefania and the household staff to raise the boy. His whereabouts were no secret for he was frequently seen at race tracks in Warsaw and in nearby suburbs in the company of women other than his wife. The Goldfeders may have been extremely pleased with their new social status but the Skarbeks' union had been in trouble from the beginning, a condition that was later reflected in Christine's two marriages.

The urban-bred Stefania, described by one relative as being rather plain in appearance, was unaccustomed to the sometimes coarse ways of local people in the countryside beyond Warsaw. She did not care much for hunting, for large rumbustious parties or for what she perceived to be the rude language and boorish antics of her husband's colleagues who trampled on her expensive carpets in their muddy boots.

Though she complained about her husband's errant behaviour her view of marriage was typical among her contemporaries who believed that marriage was forever. This was one value Christine would not share with her mother. Like her father she developed a predilection early in life for having casual affairs in and out of wedlock, and pursued a lifestyle more typical of young women of the late twentieth century. Still, Stefania could afford to soothe her wounded feelings at some of the finest shops in Warsaw and in Paris where she was always accorded the greatest respect.

Christine was born at the Goldfeder family home in the shade of Warsaw's lush Saxon Gardens at number 45 Zielna street where her grandfather had once conducted his business affairs. It must have been a desirable neighbourhood in its time, given the close proximity to the *Zamek*, the royal castle, and the historic Old Town. It seemed a peaceful setting compared to the frenetic plotting that was taking place elsewhere in the city and at a time when rumours of war in Europe were rife. Bloody street fighting between Polish rebels and Russian troops occasionally erupted in the capital and in other Polish cities. This stand-off between the upstart Poles and the Russians continued up to the eve of the first world war. A year after Christine's birth her mother purchased a modest estate some forty miles southwest of Warsaw called Trzepnica.* This was Christine's first home and apparently she remembered it so fondly that she occasionally cited it or the county seat of Piotrkow** as her places of birth. Christine's life at Trzepnica was a comfortable but solitary one. Her father, when in residence, and his stable boys were her main companions. She had no primary school education. Instead the count enriched her imagination with tales of his family's fabled ancestry, stories of men who had been knights and warriors dating back to the thirteenth century. Some of her ancestors had fought with great courage against the Teutonic knights at the Battle of Grunwald (1410) and with King Jan III Sobieski in breaking the Ottoman siege of Vienna in 1683. She must have inherited her father's talent as a raconteur, for colleagues and family members occasionally used the words 'fantasist' and 'story-teller' when describing Christine's personal qualities.

The Skarbek family were not all warriors however. Shortly before the final partition of the country by Russia and its allies, the clan divided in two. One branch*** turned its attentions to farming and social work. Their most notable member was Fryderyk Florian Skarbek who became a prison reformer in Russia and Poland in the mid-nineteenth

---

*In Polish land-registry books Stefania is listed as the owner of the family's two estates. The Skarbek's first home, however, was the estate of Mlodziesyn which the count purchased apparently with funds from Stefania's dowry. Christine was not born here, as stated in an earlier biography.

**The Germans established their first concentration camp near Piotrkow, a city known by its contemporary name Piotrkow Trybunalski.

century. He once owned the estate of Zelazowa Wola, famous as Chopin's birthplace. Fryderyk's children had been tutored by Chopin *pere* who asked his patron to stand as the boy's godfather. Fryderyk agreed and also gave the future great composer his name. He also initiated construction of Warsaw's infamous Pawiak prison. It was a bitter irony that Stefania Skarbek became one of its inmates 100 years later during the second world war.4

It was obvious from early childhood that the dark-eyed Christine preferred the rough-and-tumble of country life to her mother's more feminine pursuits. Not that she lacked femininity. She made no attempt to disguise her handsome features as early photos show and in company could be quite charming. But she preferred to spend her free time exploring the Skarbek estates and nearby countryside on horseback rather than learning the domestic skills that would make her a desirable marriage partner. Her love of riding had been encouraged by her father whose main pre-occupations had been for some time breeding and selling horses but included a passion for a day at the races with all its attendant joys and temptations. However, he did not neglect his daughter and taught her to ride when she was still quite young, a sport which she took to with great enthusiasm. Despite Count Skarbek's reputation as a womaniser, or perhaps because of it, he was once elected president of the local Horse Breeders Society.

Christine appears to have been the centre of attention within the Skarbek household perhaps because she was the more aggressive of the two children. There are few facts extant about her brother Andrzej, few recollections of his life passed on either by Christine or

---

***The Galicia line of Skarbeks holds the official title of 'count.' A decree signed by Tsar Nicholas I granted Fryderk Florian the title of count of the Kingdom of Poland. His descendant, Count Andrzej Skarbek was the most recent holder of that title. He died in 2011 in Belsize Park, London.

by her parents. Much of the correspondence that his wife Irena and her daughter Teresa carried on with Christine during the second world war was either lost or destroyed in a case of bureaucratic bungling by Warsaw social services. Those letters might have shed a more expansive light on the relationship between brother and sister.

After the dust and clamour of the Great War had settled Stefania prevailed upon her husband to extend their daughter's education beyond her knowledge of the Skarbek family history. At the age of fourteen Christine was enrolled at a convent boarding school in Polska Wies (now Pobiedziska) in western Poland, operated by the Catholic order of Sacre Coeur. It was here that she began to exhibit the sort of impulsive behaviour that would one day characterise her relationship with both British and Polish intelligence services, as well as with civilian employers.

Only one of her former classmates ever spoke about their school days together. She described the young Christine, or Krystyna as she was then, as a very active child who loved playing pranks on her unsuspecting victims. There is an apocryphal tale that she once attempted to set fire to a priest's cassock as he was conducting the Holy Mass. Fortunately for all concerned the garment did not go up in a blaze. This was the proverbial last straw as far as the nuns were concerned. Christine was sent home, not unhappily one assumes, where she must have looked forward to spending her days riding and bantering with her father's stable boys. But her parents wasted no time in finding another placement for their mischievous daughter. She was quickly packed off to Jazlowiec, a boarding school in southeastern Poland.[5]

The hard-working nuns of the Immaculate Conception, clad in their distinctive blue and white gowns, presented their new pupil with a regime more determined than the one at Sacre Coeur. They achieved the desired affect, guiding Christine towards a more serious interest in academic work with a focus on French, a language she would have been exposed to before Jazlowiec. It was still customary in the early days of the twentieth century for the gentry to speak Polish in civic and religious matters while conversing in French at home and at social gatherings. It was still considered the language of a cultured society throughout Europe and young people from the best homes spoke French to a greater or lesser degree. Christine's mother, for one, was said to be a fluent French speaker.

Her education completed without further incident, Christine returned to Trzepnica a poised and well-mannered young woman with a rather autocratic bearing. This was mistaken by some as *hauteur* but by others as a pose to conceal a deep-rooted inferiority complex. The British author and journalist Daniel Farson, upon seeing photos of her, remarked in a newspaper article: '. . . photographs of her convey a characteristic that I particularly dislike - self-satisfaction - but this is belied by all who knew her. Perhaps the look is one of self-confidence and perhaps this concealed an inner uncertainty. But here I am guessing.' **** Christine's taste for adventure hadn't been totally suppressed by the nuns. At her father's urging she rode astride in a local flat track race on a mount from his stables in what must surely have been an unusual sight in polite society. Though Skarbek was frequently absent from the estate he had nevertheless managed to impart much of his knowledge of horses to his young daughter.

The financial collapse that began in America in the late 1920s and spread to Europe

****Daniel Farson, 'Riddle of the woman pimpernel'. *Observer Magazine* 20 Oct 1974.

also put paid to the Skarbeks' comfortable way of life. Even if the count had been more astute in business affairs it is doubtful whether he could have coped with the wild fluctuations of the Polish inter-war economy. With Stefania's dowry squandered after years of high living the family had little choice but to sell their properties and prepare for the hectic pace of city life.

Christine left the family home first and arrived in a bustling Warsaw in December 1928, a few weeks ahead of her parents. Their departure from Trzepnica had been delayed by the legal entanglements that accompanied the forced and painful sale of the family home. A second property, part of Stefania's dowry, was sold off in 1929 and they then joined Christine in Warsaw where they took up residence in more modest quarters.

Before she could settle into her new life Christine had to obtain the requisite ID card. In response to the question 'place of residence,' she wrote 'unknown,' indicating an uncertain future for herself as well as for her parents. Documents - her applications for the ID card, entry for a beauty contest and her application for a British entry visa - surfaced only in the late 1990s. The discovery of her birth certificate in Beczkowice brought to light evidence of an earlier baptism. The reason for the gap between the first ceremony and second baptism may have had to do with the Russian custom of delaying the registration of birth until the child had lived for more than a year. Given the high mortality rate for infants in the early twentieth century in eastern Europe (and elsewhere), it was simply more convenient and less expensive for local authorities to wait until they were certain that a new-born baby would survive. The discovery of these various documents revealed for the first time that the 1915 date of birth on her gravestone was a hoax though one born of necessity.

Despite Poland's near-anarchic political life following the first world war, climaxed by a coup against the elected government in 1926, Warsaw was in the midst of a cultural and building boom. With people pouring in from the countryside and from smaller cities in search of work, the capital's population quickly surpassed the one million mark. A reorganised state school system led to a general increase in the nation's literacy rates, attendance at operas and theatres was up, a cabaret life had taken root and the number of poets, and periodicals seemed to grow by the day. A promising economy, if only temporary, provided Christine with her first job opportunity, at the Fiat auto garage and showroom. The company cleverly paid homage to Poland's glorious and troubled history by locating its business, whether intentionally or accidentally, between the magnificent Krasinski Square and Traugutt Park, so-called to honour a hero of the 1863 uprising. As Christine had no secretarial skills or sales experience her duties were probably limited to light clerical work and perhaps to greet customers as the friendly, attractive face of Fiat.

Her career with the automaker was not lengthy. Before the end of her first year Gustaf Getlich, the eldest son of a Polish-German family, appeared in the showroom looking to buy a new car. Vladimir Ledochowski, an intelligence officer and later one of Christine's suitors, gave a brief account in his unpublished memoir of how she and Getlich met. He had wandered into the Polski Fiat showroom having become unexpectedly wealthy when his father abruptly died leaving him in control of the family drapery business. Getlich was now a wealthy young man about town, eager to spend his share of the family's fortune. Christine's meeting with him was to lead to a new and exciting way of life for her, albeit a brief one. She and Getlich became a familiar couple in Warsaw's revived social life, seen often at some of the city's most fashionable cafes and hotel dining rooms. Getlich was an avid skier and that meant frequent trips to Zakopane. This mountain resort, less than seventy miles south of the old capital Krakow, was much more an intimate village in the nineteen-thirties than it is today. Some of Poland's wealthier families kept second homes there and often hosted salons, smart gatherings occasionally graced by the presence of one of the country's cultural icons, like the composer Karol Szymanowski or the artist and author Witkacy.[6]

Christine continued to work at Fiat until late 1929 when she fell ill with a respiratory illness. The family doctor suspected tuberculosis but that turned out to be a mis-diagnosis. Nevertheless, Christine took his advice to exchange the sulphurous air of Warsaw for the more salutary environs of Zakopane. This interlude did not disrupt what must have been for her a glamourous affair with Getlich who became a frequent visitor to her lodgings. They maintained a lifestyle similar to the one they had enjoyed in Warsaw, frequenting Zakopane's best cafes and restaurants. Christine made a quick recovery from her illness and returned to the capital in time to enter the Miss Polonia contest. This pageant, sponsored by the newspaper *Red Courier (Kurier Czerwony)*, was organised in 1929 and prominent members of Poland's intellectual class were involved including the critic Boy Zelenski.[7] The early feminist novelist Zofia Nalkowska [8] was one of its judges.

An initial field of 120 contestants, some of whom were young women from families of the aristocracy, was winnowed down to just fifteen Christine included. Her youthful beauty and charm however were not enough for her to win the crown. The sponsoring newspaper reported that she placed sixth in the judges' estimation. A thumbnail description of

Christine, based on information she herself submitted, confirms some facts of her early life along with hints at her playful nature. She gave her birth date as May the 1st, 1909 'in Piotrkow, graduated from grammar school and lives in Warsaw where she worked as a clerk in an automobile firm.' She continued with this self-description: 'She loves horse-riding and skiing. In 1926 she was awarded a prize in a horse competition. Krystyna is a tall and slim brunette with a light complexion, and big eyes full of life.'

Christine's application also confirms that she had been employed at the Fiat auto firm prior to the beauty contest and not later, after her father's death in December 1930. This dilutes the melodramatic account, part of the Christine myth, of how a young woman from a respectable family was forced to take up commonplace employment to support her widowed mother. In April 1930 she married Gustaf, called Gutek by his family, in a Catholic ceremony at the Spiritual Seminary Church with her brother Andrzej in attendance as 'best man' as the couple exchanged vows. The Getlich family hosted a grand reception afterwards at the luxurious and historic Bristol Hotel on Warsaw's Royal Way.

The Getlichs took up residence in Warsaw but spent a significant amount of time in Zakopane where Christine had become a familiar and popular figure on the social scene. Getlich, charged with the responsibility of maintaining the family business, travelled back and forth from Warsaw to Zakopane, often leaving Christine to fend for herself. In 1931 she entered an informal contest at the resort and won the title 'Miss Ski.' Others who have written about Christine conflated the two contests and for many years it was carelessly put about that she was once a beauty queen with the title Miss Polonia.

The Getlichs' marriage began to fade within a year, their once-exciting social life notwithstanding, overshadowed by the necessity of Getlich's return to Warsaw to manage the family's affairs. The demands of the business plus her reluctance to take on the role of housewife and hostess for his dinner parties created a situation that could not last. That led to a separation and eventual divorce. Because Polish Catholics were forbidden to divorce a decree was granted in 1932 in Vilno (Vilnius) in Protestant Lithuania. Christine's financial status changed radically because, according to Tomasz Getlich, his father paid Christine no alimony. Another Skarbek family source however maintains that Gutek made monthly payments into her postal account.

    Christine must have realised early on that despite her husband's wealth a marriage typical for the inter-war years was not her cup of tea. He no doubt expected that she would settle into the role of wife and mother while he attended to his business. She obviously had other ideas. The implications from the Getlich family are that it was Christine who rebelled against the constraints of a traditional marriage. No one has given her side of the story. While living with her parents she had not been encouraged to learn the skills necessary to run a home and marriage to a man of means gave her even less incentive to take on the duties of wife. Christine's lack of interest in domestic affairs did not escape the attention of her friend, Lady Livia (Pussi) Deakin.+ Her lasting impression of Christine was that of someone 'totally undomesticated. I never saw her sewing or mending, yet she always managed to look crisp and fresh. I don't think she could cook. . . she never wanted to eat at home.'

+Lady Deakin was born Livia Nasta in Romania. Interview with Madeleine Masson in *Christine, the Search for Christine Granville*. Married Sir William Deakin, SOE, knighted 1975 He was the founder/warden of St Antony's College, Oxford.

In the end she was simply too high-spirited to settle into the role of *hausfrau*. After her divorce she lived virtually all her adult life in hotels or in accommodation that did not require her to be a dedicated housekeeper. Tomasz Getlich remembered that his father seldom spoke about his ex-wife but his sister Anna Mencwel recalled that in one outburst he referred to Christine as the 'most lying person he had ever known,' without offering any explanation. Getlich described her to a would-be biographer as a 'mad-woman' who was 'continually seeking change,' comments perhaps to be expected from a vengeful former spouse. There are no surviving divorce papers that would reveal the cause and conditions of Christine's separation from her husband but their divorce was acrimonious, according to Tomasz. She did not leave behind an opinion of Getlich who later re-appeared in the narrative of her life in a most unusual and unexplained circumstance.

Christine remained in Zakopane where she had become notable for her reckless style on the nearby slopes. Her new friends, sons and daughters of well-to-do Polish families, spent much their time skiing and frequenting the resort's bars and cafes. It was bruited about that, with few responsibilities and an abundance of time and money, they indulged in a bit of cross-border cigarette and tobacco smuggling. Christine's alleged participation in this game of hide-and-seek on skis with Slovak border patrols is one of a number of unsourced anecdotes that colour her life story.

Besides the two men she married Christine received other marriage proposals in the course of her truncated life but none of her suitors ever succeeded in domesticating her. The men she selected as husbands and lovers were often as audacious as she and in that respect she saw them as partners, equals, rather than from the perspective of the swooning maiden. None ever succeeded in hanging the symbolic pinny around her neck. Christine could be as bold as any of the men she knew. Not for her a life of recipes, soft fabrics and quiet gardens. Her behaviour as a young woman, descendant of an illustrious family, signaled that she preferred a more adventurous existence than that offered by a potentially secure and materially comfortable life with Getlich. Yet she was unfocussed at this time in her life and received little guidance from her family or from anyone else.

Little is known about Christine's political preferences even though by the mid-1930s Warsaw had become a hot-bed of political intrigue following the death of Marshal Jozef Pilsudski.[9] He had carved Polish independence out of the chaotic aftermath of the first world war but what opinions she may have held about the often abrasive Pilsudski were not recorded for posterity. In fact there is nothing in Christine's background that would suggest an interest in politics or involvement with any movement. That was a reflection of the manner in which she lived her life, a person who followed her own instincts and kept her own council. Given her distaste for authority she could not have been happy with Pilsudski's autocratic regime. He had seized the reins of power in 1918 and cemented his position as Poland's saviour when he lead a smaller Polish army to victory over the Red Army during the abbreviated Polish-Russian war of 1919-20.

In 1926 he orchestrated a coup against the democratically government that led to several days of gun battles in the streets of Warsaw and the deaths of a number of bystanders and cadets from the military academy. Afterwards he personally approved the deposed president's successor.

Pilsudski's principal opponents were the right-wing National Democrats, known also as the ND or *Endeks*, whose core support came largely from Poland's merchant class. Christine's uncle Alexander Skarbek had been elected senator to the Polish parliament (*Sejm*), representing the ND but with his party's determination to consign all Jews to Palestine it certainly would not have appealed either. Not least because she was the child of a Jewish mother. But the senator and his cousin did have one thing in common and that was their penchant for rebelliousness. Skarbek's term in office was characterised by clashes with Pilsudski as well as with Roman Dmowski, his own party leader.[10]

There is no indication which political party Christine favoured out of the many vying for power. In her Personal File (PF) at The National Archives she is quoted only once as having hinted at a preference and that was a single favourable comment about the Polish Socialist Party (PPS). Whatever the politics of her youth she gave every impression of being a Polish patriot though during the war she seemed quite pleased to be in the service of the British government. Politics appeared not to be a subject that troubled the Skarbek family nor were there any serious problems with the fact that the Catholic count had married an assimilated Jew. An insulting bit of doggerel about Christine's parents was briefly circulated in Warsaw but had little effect on their marriage. When Pilsudski became the dominant political figure in Poland he offered the Jews some relief from the formerly oppressive regimes of the Russians. The Jews had voting rights too and between the wars were served by no less than five political parties, some of whom were elected to the Sejm. Jews also figured prominently in Warsaw's cultural and commercial life though they were barred from joining the civil service and the military despite Pilsudski's benevolent attitude towards them. Nevertheless, there was still a certain amount of hostility towards Jews in the country, thus those who had assimilated were not always forthcoming about their family history.

Neither of Christine's parents was especially religious and perhaps they passed on this attitude to their daughter. The count was much too fond of gambling, horse racing and women to spend time in a church. Christine's cousin Jan Skarbek characterised him as a 'playboy' and 'ne-er-do-well.' Stefania was not a strong Catholic either and remained close to the Goldfeder family. However, it seems she made no attempt to influence her daughter in the direction of Judaism.

Because Christine had been baptised into the Church she never thought of herself as anything but a Catholic. Like many Poles and millions of tourists she made the ritual pilgrimage to the shrine of the Black Madonna of Czestochowa near Krakow.[11] For many years she carried with her a medallion bearing the image of the Black Madonna, found among her belongings after her death but she was not known to attend church services. In the eyes of the Goldfeder family however Christine was still a Jew. For years she maintained a discreet silence about her bloodline and even her friends, often the children of aristocrats, seemed unaware of it. Thanks to the Skarbek name she was able to blend effortlessly into their milieu without any questions being asked. They remained ignorant of her background until she was publicly but unintentionally embarrassed by a member of the Goldfeder family in an incident that occurred just before the second world war.

The author Witold Gombrowicz [12] witnessed a chance meeting on the veranda of her lodge in Zakopane between Christine and one of her Jewish aunts. When the aunt called out to Christine who was in the company of friends she tried to ignore the older woman, clad in the sort of clothing usually seen in Jewish enclaves rather than at ski resorts. When the visibly embarrassed niece finally acknowledged her aunt's persistent shouts, a silence descended upon the group as if they had discovered her guilty secret.

Despite the many improvements in Poland's public health services tuberculosis was still prevalent throughout the country and in many European cities. Warsaw was no exception. In December 1930 the disease claimed the life of Count Jerzy. His demise had been hastened by the humiliation of bankruptcy and the compulsory sale of Trzepnica, as well as by his continuing profligate lifestyle.++ Skarbek was not living with his wife at the time of his death but was in the spa city of Baden near Vienna with another woman, identified only by the surname Krzesiolowska. He may have gone there to be treated for consumption but whether that woman was merely his traveling companion or his mistress is a matter for conjecture. In any case the count never divorced or formally separated from his wife who remained stoically loyal to him in the face of his numerous adulterous affairs.

Upon receiving the news of his death Stefania and her children inserted a headline-notice in the newspaper *Warsaw Courier* (*Kurier Warszawski*), expressing heartfelt grief and signed by 'his wife, children and family.' He is buried in the Skarbek family plot in Powazki cemetery. Only two family members are missing, Christine and her mother.

++The Goldfeder bank (*Dom Bankowy*) declared itself bankrupt in 1932. Source: *Polacy-chrzescijanie pochodzenia zydowskiego, tom II* (Warszawa: Wydawnictwo M. Fruchtmana 1938). [Polish-Christians of Jewish origin, vol II]

Chapter 2.
Secrets and Lies

After her sojourn in Zakopane Christine returned to Warsaw and moved into a flat of her own on Filtrowa street, a crosstown thoroughfare in the southern half of the city. She did not return to Fiat and it appears that she was not employed elsewhere. There is a lingering but brief account, source unattributed, of Christine's affair with a man remembered only as Adam. They became engaged but Adam's mother, dismayed at his fiancee's lack of a proper dowry, intervened before the couple could marry. This aside, there are few anecdotes told by friends or family that might shed some light on her activities for the years 1933-37, a time-span during which events in Germany were about to change the course of history.

During the 1920s and '30s Poland, and especially Warsaw, experienced a brief golden age. The city's cultural life was positively thrumming with activity in contrast to the nation's unruly politics and an economy that was always on the verge of collapse. The city's opera company and symphony had been re-invigorated. Paderewski (briefly Poland's prime minister), Artur Rubinstein, Karol Szymanowski and the Russians Rachmaninov and Prokofiev occasionally appeared in concert. Films, especially American, were all the rage. By 1939 there were nearly seventy cinemas in the capital. One of the more popular Polish-made films was 'The Masked Spy' (*Szpieg w Masce*) starring Poland's premier cabaret and recording singer Hanka Ordonowna.

A young woman as attractive as Christine with an distinguished family pedigree, must have been a desirable partner despite her divorce. Warsaw's social life would have offered women like her multiple opportunities to meet attractive and eligible men. Arthur Barker, *The Times* correspondent, attended the many social functions at the Royal Castle to which government officials, members of the Polish aristocracy and the *corps diplomatique* were invited. These sometimes raucous occasions attended by the elite of Polish society were called 'routs' by those fortunate enough to be invited.

Because of her brief marriage to Getlich and subsequent divorce, coupled with her uninhibited behaviour at Zakopane, Christine had achieved a certain notoriety. Nevertheless, the Skarbek name still counted for something in Warsaw society. Though she never had a career as a journalist she had friends who were and who were part of this heady mix of diplomats, politicians, foreign correspondents and aristocrats. There is no definitive account of who might have recruited her to the British secret service but this seems to have been an opportune moment for her to have met members of the British consulate. SIS had established its presence in Warsaw at the conclusion of the Polish-Soviet war in 1920, inserting one of its agents into the consulate's Passport Control Office (PCO) in New World Avenue (*Nowy Swiat*), standard procedure for PCOs throughout Europe. From the vantage point of Warsaw SIS kept a close eye on political activities in Germany and the USSR but they also maintained a file on Poles suspected of involvement in espionage.

Nineteen thirty-four appears to have been the year during which Christine suddenly matured, making the leap from her impulsive carefree existence to that of a more concerned citizen with a strong interest in her country's fortunes. In her initial interview with Section D* in the autumn of 1939 she offered without prompting the statement that she had known the journalist and covert SIS agent Frederick (Freddy) Voigt for nearly five years but did not describe how they had met. Her second husband Jerzy Gizycki seemed to confirm that date when he let slip in an interview with British intelligence officers that she had visited London once before their marriage. He thought it was either in 1934 or 1935.

Coincidentally, in November 1934 British and Polish intelligence officials convened a meeting at the Grosvenor Hotel in London. What the British goals were is unclear but the Poles were hoping to establish a joint cell in Persia (Iran). SIS however were not keen on the suggestion and Polish hopes were dashed. Despite this setback there was a obviously a move on the part of both governments for closer intelligence cooperation and an ideal time for the British to recruit Polish operatives.

Freddy Voigt also visited Poland several times in the early thirties from his base in Berlin. This places him and Christine in Warsaw at the same time, a convenient moment for the two of them to have met at one of Warsaw's many social functions. This chronology is significant in that just two years earlier Christine was last seen cavorting on the ski slopes near Zakopane, a world away from the artifice and skulduggery of secret agents. Somewhere there is a missing link that would explain how she made the transition from the life of a carefree young divorcee to British operative. After leading a seemingly ordinary but comfortable existence in Warsaw she suddenly turned up in Whitehall nonchalantly describing her prominent role in an espionage ring. It was an audacious claim to be made by someone who heretofore had not shown any interest in international affairs.

In earlier versions of Christine's story it was stated that she had somehow found her

---

*Section D, a bureau of the War Department, became operational in November 1938. Its remit was to produce anti-German and pro-British propaganda for distribution in Europe, and to help organise resistance movements in countries in danger of being overrun by the German army.

way to Section D headquarters in the autumn of 1939 and 'demanded' to be taken on as a British agent. It beggars belief that a young woman lacking any military or political experience, and who barely spoke English, would be employed at such a precarious time with such a show of impertinence. The sources for these comments did not explain how she knew where to find Section D headquarters in the first instance. Christine was known to act impulsively at times but there is sufficient circumstantial evidence in SOE documents and in statements given by former agents to reveal the more conventional manner in which she was most likely recruited.

One clue to her pre-war activities was offered by Tadeusz Horko, correspondent for the *Polish Daily (Dziennik Polski)*. He also provided just a modicum of substance to her claim that she'd worked as a journalist before the war. Horko recalled seeing her in the hotly disputed territory of Teschen working as a 'young reporter.' This territory, situated at the juncture of Austria, Czechoslovakia and Poland, had long been a bone of contention especially between the Czechs and the Poles. It was about to become a target for German aggression as part of the Hitler's plan to seize all of Czechoslovakia.

With Austria securely in German hands as a result of the *Anschluss* of March 1938 Hitler began a scurrilous propaganda campaign against the Czechs, aiming first to hive off the Sudetenland with its large minority population of Germans. Under fierce pressure from Nazi officials as well as more diplomatic urging from the British government, the defenseless Czech government yielded and signed the Munich Accords in September in order to avoid war.[1]

Cieszyn, as it was originally known, had been part of the Piast dynasty for centuries and was passed on successively to the Hapsburgs then to Austria. At the end of the first world war, with the Austro-Hungarian empire shattered, troops of the new republic of Czechoslovakia seized Cieszyn with its large population of ethnic minorities and re-named it Teschen. But before Hitler could act against the territory the Polish government embarrassed itself by claiming Teschen on the spurious grounds that the Polish minority needed its protection. When the Czech government challenged the Poles' assertion Colonel Jozef Beck, also the foreign minister, led a contingent of Polish troops into Teschen in mid-October and occupied a portion of it. The Czechs responded by sending in their own forces. After several weeks of fighting in January 1919 a compromise was agreed. Beck's actions were condemned by governments usually well-disposed towards Poland as well as by segments of the nation itself. His belligerent behaviour left a residue of resentment between the Czechs and Poles that was resolved only by the necessity for cooperation against the Germans.**

Horko's sighting of Christine in Teschen remains unexplained and served only to stoke the rumour mill. This heavily industrialised area had no tourist attractions (though there was a ski resort in the nearby mountains) and she had no known relatives living in Teschen. There is only Horko's word that she had been present, attracted perhaps by the possibility of an armed clash between Czech and Polish forces. If she wrote anything for publication about Teschen, or any other subject, her bylines have yet to be discovered in any archive.

Infrequent appearances by Christine such as this only served to generate rumours that lingered long after her death, whispers that she had been working either as a spy or as a journalist for as much as four years before the German invasion of Poland. She told Patrick Howarth, her SOE section chief in Cairo, that she'd once been a reporter in Paris but was noticeably chary about the details. When asked about his source Howarth replied that Christine had volunteered the information without further explanation. He was inclined to think that she was 'romancing a bit.' ***

Christine also told Lady Deakin that she had lived in Paris but omitted any mention of past experience as a journalist. Her aunt, Helena Zaranska, a member of the Polish diplomatic corps, lived there and it's reasonable to assume that her niece may have enjoyed lengthy visits. But there is no proof that Christine was ever employed as a reporter in the French capital or elsewhere. She made no secret of her dislike for the boredom of office routine and readily admitted to her inability to type, rendering her claim to be a journalist all the more dubious.

Christine's vague allusions to employment as a reporter were part of a pattern in which she gave only the slightest glimpse into her personal life, an ideal background for someone who was to become deeply involved in the murky world of British espionage. In her wartime role as an intelligence operative she cultivated an aura of mystery that gave rise to a rash of stories about her which she would neither confirm nor deny. At times it seemed that she enjoyed the admiration and curiosity that later came her way.

With the crisis in Teschen resolved, unhappily for the Czechs, Christine returned to Poland where she married Jerzy Gizycki, author and diplomat. They had apparently been

---

**Efforts to resolve ownership of this strategic rail centre in 1920 reached ludicrous heights when a white line was painted through the center of the city, leaving the rail station on the Czech side and the Market Square on the Polish side. See Norman Davies' *God's Playground, a history of Poland. vol II 1795 to the Present.*

introduced before Teschen by the literary critic Tadeusz Breza who had reviewed Gizycki's book *The Whites and the Blacks*.2 There is a more exciting but apocryphal version of how the two met which is that while careering down a slope outside Zakopane she lost control of her skis. Gizycki somehow managed to save her from a sure collision with another person or stationary object. This version, more colourful than mere hand-kissing at a party, has been generally accepted without question for it was known that Christine was not a graceful skier. On the slopes as well as on horseback she displayed a quality of recklessness, a determination to reach the finish line regardless of the consequences. It was this same quality of impatience that disqualified her from becoming a spy in the conventional sense of the word. She was not the sort who could lie doggo for weeks or months behind enemy lines, not nearly as smooth or deceptive as a Kim Philby. She always insisted on being in the thick of the action and her missions into enemy territory were the sort that required action and movement, not patience.

Christine was nearly thirty years old and still single when she was introduced to Gizycki who was of an entirely different species from the frivolous young men she had known to date. He was to play a pivotal in her life for it was his insatiable desire for travel and adventure that provided her the opportunity to break free from a heretofore aimless existence in Poland. Much of what is known about Gizycki is contained in his unpublished memoir *The Winding Trail*.2 He wrote that he'd been born into the eastern European landed gentry, a family of small estate owners in what was then Bessarabia (now sub-

***Interview with Howarth at his Sherbourne home in December 2002.

sumed by the Ukraine and Moldova) and later moved to Russian-controlled Warsaw while still a boy. He left school at an early age and travelled through Europe and America, supporting himself by taking on odd jobs, including stints as a cowboy, a miner and a Hollywood film extra. After the first world war he joined the Polish diplomatic service and was posted to Africa, returning to Warsaw to become part of the entourage that accompanied the Polish team to the Paris Olympics of 1924, portrayed in the film 'Chariots of Fire.'

Physically, Gizycki was well-suited for a life of adventure. He was a stocky, muscular man with a deep reserve of energy. Those who met him inevitably commented on the startling effect given off by his grey eyes which revealed little emotion. He was also known to have a short fuse and his SOE colleagues were well aware of his tendency to explode over what were sometimes minor issues. Like his new companion he'd also lied about his age when he applied to join Section D. His physical strength however belied an internal weakness, for he suffered recurring bouts of malaria, a souvenir of his African adventures. During periods of recuperation he considered taking up the more sedentary career of a writer. By retiring to Zakopane he combined his need for rest with his desire to write.

In this same memoir he glides over the circumstances of his first encounter with his future wife. He would only say that Christine became his 'constant companion.' His sole concession to emotion was to admit to a high regard for his new friend who was, 'an excellent horsewoman, fair skier, and the most intrepid human I have ever met - man or woman.' He was widely read, spoke several languages and had just published his first book when he met Christine. She was immediately impressed by his depth of knowledge which he was more than happy to share with her. They soon became regular guests at Zakopane's literary salons where they mingled with other writers, artists and their wealthy hosts.

Through his intermittent service with the Polish diplomatic corps Gizycki had become acquainted with a number of ministers and civil servants. Foremost among them was General Wladyslaw Sikorski, the future prime minister. He became an occasional visitor to the Sikorski household in Warsaw, played tennis with the general and taught his young daughter Zosia to ride. (Sikorski and Zosia, his only child, perished in an unexplained plane crash off Gibraltar in 1943. In the blizzard of conspiracy theories that followed Christine's name was mentioned though she was never implicated in any plot.)

Gizycki's friendships with such men of status gave him entry to the drawing rooms of Warsaw where Christine's reputation for fast living sometimes preceded her. Their courtship was brief, and for Christine, must have been exciting. Despite their age difference, some nineteen years, she and Gizycki were immediately attracted to one another. Each possessed a restlessness, a hunger for new experiences that kept them on the move. She must have suspected with good reason (it may have been explicit) that with him she would not be expected to settle into a life of domesticity.

The autumn of 1938 was a memorable time for Europe, for Poland and for Christine. The most significant and shocking event took place in Germany where Nazi thugs went on a bloody rampage against the Jews in what has become known as the infamous *Kristallnacht*. In October with the *debacle* at Teschen settled, Jozef Lipski, the Polish ambassador to Germany, was summoned to a meeting with Joachim von Ribbentrop, Hitler's foreign minister. Lipski was presented with a list of demands, foremost of which was the 'return' of the city and port of Danzig (Gdansk) to German control. Poland refused to accede to the demands and the stage was set for the German invasion of 1939.

Unperturbed by these events or by rumours of war, Christine married Gizycki in Warsaw's Evangelical Reform Church on Aleje Nalewki (now part of Solidarity avenue). The ceremony took place just a few streets away from the Bristol Hotel where she and her first husband had celebrated their own marriage. The church was destroyed during the second world war and never rebuilt. The Bristol had better luck though it took several decades to fully rehabilitate it.

Between them Christine and her new husband had enough money so that settling down to enjoy domestic bliss was neither a priority nor a desire. After a leisurely honeymoon in Zakopane they spent the early weeks of 1939 traveling, playing tennis and skiing in Switzerland where Gizycki broke his collarbone. The damage was repaired at a clinic in Geneva but he re-injured the broken bone and had it re-set by a surgeon in Paris who fitted him with a plaster cast.

Christine's relationship with the diplomat Gizycki gives rise to the conundrum, who recruited whom. He obviously would have had connections with certain government departments and she had already aroused whispers about a connection to SIS. If both she and Gizycki were entirely innocent then how to explain their meeting in Geneva with Stefan Witkowski, an engineer, inventor and soon-to-be resistance leader? This meeting is mentioned within the context of a lengthy intelligence report discovered in a little-known Polish archive in London. (A note in another Polish document reveals that Gizycki and Witkowski had met once before, in Paris.) That second report provides no explanation of how the three had come to meet or why but in view of subsequent events it would be reasonable to assume that their conversation strayed beyond inventions. In the autumn of 1939, only weeks after the German invasion of Poland, Witkowski turned up in Warsaw as leader of a renegade intelligence cell known as the Musketeers (*Muszkieterze*). This revelation undermines the innocent claim that when Christine slipped into Warsaw in early 1940 'friends' introduced her to him for the first time.

There are other clues as to how she spent those last pre-war years but nothing that confirms the date of her introduction to SIS. A summary of her initial interview with Section D in December 1939 reveals a more mature woman insofar as she appeared to be seriously concerned about the dangers facing her country. Her aroused sense of patriotism and desire to join the fight to liberate Poland may have been stimulated by the well-travelled Gizycki whose interest in international politics was much more developed than hers.

Their honeymoon at an end, the couple were preparing to return to Poland when Gizycki received a call from the foreign office summoning him back into service. He was asked to open and maintain a consulate in Addis Ababa that would also serve Polish interests in Uganda, Tanganyika, Nyasaland and Zanzibar. The government made it clear that, like the Germans and the Italians, they too wished to have overseas colonies. The administration of President Moscicki was beginning to flex its martial muscles in a bad imitation of its belligerent neighbour. Less explicitly they wished to observe at first-hand how the Italians had organised their newly acquired possession, Abyssinia (Ethiopia).

The Polish government, incidentally, were not as naive as is often depicted about the seriousness of their situation in the run-up to the German invasion. Their economy was doing moderately well, underpinned by high expenditures on the manufacture of arms and military hardware. The Fiat corporation, Christine's erstwhile employer, played a dual role in giving the economy a boost. Prior to 1932 Fiat cars were seldom seen in Poland. While the company had been licensed to provide family cars - and it did - the government had concluded a covert agreement with Fiat to produce a line of military vehicles.

Though Gizycki disliked desk jobs and the routine of consular life, he could not ignore the prestige of government office plus the opportunity for more travel. He was assured that in Africa he would have ample time to pursue his favorite pastimes, hunting and shooting. Traveling under the auspices of the government (and at its expense), he could also provide his bride with an extended exotic honeymoon. The couple sailed first to England where they remained for an unspecified but longer than expected time while 'the usual formalities' were taken care of. Gizycki, in his sometimes cryptic manner, did not elaborate on what those formalities were but he managed to create the impression that he had been asked to take on an intelligence-gathering assignment for the Polish government. If he had, nothing much seemed to come of it. They then traveled to Southampton where they booked passage on a ship taking them to South Africa.

There are two versions of what happened on the next and final leg of their journey. Gizycki's account of their African sojourn omits any description of time spent in Addis Ababa. There are no reports on what his consular duties were, who he met, what official business he might have transacted. In fact Gizycki maintained that he and Christine disembarked in Capetown, a long way from their official destination. Driving a station wagon they had brought along, they spent much of their time touring South Africa and arrived in Jo'burg in time to hear the devastating news of the German invasion of Poland.

The second published version, source unknown but probably Andrew Kennedy, describes the couple arriving in Mombassa, an exotic port city then, swarming with all manner of traders and merchants as well as an exciting mix of people of all colours and faiths. Kenya was also home at the time to a group of well-to-do British ex-pats, the Happy Valley set, notorious for its consumption of alcohol and casual sex. After a stay of indeterminate length the Gizyckis travelled by rail to Nairobi and set up housekeeping, if it can be called that, at the Salisbury Hotel. Neither Christine nor her husband remarked on the details of their daily life but it can be safely assumed that she remained at the hotel or indulged herself sun-bathing, one of her favorite pastimes, while he attended to his diplomatic duties.

The most likely explanation for this lack of detail, or for the perhaps misleading version of their travels, is that Gizycki was writing his memoir at a time when British authorities were wielding their Official Secrets Act with a vengeance, and while many of his former British and Polish colleagues were still alive who might challenge his version of events. It cannot be because he had access to state secrets for he never rose that high within the ranks of SIS.

Regardless of where the Gizyckis were when the news of the German invasion of Poland on September the 1st reached them, they instinctively made plans to leave Africa as soon as possible. Each had family in Poland and their thoughts must have been for their safety as well as for what was happening to their country. Over time their worst fears were to be tragically realised.

Chapter 3.
'Notes on Madame G'

Travel to Poland in those early hectic days of the war was out of the question for the Gizyckis. Given the uncertainty of life in Europe, England seemed to be the best destination, a safe distance from the fighting yet close enough to the continent to access information from home. They left Africa as soon as they could secure passage on a ship bound for Southampton, arriving on October 6th aboard the *Capetown Castle*. Under the category Alien Passengers they registered as Gizycki, Jerzy [George], age 50, profession: Polish consul. Gizycka, Krystyna, age 30, a second reference to 1909 as her birth year, occupation: housewife, a designation she must have found amusing for she was anything but. Upon arriving in London they contacted the Polish Consulate-General who found them temporary accommodation. Separately they each sought ways to enlist in the fight to drive the enemy out of Poland. But the onset of war also marked the beginning of the end of their brief marriage.

Christine and her husband arrived in a city preparing for an invasion that never came. There was a tangible air of anxiety in London but no widespread panic. Shopkeepers and home-owners had quietly set about taping their windows as a precaution against bomb blasts. Refugees had begun arriving from the continent, disembarking at rail terminals crowded with men in uniform and parents who had already begun the discomfiting process of evacuating young children to the countryside.

He was still a Polish diplomat despite having abruptly resigned his post in Africa and had no difficulty in obtaining a position at the consulate. While Gizycki reported to his office each day Christine was left adrift in a city where she knew few people, marooned in a country whose language she had not yet mastered. But if the hints dropped by her and by Gizycki can be relied upon there was at least one person in London she'd met before, a man who was to become the key figure in recruiting her to Section D. That was FA Voigt, called Freddy by friends, former diplomatic correspondent for the *Manchester Guardian*. It has been generally accepted that she had been brought into Section D by Robert Vansittart, chief deputy to the Foreign Office. But it is unlikely that a minister of his status would do any more than conduct an interview or give approval to employ someone afterwards.

 Until now no one has been able to piece together the process by which Christine had been recruited by the British, because after the war successive administrations had thrown a cloak of secrecy over the remaining SOE files. Those documents were to have been destroyed, virtually eliminating any written record of the Executive's existence.[1] Despite a directive from Winston Churchill in 1945 ordering the destruction of the entire archive a significant number of files survived because of the haphazard manner in which civil servants carried out that order.* (This process was never completed and SOE was formally wrapped up in early 1946). The secret papers, copies of letters and telegrams, intelligence reports that survived, are considerable in number despite the attempt to dispose of them. These, plus the memoirs of former SOE operatives, have provided a road

---

*A former SOE officer wrote that he observed a group of clerks sitting in SOE's offices after the war, playing a makeshift game of basketball by crumpling documents into paper balls and hurling them into a waste paper basket placed in the center of the floor.

map of sorts by which the process of Christine's introduction to Section D (later SOE) can be traced. They leave no doubt that Voigt was most influential in recruiting her.

In a post-war interview with a Polish newspaper, Christine's niece Teresa Szulczewska revealed that Florian Sokolov, correspondent for the Polish news agency PAP, had introduced her to Voigt. Unfortunately Szulczewska didn't mention the date and place of that initial meeting during her interview. Though Voigt spent most of his working days in Berlin he managed several trips to Poland. Afterwards he wrote scathing accounts of how the Pilsudski government were mis-treating Ukrainian rebels who were attempting to wrest the western Ukraine from Poland's grip. If he and Christine met on one of his visits neither of them recorded it for posterity. But there can be no other explanation of how she managed to contact him once she and Gizycki arrived in London five years later.

A detailed account of how Christine came to the attention of Section D involves a cast of characters gathered together by Voigt who had been a covert SIS operative for several years. His only daughter however maintains that there is nothing in the personal papers he bequeathed her to indicate his involvement with SIS. Documents in TNA tell a different story. By the time Christine arrived in London Voigt had resigned from the *Manchester Guardian* and was writing propaganda tracts for the government. He was a proponent of what was known as 'white' propaganda, that is, material produced at home with a positive one-sided view. In contrast, 'black' propaganda was designed to appear as if it had been produced in occupied territory, planting in the minds of the enemy the fear that there was a resistance movement in their midst.

Christine's Personal File contains, among other documents, a memorandum dated

December 1939 titled 'Notes on Madame G [Gizycka]', written by a Section D operative known only as Fryday who conducted that initial interview. These surviving notes had been sent for review to a Section officer, George Taylor,** formerly an Australian textile executive with extensive corporate experience in Europe. He was described by one colleague as 'always belligerent, persistent and ingenious.' Taylor had been recruited into Section D in 1939 with the rank of captain. He was the first of many business executives to be employed by the British and was instrumental in attracting other talented civilians to the Section.

Fryday described Christine in this often-repeated quote as '. . . a very smart looking girl, simply dressed and aristocratic. She is a flaming Polish patriot. She made an excellent impression and I really believe we have a PRIZE.' Fryday seems to have accepted without comment Christine's unsolicited claim about her relationship with Freddy Voigt. More importantly Fryday noted that it was Voigt who introduced the new recruit to Vansittart (later knighted) and to another anonymous operative known only as Colonel Williams. The name is a cryptonym and the officer's true identity has yet to be revealed.

A name not mentioned in Christine's round of interviews was that of Selwyn Jepson, novelist and short-story writer. He had been recruited by SIS in the 1930s, valued for his expertise in personality assessment. When meeting potential agents Jepson never revealed his real name but employed pseudonyms and liked to call himself Mr Potter. The interviews usually took place in a sparsely furnished office in a Northumberland Avenue hotel. Jepson claimed to have interviewed a number of female agents including Christine.

**Taylor's personal file was one of those destroyed at the end of the war, thus limiting what is actually known about his intelligence activities.

Near the end of the report Fryday appears to have accepted, also without comment, Christine's surprising claim that she 'is able to get regular reports from the interior of Austria and from Poland. The former will come through Slovenes who have lived for years in Vienna. The latter will be smuggled out by *my people* [my italics].'[2] These statements, coming from Christine herself along with Gizycki's comment that she'd been in London in 1934, seem to resolve the question of her pre-war status, that is to say, whether she actually had been a British operative at that early stage of affairs. That being said, the casual manner in which this information was presented to Fryday begs the question, was she exaggerating or was she telling the truth?

It seems extraordinary that George Taylor apparently took no interest in this revelation, for nowhere in SOE files is there any comment from him or from any other official on Christine's alleged pre-war covert activity. Given that virtually everyone in government expected war to explode imminently, Section D and SIS should have been excited at the prospect of having on board someone with an intelligence-gathering cell at work in Poland and informants in the midst of the Nazis in Austria.

Christine has been described by more than one person as a fantasist but the notion that she concocted a tale in which a group of Poles and Slovenes were acting as her operatives is stretching things a bit, even for her. If true it would mean that after her divorce from Getlich she had suddenly become aware of Poland's precarious situation *vis a vis* Germany and had decided to do her part for *Ojczyzna,* her homeland. There is also the real possibility that Section D, in its haste to recruit staff, allowed her to blag her way into its service, adding her name to a roster that already included Kim Philby, the notorious Third

Man, and Guy Burgess, two of the four Cambridge traitors. This revelation describes a woman more mature and more earnest than the carefree girl who once smuggled cigarettes across the Slovak border.

Because of the loss of Taylor's Personal File (PF) we cannot know for certain how he reacted to this news but signals sent to his operative in Budapest, even after he had agreed to employ Christine, reveal an obvious skepticism about her claims. How and who might have recruited her may never be precisely known but this is the most documented information uncovered so far. What is certain, coincidentally, is that Voigt was still at his post of diplomatic correspondent in central Europe during those years which are unaccounted for in Christine's chronology.

In her desire to become involved in the war effort Christine either told a rather audacious story to Fryday or else she was telling the truth. Her self-assured responses during interviews with Section officials were nevertheless enough to convince them to employ her. This is the first in a number of instances in which she used her remarkable powers of persuasion to bend someone, whether intelligence agents or even a Gestapo officer, to her will. Among the opinions that Christine apparently offered Fryday included the statement that 'sabotage [in Poland] is absolutely essential as it is necessary to intimidate the Germans who are great bullies but not brave when attacked singly.' She also voiced her concern at the spread of bolshevism. Having grown up in the shadow of the Russian bear she had good reason to be apprehensive.

As if to enhance the new recruit's qualifications Fryday mentioned her madcap fling with tobacco smugglers along the Polish-Slovak border, and added that she 'knows every man in the place [Zakopane]. She is confident that these men will help her now. She is absolutely fearless herself and certainly makes that impression.' Fryday closed the report by urging Taylor to meet with Christine, still known as Krystyna, but inserted the caution that he should use an assumed name indicating that Fryday hadn't been completely taken in by the new applicant. How she came to know so many men in Zakopane was not explained.

Christine's claim to have contacts in Vienna is of particular interest in light of the fact that some in Voigt's close-knit circle had been SIS operatives in the Austrian capital as he himself had been, if only briefly. He was one of the more interesting characters among her friends in what was a brief and platonic relationship. Frederick Augustus Voigt served with SIS for only a short time and by the end of 1940 had retired from active service to devote his time to writing political tomes. He was born of German parents living in Hampstead (Voigt was his mother's family name) and was educated at schools in London. After serving in the British Army (Royal Garrison Artillery) during the first world war he became a journalist. Not long afterwards he was posted to the Berlin of the Weimar Republic and was one of the first reporters to become openly critical of the Nazis. This had its inevitable repercussions, a flurry of death threats which caused him to hurriedly leave Berlin for Paris in 1933.

When the threats continued Voigt returned to London and in 1938 joined a newly created department of the Foreign Office known as Electra House, named after the government building in Whitehall that housed its offices. It had only one function and that was to produce propaganda and counter-propaganda, a remit that gave it a certain amount of authority over even the BBC. The efforts of EH, however well-intentioned, duplicated work being carried out by Section D. Conflict between the two departments was averted when EH was folded into the larger section in 1940. That union was in turn swallowed up by Special Operations Executive which became operative in July.

Christine's own connection to Vienna, in the form of her Slovene cell and her possible earlier meeting with Voigt, strongly suggest that when she arrived in London they were already known to one another, hence the ease with which she was taken on by Section D. It has been assumed in virtually everything ever published about Christine that she met first either George Taylor or Vansittart. Whoever was responsible for this version of events did not explain how she had come to meet one man or the other in the first place. But Voigt, in his role as diplomatic correspondent, had developed a string of contacts among highly placed politicians one of whom was Vansittart. That is the more plausible explanation of how Christine became acquainted with those two officials.

Voigt had returned to London from Vienna just a few years before Christine and her husband arrived after their voyage from Capetown. He'd been working as a journalist since the late 1920s before being recruited by Claude Dansey, the controversial deputy directory of SIS (also known as MI6). Shortly before war broke out Dansey, as much a renegade as Christine, had established a network of covert operatives across central Europe which he named the Z-Network. There was to be one operative in each capital city known by the initial Z followed by their location. Voigt's cryptonym was Z-Vienna. Others were known as Z-Budapest and Z-Bucharest, among the several cities represented. Dansey himself took the title Z-1. [3]

Impressed with Christine's patriotic fervour Voigt arranged for her to meet Vansittart at the home of an English woman who operated on the periphery of the intelligence community, one Evelyn Stamper (later Mrs Lefeuvre). She had been employed for several years at the British Passport Control Office in Vienna, also the official cover for the SIS station. Passport Control Offices (PCO) throughout Europe had doubled as British intelligence-gathering centers ever since their inception. The Nazis eventually became aware of their dual nature and, one by one, pressured the host governments to shut them down. The Vienna office was the first to go and by the early 1940s most of the PCOs in Europe had been shuttered.

Evelyn Stamper was among those who returned to London where SIS assigned her to its German-Austrian sub-section. To provide her with cover they created the Austria Club in Ebury Street, installed her as its president and deposited £300 in a South Kensington bank in the club's name but for Stamper's use. She and her colleague Marguerite Holmes were ostensibly to provide a rallying center for exiled anti-Nazi Austrians in England but the two women also kept an eye out for potential recruits to Section D.

Once a cease-fire had been agreed between the Polish and German forces, the British government found itself without an intelligence source in Poland. Section D then began the search for a recruit to covertly enter the country and assess the situation. This mission required a Polish speaker who knew the country well. Voigt thought he had such a candidate in Christine and a meeting was convened to introduce her to Section D's top officials. It has been said that she volunteered for the assignment but the Section's archives, and her relationship with Voigt, indicate that she had been recruited and quite readily too.

Christine went along to Stamper's flat one chilly day in December for her initial interview. Voigt arrived shortly afterwards in the company of Vansittart and at some point George Taylor joined them. More than a year later Christine wrote a report on her work to date that began with a description of that meeting. When a copy of this document was first shown to me the names of the other persons present had been scissored out by government officials except for Taylor's who is identified only as T. It was only after her PF was opened to researchers that the names of the other officials present were revealed. What Christine brought to the table was a deeply felt desire, almost a desperation, to strike a blow for Poland. Her enthusiasm convinced the Section's leadership that she had just had to be brought on board. It seems that her apparent sincerity and her persuasiveness made more of an impression than did her claim to an affiliation with freelance operatives in Europe.

Vansittart reportedly was impressed by this attractive Polish woman and by her heartfelt desire to do something for her beleaguered country. But she had more hoops to jump through before signing on with Section D. A note in SOE files addressed to Taylor and signed only with the initial F, describes a telephone conversation between Christine and the anonymous F, written after that first gathering. The author of the note must have been Freddy Voigt who occasionally signed his letters with that epistolary flourish. The content concerns information only he could have had. He reported that Christine's visas were in order and that 'she is anxious to leave 'le plutot possible,' apparently quoting her as she preferred speaking French since she had yet to become fluent in English.

She had asked to speak to F alone, 'probably about something she wants me to do for her through you.' The proposed subject of their meeting was the disposition of her salary cheques, confirmed in a Section D document. F closed the letter by saying that she would be delighted at the prospect of seeing Taylor again. Thus Voigt presented Christine with an opportunity to join the battle. But her decision to cast her lot with the British, however well-meaning, put her into immediate conflict with the Polish government in London and with its intelligence services.

Though Fryday's identity remains a mystery there was someone else who lent at least logistical support to the effort to recruit Christine. The discovery of this woman's identity was quite accidental. Voigt's note to Taylor had been written on letterhead stationery bearing the address but not the name of a Mrs Forbes Dennis. The introduction of her name into the drama describes the intricate net which SIS had spun to draw civilians into its intelligence-gathering apparatus.[4]

Mrs Forbes Dennis was perhaps better known as Phyllis Bottome, a minor novelist once described by an Oxford academic as 'a masculine type, half-American.' Her husband, Captain AE Forbes Dennis, had served in the British Army (7/8 KOSB) during the first world war and had been grievously wounded. After the war, fully recovered from his wounds, he joined SIS and in 1927 he too was employed at the Vienna PCO. During the early 1930s he and his wife established a kind of finishing school in Kitzbuehl for young men destined for employment in the upper echelons of government. One of their pupils was the young Ian Fleming, sent to Kitzbuehl by his mother who despaired for his future, and with whom Christine was romantically linked after the war. Mrs Forbes Dennis was prolific but not entirely successful though she did publish a number of novels and books of nonfiction. She also contributed articles to local newspapers and to church bulletins. Shortly after the Germans had crossed the Polish border she wrote to Vansittart, offering her assistance towards the war effort. Vansittart was in a peculiar position for he advocated a non-interventionist policy in Europe as Britain's official stance though he was in opposition to the Hitler government.

Besides lending her house in Lexham Gardens, Kensington, to friends doing 'important war work,' Mrs Forbes Dennis offered to return occasionally to the United States to gauge the level of support the British could expect from the Americans. She and Vansittart then embarked upon a lengthy correspondence and by war's end she was addressing him as 'Dear Van.' Stamper's name also crops up in the Forbes Dennis papers. Prior to setting up the Austria Club she and her husband, called Sergeant Bill, had been part of the Forbes Dennis social circle and had even taken rooms at her home. It seems that this apparently innocent cluster of friends were not simply meeting for tea and biscuits but were actually hard at work recruiting staff for Section D and writing propaganda tracts for the government. Ironically, Christine would one day meet her gruesome fate just a few doors away in this same pleasant Lexham Gardens. But in the autumn of 1939 it provided a safe gathering place for Voigt and his secretive little group.

After two meetings with Christine, George Taylor was suitably impressed with her and a working arrangement with Section D was agreed upon. Preparations for her departure for Budapest were now set in motion. Referring to her formally as 'Madame Gizycka', Taylor wrote to Vansittart restating the terms of her employment: a period of six months for which she would be paid £250. Voigt arranged her cover story, describing her as a travel writer doing research for articles on Hungary. He was also assigned the role of paymaster.

Because her assignment was defined only in general terms Christine received no training. She was not taught to use weapons or explosives and it was only much later that she trained as a wireless operator. Nevertheless, she seemed a perfect fit for a Section which had a large intake of civilians in its recruitment, many of whom had either a special knowledge of Europe or its languages and sometimes both.

The parameters of Christine's mission were finalised in December 1939. After their last meeting Taylor wrote to Lieutenant Colonel Lawrence Grand, Royal Engineers, known by the cryptonym 'D' as well as being head of Section D. He reiterated the authority which Grand had given him on December 16, authorising him to employ Christine. Grand thought it a good idea and incidentally, found himself attracted to her. They had been introduced by Robert Vansittart and Grand, like most men who knew Christine, found her quite charming. But he never pursued her and nothing came of his infatuation.

Christine's close relationship with Voigt is also borne out by her written request to her supervising officer just prior to her departure for Hungary. She asked that her monthly salary of £41, 13 shillings and six pence be paid into the account of 'F.A. Voigt, Westminster Bank, Willesden Green Branch.' The instructions regarding the disposition of her salary added the caution that '. . . no mention whatever should be made of Madame Gizycka.' This caveat was no doubt included to prevent the disclosure of her true identity. No explanation was offered as to why her husband was not to be entrusted with her salary cheques.

Gizycki was presumably cut out of the picture for reasons of security. But this arrangement proved to be an accurate reflection of the state of their brief union. According to SOE colleagues she realised while still in Africa that their romantic relationship had run its course. Her cavalier treatment of him, and other lovers, amply demonstrates that she could be terribly cold-blooded when it came to terminating an affair.

Voigt probably knew more about Christine's relationship with her husband than anyone else for when Gizycki himself was posted to France, Voigt became his controller too. Christine had actually introduced him to her husband who patronizingly described Voigt as 'simple in his ways . . . tall, with a round head completely bald at the top, and the rosy cheeks of a young boy.'[5] Gizycki was more flattering when it came to Voigt's writing, for in addition to his role as diplomatic correspondent for the *Manchester Guardian* he also edited a series of political monographs titled *The Nineteenth Century and After*. Gizycki called this series the 'best English political magazine.'

Patrick Howarth recalled that Christine admired Voigt though there was no implication that her feelings for him resulted in an affair. Howarth also confessed to having been very fond of her too but protested in one of the last interviews he gave that nothing unseemly had occurred between them.**** A fellow officer's comments about Howarth's undisguised affection for Christine is underlined in an SOE document, implying that he often spoke of her without hesitation. But in April 1944 Howarth met another Polish woman, Clara Potocka, who replaced Christine in his affections. Major Henry Threlfall wrote, 'All his [Howarth] sentences, instead of beginning with the word "Christine" as formerly, now start with "Countess Potocka" ' whom he married after the war. It was to be a stormy marriage and ended in divorce.

While his wife was being interviewed by Section D officials Gizycki was hard at work

****Interview with Howarth at his home in Sherbourne in 2003 with Diana Hall.

at the Polish consulate. He had hoped, perhaps naively, to join the Polish army regrouping in France under the leadership of General Sikorski. His request was rejected however because of his age and chronic phlebitis. He complained bitterly in his memoir, 'that leg didn't keep me from skiing, mountain climbing and covering several hundred miles on foot across African colonies.' He had to settle instead for the colourless job of labour mediator.

The Section D files reveal that in the days prior to Christine's departure for Hungary, Taylor began to have doubts about her suitability for the role of British operative. Accustomed to making executive decisions in civilian life, he found himself questioning his decision to send a novice spy into a potentially dangerous situation with little preparation. Though Hungary was straining to maintain some semblance of neutrality it was known in certain quarters that the Gestapo had infiltrated the Hungarian Ministry of the Interior. There was a personal danger for Christine too. In 1935, in a maneuver patently designed to placate Hitler and ease German pressure on Admiral Horthy to form an alliance, the Hungarian government passed into law its own version of the despicable Nuremberg Laws, an overt threat to its Jewish population.

The state of Taylor's indecision is obvious in the flurry of telegrams he sent to his man in Budapest, Hubert Harrison. On December 20 he sent Harrison a wire in which he stressed the need for pro-British propaganda to be smuggled into Poland. The text would be prepared and printed in London but it would be up to Harrison to see to it that the leaflets were effectively distributed. But Taylor and Fryday were at odds over what Christine's priorities should be once she had established herself in Budapest. Fryday had reported that 'her [Christine] idea is to bring out a propaganda leaflet in Buda and to smuggle it over the frontier herself.'⁶ However, Taylor's message to Harrison includes the suggestion that this [distribution] perhaps could be done by 'the Poles with whom you are already in touch.' The reference could not have been to Christine for they had yet to meet.

In that first signal to Harrison, Taylor added almost as after-thought, that the Section had decided to 'subsidize' a certain Madame Gizycka 'who has special facilities for working into [sic] Poland,' and that in future she would be referred to in all correspondence as Madame Marchand, a name selected by Voigt. Taylor instructed her to contact an operative in Budapest using the cryptonym AH1. This was the Polish journalist Jozef Radzyminski+ with whom 'she [Christine] has worked previously.' Taylor did not say exactly where or when the two had worked together but the employment of yet another journalist underlines how heavily the Section depended upon them. In this case however her relationship with Radzyminski was to have disastrous effects.

It was Fryday who had alerted Taylor to Radzyminski's presence in Budapest and to the fact that he had met Christine in Warsaw. Fryday wrote: 'The young man R is a distant connection. I understand he will do anything for her or with her.' What is apparent in hindsight is that Radzyminski had fallen in love with Christine before the war while both were still living in Poland. Christine thought she had made it clear then that she could not, would not share his passion. Fryday knew of Radzyminski's presence only from a distance

---

+This is almost certainly Jozef Radzyminski, journalist and foreign correspondent for Polish newspapers whose name has been misspelled in SOE files. He has an entry in the *Dictionary of Polish Journalists (1661-1945)* whereas Christine's name in any of its forms is absent from this compilation, despite hints of a journalistic career.

and could not have known that he would become seriously unhinged over his unrequited love for Christine.

Taylor's signal to Harrison also makes it crystal clear that she was not to be trusted with the job of smuggling *agitprop* into Poland. Perhaps he felt that given her lack of experience in these matters she might give the game away if she fell into enemy hands. Instead, she was to quietly slip into the country, make contact with resistance cells and map out a route by which the propaganda materials would be delivered to them. Once this plan had been agreed upon the leaflets would be sent from London to Budapest, probably by diplomatic pouch, after which distribution would become Harrison's responsibility.

In re-telling this episode years later Andrew Kennedy added to the confusion by claiming that Christine offered to produce pro-British propaganda and smuggle it into Poland herself. Her account however remains the only version of who offered to-do-what and it differs slightly from Andrew's second-hand account. She had actually proposed broadcasting morale-boosting messages to the Poles but had said nothing about producing and distributing written material.

In what was a near-fatal decision Taylor had cautioned Christine against making direct contact with Hubert Harrison or any member of his organisation but to use Radzyminski as their go-between. He was as unaware of the journalist's state of mind as Fryday had been. Taylor's detailed instructions to Harrison included the suggestion that while in Poland, Christine might acquire information that could be of use to the British such as the locations and numbers of German forces. Though Taylor had recommended Christine for this mission he also appears to have been ambivalent about her chances for success.

He reminded Harrison that their new recruit was on a six-months' trial after which Harrison would be asked to assess 'her usefulness' to Section D, and whether he wished to continue working with her. However, in the very next sentence Taylor expressed the fear that she might not be of use after all and asked Harrison for suggestions on how Christine might be best employed. Section D were anxious for her to play a part in their efforts to stir unrest in Poland but on the eve of her departure Taylor in particular was still unsure of what her role would be and if she was actually cut out to be a Section D operative.

As it turned out Christine far exceeded Taylor's and the Section's expectations. She returned to Budapest with a lengthy and detailed report of the locations and movements of German troops, a report that justified their original decision to trust her with such an important mission. Of equal value perhaps, she provided the first significant link between Polish resistance and MI6 by establishing a regular and relatively safe courier service, operating between Warsaw, Krakow and Budapest. Christine received no recognition for these achievements. Nor did the Musketeers who are seldom mentioned in SOE's archive.

After all the confusion and double-talk over who would do what with the propaganda leaflets, Harrison reluctantly had to entrust Christine with the distribution of his subversive messages, having been rebuffed by the Polish group with whom he'd been working. This comes as no surprise for even in their desperate situation the Poles in Budapest were divided, argumentative and suspicious of one another. Christine's decision to work with the British rather than with Polish intelligence or these splinter groups resulted in a permanently frosty relationship with the Poles' London government and their two intelligence bureaux, the *Deuxieme Bureau* and the *Seizieme Bureau* (the 2nd Bureau and the

6th Bureau). This barely disguised, and mutual, hostility lasted the duration of the war.

By mid-December all formalities necessary for Christine's mission had been completed. She left London on December 22nd bound for Budapest via Paris and Italy. Her husband described their parting thus: 'I put Krystyna on the bus taking her to the airport [at Croydon] and saw, through the window, how she was trying to hide the tears running down her cheeks.'[7]

The Gizyckis' marriage had lasted for just a year before their individual assignments forced them apart. Though they were not divorced until 1946 they lived separate lives during the war and met only twice in those six tumultuous years. The war had unexpectedly provided Christine with the perfect opportunity to detach herself from her faithful husband whom she had once described as her Svengali.

Within SOE files there are comments by officers who knew both husband and wife, describing their marriage as having been in trouble from the beginning. That being said, it's unlikely that someone as independent as Christine could have ever had a successful marriage. She moved about almost as she pleased, undomesticated and nomadic, with few life-long attachments and few possessions. One can only speculate about the effect her parents' passion-less union had had upon her. She eschewed convention, preferring instead what she perhaps imagined to be a romantic, peripatetic way of life, unencumbered by domestic responsibilities, a lifestyle more often associated with dashing men who roamed the world performing heroic deeds in fiction if not in reality.

Part II. 1940
Chapter 4. An Obstreperous Pupil

Budapest, in late January 1940, experienced its coldest winter in sixty years. Temperatures had plunged to a record low of thirty-three degrees centigrade and the waters of the Danube remained frozen for days at a time. In such conditions few people were outdoors to observe the rather tall brunette as she moved into her flat in the old town of Buda on Dereck street.

In appearance the dark-eyed Christine could easily pass for Hungarian though her neighbours were unaware that she spoke not a word of their language. Her cover of travel writer suited Christine perfectly because she had long held pretensions to being a journalist as she had once claimed to her superior officers. Her command of English was also lacking but her controllers in London were gambling that their new recruit would be discreet and avoid being noticed by the police.

Budapest had been selected for Christine's base of operations ostensibly because of its declared neutrality and because it probably hadn't yet appeared on Hitler's 'hit' list. From there she would attempt to enter occupied Poland to make contact with resistance groups and report on the movements of German forces. Just prior to departing on her first mission she was enlisted to carry anti-German propaganda sheets to Warsaw because the fractious leaders of the Polish refugee cells had declined to assist Section D in that British-led operation.

The Hungarian government, led by Admiral Miklos Horthy,[1] clung precariously to its flimsy neutrality in those early days of the war. Horthy was in a difficult position for he was all too aware of the looming presence of the Nazis in neighbouring Austria, yet he wished to retain cordial relations with Britain. Under his leadership Hungary was struggling to maintain its new-found independence after having languished for decades as the junior partner in the Austro-Hungarian Empire. Its economy was still largely agrarian but change was coming and was most noticeable in the nation's cities. Budapest itself was gradually succumbing to modernisation. The wide boulevards of Buda were still dominated by the Baroque architecture of the old Empire but here and there new western-style structures had begun to appear. Major thoroughfares were decorated with French-style advertising kiosks and glass telephone booths. Boulevards and main streets were lined with wastepaper baskets as if to underline the government's boast that its capital was one of the cleanest in Europe. New cars mingled with horse-drawn carriages and sidewalk cafes were almost as numerous as those of Paris. In many of these establishments one could read newspapers from countries as far away as the United States.

While the government kept an anxious eye on events unfolding in Germany, urban Hungarians coped well with the shortages brought about by increased exports to that country. Coffee and tea were heavily taxed while Mondays and Fridays were 'meatless' days. The government relieved this latter hardship by ruling that '. . . game, venison and such things as liver are not classified as meat.'[2]

Hungary's drive to assert itself as a modern republic had been brought up short by the opening salvoes of the second world war. That catastrophe brought floods of refugees into the country from across Europe, many of them desperately en route to other destinations. Czechs and Poles were the most numerous in a nation ill-equipped to shelter them. Concealed among their numbers were scores of intelligence operatives, some legitimate, others mere chancers. Christine thus found herself in a milieu teeming with spies and other shady characters. They often met quite openly in fashionable cafes like Florisch's and Hagli's, as well as in seedier locales. Even the large confectioner Gerbeaud's was occasionally the site of a clandestine meeting.

Numerous European governments had agents in place in Budapest by early 1940 and even the Americans, still a considerable distance from war, had their sources. Their agents were not active but their government was kept well-informed about political matters. The British Consul-General in Hungary, Owen Saint Claire O'Malley* reported '... the American Counsellor in Budapest is a shrewd and helpful person, and his Military Attache, Partridge, knows a great deal about all the underground organizations which operate(d) there.'[3] Operatives from Poland cautiously sought out fellow refugees, always having to be on guard against the Hungarian secret police and the Gestapo whose agents had already infiltrated the government at the highest levels.

Beneath the city's placid surface lurked another danger for Christine, and anyone with a Jewish relative in the family tree, and that was the Hungarian government's anti-Semitic Nuremberg Laws. Hungarian Jews were defined in racial terms, excluded from employment in civil service and forbidden to marry non-Jews. Nevertheless, ordinary

---

*O'Malley's (1887 - 1974) official title was Envoy Extraordinary, Minister Plenipotentiary and Consul-General. Knighted in 1944.

Hungarians were generally receptive to the Poles regardless of religion. A Hungarian-Polish Committee for the Welfare of the Refugees was organised soon after Germany's assault on Poland and established a network of catering stations on Budapest's main streets. The local Red Cross gave what help it could. In order to cope with the influx of refugees the government herded the bulk of them, including military personnel, into hastily constructed camps. Access to them was permitted but this only gave some of the more astute Poles the opportunity to bundle their key people out of detention and send them on their way to France and to London.

Christine gradually eased herself into the city's daily life, frequenting small nondescript cafes while discreetly gathering together a group of Polish operatives, as much an amateur as she was. It was important for her and her colleagues to remain inconspicuous for more than just the obvious reasons. Aside from the threat of arrest, any suspicion on the part of the Horthy government that the British were using Hungary as a staging post to enter Poland might have undermined their tenuous relationship and might well have driven him into the arms of the Nazis. A much more serious threat to the Hungarians would have come from Berlin if the Germans suspected that Horthy was secretly cooperating with the British. That would have effectively brought about the end of his rule. Hungarian authorities must have suspected that British agents were already at work in the capital but in the early days of 1940 were unable to identify them.

Once settled, Christine quietly began contacting individuals within the Polish refugee community, hoping to establish a rapport with its leaders. Her hopes for cooperation were rudely dashed however when none offered assistance despite the obvious fact that they were all on the same side. Operatives from the Seizieme Bureau were too pre-occupied trying to establish and maintain lines of communication with colleagues in Poland to notice Christine. Furthermore, they were not about to share their precious bits of information with someone completely unknown to them. She was not welcomed either by the remnants of the Deuxieme Bureau of the Polish General Staff, charged with establishing in Poland 'an organisation capable of undertaking propaganda, sabotage and other underground activities likely to embarrass the Germans.'

To complicate matters for the British at least half a dozen freelance intelligence cells appeared in Budapest after the fighting had ended in Poland, funded by high-ranking Polish army officers. Co-operation between this bewildering array of official and unofficial cells was minimal at best as Christine was to discover. Minister O'Malley observed that, 'The Polish organisations in Budapest were manifold and worked with varying degrees of secrecy.' Of course everyone claimed to be working in the best interests of Poland.

The optimistic Poles, sustained by their religious faith, were busily planning for the future, convinced that the Germans would soon be defeated after which they would all return home to rebuild their country. The only question was, which political faction would prevail. The dominant attitude within the British intelligence community was optimistic too, holding to the assumption that once the war ended, with victory for their side of course, the pre-war status quo in Europe would be reinstated. In other words all those kings and queens sheltering at the London Ritz and at the Savoy would be returned to their thrones. Normal life as they had once known it would be resumed.

Christine's presence in Budapest had unwittingly complicated matters for Section D almost as much as it did for Polish officials. The implications were pointed out in a memo dated February 1st, 1940, written by Arthur Goodwill, a senior desk officer known within the Section by his cryptonym D/H1. He noted '... there appears to be a danger of a deadlock... The Poles have a very efficient organisation of their own, and it would be injudicious on our part to attempt to force our own members [namely Christine] into their organisation....' Major Harold Perkins concurred. After the war he wrote, 'the contribution of Polish intelligence to the victory of WW II was one of the most protected secrets of British intelligence.'4

Goodwill wasn't the only one to cast doubt on Christine's role. The British Consul O'Malley also had misgivings about the presence of a Section D operative in Budapest. It was his responsibility to maintain the delicate balance between the British and the Hungarian governments. He held to the Foreign Office line that the status quo should be respected in neutral countries and was openly opposed to British agents lobbying to perpetrate acts of sabotage in Hungary.

Even before the Germans had settled into their nightmar-ish role of occupier of Poland, a split had developed among the exiled Poles. The remnants of Pilsudski's deeply unpopular pre-war regime and General Sikorski's supporters distrusted one another. Cooperation on tactics was given only grudgingly. In an attempt to coordinate the actions of so many independent and opposing groups, Sikorski, newly appointed as prime minister of a government beyond Poland's borders, established an organisation known as Continental Action (CA) within the Ministry of Internal Affairs. Under the CA umbrella each cell would be permitted to carry out sabotage missions only after having obtained clearance from central command. Everyone agreed to this arrangement except the Musketeers in Poland who would continue to be an unwanted distraction for the next two years, though they occasionally provided the British with valuable information.

There was also disagreement between the British and the Poles over their propaganda targets. Christine and Taylor wanted to appeal directly to the Polish population to demonstrate that the British had not forsaken them. Professor Stanislaw Kot, appointed by Sikorski to head CA, believed that the pro-British messages could be dangerous to those found to be in possession of them. He suggested that such material should be addressed instead to enemy troops of the lower ranks whose morale could be easily undermined.

Christine was not warmly received by the jumble of Polish freelance operators. With their penchant for secrecy the Poles immediately distrusted her because she represented British interests. Furthermore, she was new to the job, had not been active in Polish politics before 1939 and was therefore an unknown quantity. There was a sense of unease about her within the Polish exile community, the fear that if she were to be arrested she might betray the AK's recently established base in Budapest, code-name Romek. It was perhaps naive of them to believe that the German counter-intelligence *apparat* did not already know of its existence.

When O'Malley was later posted to London he wrote of Christine that, '. . . she has a special set of grievances against the Polish authorities which weigh with her more powerfully, and I think it possible that in case of a clash of interests she would work for the British interest even if she considered that it was against the immediate but in the ultimate interest of her own country.'[5]

O'Malley did not explain what these grievances were but he was quite prescient in his estimation of her intentions. When the Seizieme Bureau were considering her for a mission to Romania in 1944, she told her controller Patrick Howarth that if she accepted the assignment she would send her reports to him and not to the Poles. This seems a petulant attitude, especially in such desperate times but she was a stubborn woman who usually got her own way. The Seizieme Bureau inexplicably cancelled the mission, sparing Christine the embarrassment of betraying her own people. Nevertheless, the tension between her and Polish intelligence remained strong throughout the war and until her death in 1952.

Before Christine could proceed with her own mission she was caught up in the on-again off-again relationship of the two Allies. Each was desperate in its desire to defeat the Nazi regime. The British priority was to prevent the Germans from launching an invasion of their island kingdom while the Poles' immediate concern was to drive Hitler's armies out of their country as quickly as possible. The British however were in no position to intervene militarily and without their assistance any Polish attempt to fight the Germans was bound to fail.

Though British intelligence bureaux desperately needed reports on conditions inside Poland, Section D officials were skeptical regarding the accuracy of the reports they could expect from those who had escaped the German onslaught. Signals sent to London from operatives in Europe occasionally contained unflattering descriptions of Britain's only active ally in that first full year of the war. In a separate, later report Hazell who was fluent in Polish continued his criticism by writing that, 'the Polish agencies in the other Balkan countries, namely Hungary, Bulgaria, and YugoSlavia, were also simply hot beds of intrigue and all that ever came out of them were the famous XYZ trio.' [Christine, Andrew Kennedy and Jerzy Gizycki] He offered this unflattering comment about the trio of Polish spies: '... the work that these people did had nothing to do or hardly anything to do with the Poles and should be covered in other Sections' histories,' ** contradicting Perkins' postwar assessment.

Hazell's jaundiced attitude toward the refugees was strengthened by reports that many Poles were homesick and wanted to return home in the face of the German occupation. British observers reported that large crowds of Poles gathered daily outside the German Legation seeking visas for their return. Minister O'Malley discovered that, under pressure from the Germans, the Horthy administration would permit civilians to leave the country provided they signed a document saying they wished to return to Poland. O'Malley was rebuffed however when he suggested that those seeking to join the revamped Polish army in France be granted similar consideration. He speculated, correctly as it were, that many of the refugees leaving Hungary were destined for concentration camps while the lucky few would be pressed into German labour battalions.

While the rival Polish factions wasted precious time with their stumbling efforts to mount an opposition to the Germans, Christine managed to gracefully navigate the political road blocks that had been placed in her path. Rather than be drawn into their internecine quarrels, she settled into the more serious business of preparing for the return to her beleaguered homeland. She began to frequent the Polish consulate on Verboczy street. She arrived one evening to find a small gathering being addressed by a handsome officer,

---

**See* 'Balkans and Middle East' in Polish Minorities Section, section IV, part 1. TNA.

Andrzej Kowerski, later known as Andrew Kennedy. Afterwards, the two of them struck up a conversation during which they realised that they not only had friends in common but had met twice before. (Another version has Christine meeting Andrew at the popular Cafe Floris.) They had first met as children on the Skarbek estate, accompanied by their fathers who discussed business matters. The two children stood by politely throughout the conversation. Their second meeting had taken place quite by accident in a ski shop in Zakopane just before the war. Christine had by then married the diplomat Jerzy Gizycki. They exchanged pleasantries with Andrew then left Zakopane and went their separate ways. Now, circumstances had brought them together again, this time in less salubrious surroundings. Besides their landed gentry roots the three of them had in common a nonchalant attitude towards danger and a tendency towards tongue-in-cheek boasting often found among those who have faced death on the battlefield.

Andrew was a bona fide hero who had proved himself in battle despite the loss of a leg in a pre-war accident. He had been an officer in the Horse Artillery at the time and as a result of that ghastly incident had to leave military service. Always an active young man, he had frequently participated in hunting parties on his father's estate. At one of these gatherings a guest stumbled and fell, causing his weapon to discharge. The bullet struck Andrew behind the knee. Local doctors lacked the expertise and the penicillin to treat the wound. He was then tranferred to a hospital in Lwow where the leg was amputated and where he remained for a year. Afterwards he was taken to London and fitted out with an artificial limb. During the course of his long life the remaining stump frequently required treatment.

Nevertheless, his sense of humour remained undiminished. In re-telling the story of the shooting he recalled that only twelve guests had been invited to the party. A thirteenth man had arrived indignant that he'd not been invited. It was this man's weapon that had gone off, crippling Andrew. Members of the Skarbek family, unimpressed by his bravado, suggested that perhaps the shooting was self-inflicted, implying that his gun had gone off while he was loading it.

Andrew was universally admired though one of Christine's relatives thought he was a bit full of himself with his robust attitude towards life, sometimes bordering on bragging. He was cut from the Hemingway cloth of masculinity, a big, barrel-chested man with a full mustache, heroic and contemptuous of his handicap. He once described to the author Patrick Leigh Fermor an incident that occurred in the heat of battle in the final days before Poland fell. He was at the time wearing a metal prosthetic device. During the fighting the new leg became jammed within the treads of a vehicle. When someone shouted for a medic Kennedy retorted, 'I don't want a doctor, I want a blacksmith!' He also told Leigh Fermor that he survived his student days in Krakow living only on vodka and raw meat.+

Once the German invasion was under way the Polish army needed all the help it could get and reactivated him with the rank of lieutenant. He was assigned to the Mechanised Brigade under the command of Colonel Stanislaw Kopanski with whom he would be reunited in Cairo in a few years' time. Andrew distinguished himself in the fierce fighting around Warsaw and was awarded the Virtuti Militari, Poland's highest military accolade.

+Both anecdotes were part of a longer tribute to Andrew Kennedy by Patrick Leigh Fermor. Published in the *The Spectator Magazine*. January 1, 1989,

When it became clear that the Germans were about to overwhelm the Polish forces Marshal Edward Smigly-Rydz commander-in-chief of the army, slipped away leaving his troops leaderless. An order went out for army units to disperse and to defend themselves as best they could. It was acceptable to leave the country if necessary and regroup but first caches of weapons were optimistically hidden to await use at some future date. Facing overwhelming odds, Andrew decided it would be better to live to fight another day. He led his remaining troops out of Poland, reaching Hungary by sometimes quite circuitous routes.

Following their meeting at the Legation, Christine and Andrew met for dinner at her suggestion. Afterwards she invited him to her flat where they became intimate. It was the beginning of a relationship that survived the war and continued until her tragic death. Though he shared a flat with his cousin Baron Adam Konopka in the city's red-light district, he began to spend much of his free time at Christine's place. Theirs was an unusual relationship in that they spent much of their time together discussing politics and tactics. Budapest's night life continued unabated despite the war raging across Europe but these two had little time for such distractions. They preferred instead to dine inconspicuously at local cafes with Polish emigrees where they would not attract unwanted attention. Even their shared passion did not divert them from their determination to see Poland freed from its German oppressors.

Though they had separate assignments, Christine eagerly joined Andrew in the hazardous work of exfiltrating downed aircrews from German camps and prisons. It was a mission that required great patience, knowledge of the Hungarian countryside and the ability to outwit enemy patrols. It has been erroneously reported that she recruited him to set up exfiltration routes out of Poland but he'd been at work on that very same project months before she arrived in Hungary. She did however succeed in urging him to add captured British airmen to his list of prisoners to be rescued. Not everyone saw this as an heroic gesture. The acerbic SIS deputy chief Claude Dansey considered escaping prisoners and shot-down air crew as nuisances. 'More trouble than they were worth,' he complained.

Initially, Andrew had organised the escape of Polish military personnel interned in Hungarian camps and sent them on their way to France where Polish forces had reconstituted themselves. He then turned his attention to the detention camps in Poland which held Czech and British prisoners as well as Poles. Thanks were due in no small part to Owen O'Malley who, by chance, had discovered a postcard sent by a POW that had found its way into a diplomatic bag delivered to the consulate. O'Malley arranged for a reply to be sent to the prisoner in Oflag VII C and thus discovered that communications between POW and those outside the camps were fairly relaxed. O'Malley claimed that he once posted a guitar to a prisoner.

Andrew's escape routes began at the Poland-Czechoslovak and Hungary-Yugoslav borders. At an appointed rendezvous he would greet the escapees and direct them to a safe house in Budapest. There they would be given food, medicine and money then sent on their way to France and or to England. His work however was not without its hazards. He was arrested at least four times by Hungarian police. On one occasion he was knocked about but released, arguing that as a one-legged man he was not much of a threat to

Hungarian security. It helped that he'd established a rapport with the officer leading the interrogations.

In spite of these occasional setbacks he and his colleagues continued their rescue efforts. A British source commented that he rescued so many Poles that it was impossible to compute the exact number. His post-war recommendation for the OBE (which he did not receive) states that he rescued 5000 Czechs and Poles from captivity but the exact number will probably never be known. That same official wrote, '. . . in the course of doing so (he) ran every kind of personal danger.'6

Christine was now riding two horses. Her priority remained to gain entry into Poland to conduct surveillance of German forces. Nevertheless, with her inexhaustible supply of energy she found time to help her lover in his vital work. But if Andrew harboured any thoughts of playing the role of tutor to her novice he would have encountered an obstreperous pupil. He was very protective of her, almost paternal, from the very beginning of their relationship and while there is little doubt of her love for him, she rebelled against the restraints he tried to place upon her, insisting on leading her own devil-may-care existence. Eventually, he realised that she was indomitable and their relationship settled into a partnership, cemented by mutual love and respect.

Preparations for Christine's first mission as a British operative came perilously close to failure, and at times resembled a comedy of errors. Taylor's cautious instructions, to use the journalist Radzyminski as her contact with other agents came undone when his irrational love for her took a dramatic turn. When she made it clear that her feelings for him were not to be reciprocated, he threatened to shoot himself in the genitals but succeeded only in wounding his foot. He was sent back to London to recuperate but she hadn't heard the last of him.

Ignoring Radzyminski's theatrical antics, Christine made contact with Section D's operatives already active in Budapest. Two of them had been discreetly insinuated into the capital months before she arrived. Hubert Deacon Harrison had seen action as a young officer in the British army during the first world war. Having survived without injury he took up a career in journalism and was employed by the *News Chronicle* at the time he was recruited by George Taylor in 1939. Harrison was a particularly valuable asset to the Section because he had spent a great deal of time overseas, mostly in Italy, Yugoslavia, Germany and in Abyssinia as correspondent for his newspaper. He had, however, lately been barred from Italy because of his criticism of its fascist government. The Yugoslavs were not enamoured of him for similar reasons but had not banned him.

Harrison's assignment was to liaise with Polish intelligence groups to whom he was known as 'Braun.' Christine had refrained from contacting him as instructed by Taylor, but after Radzyminski's emotional collapse she had no choice but to get in touch with him directly.

Edward Howe was the Section's other man in Budapest. He'd been in Hungary and the Balkans since the beginning of the war and knew Central Europe well, the territory he covered as correspondent for *The Times* and for Reuters. Though he and Christine eventually met they never worked together. In common with the Forbes Dennises in London, Howe was also acquainted with Ian Fleming and his name figured as well in post-war rumours of the author's alleged affair with Christine.

She did not immediately disclose to Andrew the details of her mission to Poland. But when she revealed her intention to cross the mountainous Slovak border with Poland, he strongly objected. To attempt to hike over the Tatra mountains, the shortest of the Carpathian ranges, in late winter seemed to him complete madness. She would not be dissuaded however and stubbornly insisted that she would make the journey with or without assistance.

For her first mission she was to have a guide known only as Johan. At the last moment his courage seemed to have failed him and he refused to go. Her irate view was that he belonged to a loose-knit group of Poles who were constantly 'intriguing against something or someone.' Apparently these unnamed people had convinced Johan that, because she was on the British government's payroll she was no longer 'a trustworthy Pole.' Christine attempted to defuse the situation and prove her loyalty by suggesting to leaders of the Polish freelance cells that she would organise a separate entity whose only function would be the production and distribution of anti-German propaganda. This offer met with undisguised contempt. One of her detractors is alleged to have declared, 'any movement in Poland which is not our movement is an enemy.'

Christine was not one to take this snub lightly. Her lifelong refusal to knuckle under to authority was a major influence in her rebuff to the new government. Polish conservatism, with its need to control, did not appeal. She had grown up in a country dominated by the Catholic Church and by an autocratic regime but had survived with her high spirits undiminished. She was not now going to submit to the restrictions of any political organisation unless it offered her the widest possible latitude (provided her actions would not harm the Polish cause). She had always preferred to act independently and would never harness herself to the demands of any group dominated by the sort of men who insisted upon unswerving loyalty. Vera Atkins, 'house-mother' to female agents, described her as 'a loner, a law unto herself.'+++

Christine could be fiercely loyal but only when she chose to be, not because it was expected of her. Ultimately, her allegiance was to her country not to ambitious politicians. Relations between her and those free-wheeling self-appointed operatives on the loose in Hungary were severed permanently when Johan refused to give her the names of his contacts inside Poland. Even in such dire circumstances the Poles displayed an astounding lack of unity.

For the remainder of the war, indeed, for the most important years up to and including its conclusion, the Polish government-in-exile treated her with suspicion. Its intelligence agencies not only refused their cooperation but several of its officers openly intrigued against her, initiating rumours that she was a double agent working for the Germans while ostensibly fulfilling her duties as a British operative.

Some forty years after the end of the war the files of Special Operations Executive were finally opened to the public. Correspondence between three of its Middle East officers revealed that Christine really had been acting as a double agent of sorts, reporting to SOE not only what the Germans were up to but what was being said within the Polish community in Cairo.

+++Atkins was born in Romania. She became Buckmaster's assistant in France and after the war discovered the fate of many of the missing female SOE agents. See her biography *A Life in Secrets* by Sarah Helm (New York: Little Brown 2005)

Chapter 5.
To Poland and the Musketeers

The chronology of Christine's missions to Poland has been purposely obscured, both by her and by SOE, for reasons of security. She was deliberately vague about the dates, naming only the months of three of the attempted trips and wrote only one report, a synopsis of her first mission. The need for secrecy within SOE, theatrical at times, suited Christine perfectly. She was not a garrulous person and though friendly enough, seldom revealed her innermost thoughts even to her closest friends.

Colleagues and journalists have speculated about the number of times she attempted to enter Poland, perhaps exaggerating to enhance the suspense of their own tales. Unfortunately these mythical numbers continue to distort the truth about her forays into Poland. She crossed into the country only twice. One SOE officer claimed that she had penetrated the Polish-Slovak border fifteen times, an utterly baseless claim.

These embellishments do not take into account the logistics of making the arduous and time-consuming journey from Budapest to Warsaw. Christine spent a total of just twelve months in the Hungarian capital whereas the zig-zag trip from there to her destination could take anywhere from five days to six weeks. Success or failure depended upon several factors - weather conditions, train reliability and the presence of enemy border guards. It would have been almost impossible within that time frame, and with those hazards, for her to have made the return trip from Budapest to Warsaw with any frequency.

Aside from the danger of enemy patrols couriers could not always count on meeting friendly faces within the civilian populations of Hungary and Slovakia. Some informers acted out of spite while others may have harboured a misguided loyalty to the Germans and to Hitler. Those with no loyalty to either side had simple venal motives, hoping for a financial reward from the local Gestapo.

Christine's first and longest incursion into her own country was made in early 1940. She remained in Poland for approximately six weeks. She next attempted to cross the Hungarian-Slovak border in the spring either in May or early June - the date is uncertain - and again in mid-June. The details of her third journey across Slovakia are well-documented. Her fourth and last successful attempt to enter Poland took place in November 1940. Prior to that final mission she had spent the summer in Budapest assisting Kennedy with his exfiltration schemes. That too is well-documented.[1] Christine simply did not remain in Hungary long enough to make as many return trips as has been alleged in some quarters, given the distance to be covered and the many obstacles to be overcome.

Christine slipped across the Polish frontier in February 1940. Her mission was twofold, to conduct surveillance of German troop movements and to contact the Musketeers. It's safe to assume that the inventor Stefan Witkowski, whom she'd first met in Geneva, was high on her list of people to see. She had also volunteered to carry Harrison's propaganda sheets after he'd been rebuffed by the Polish cell with which he'd been working in Budapest. With Jozef Radzyminski still unsettled, to say the least, Christine asked Andrew to maintain contact with Section D in her absence even though he was not officially a British operative.

At the last minute an experienced mountaineer named Jan Marusarz volunteered to accompany her as far as Zakopane. He came from a family that skied and trekked the Tatras and was familiar with the territory that Christine would have to cross. Jan's brother Stanislaw had been named Polish athlete of the year for 1938 and his account of Christine's first journey identifies her as 'Krystyna P.' This is either a mistake on the author's part or a typographical error.

The distance to be covered from Budapest to Zakopane was daunting. Christine and Jan traveled by train to the Polish-Slovak border, some 270 kilometers northeast of Budapest. They spent the night in the border city of Kosice at a safe house secured by the Armia Krajowa. Zakopane was approximately 170 kilometers *west* of Kosice and could only be reached by crossing a Slovakia that had recently passed into Germany's orbit. When Hitler severed the Czechs from the Slovaks after Munich he tacitly allowed Hungary to seize Ruthenia, the eastern-most province of Slovakia in a naked attempt to coax the Hungarians into entering the war as a German ally. The Slovaks, hoping to retain a modicum of independence, attempted to appease Hitler by applying to become a German protectorate after which the Nazi dictator wasted no time in positioning troops on their territory.

Still, the Slovaks continued to encourage tourists to visit and claimed not to be an occupied country but the Gestapo presence was obvious in Bratislava. Though the route from Budapest to Kosice to Zakopane described an extreme detour, at the time it promised the safest route for couriers to transit Slovakia because that country's eastern borders had remained lightly guarded well into the spring of 1940. From Kosice, Christine and Jan took a second train across the eastern tip of Slovakia, disembarking just before reaching the Polish border. Once in familiar territory they continued their trek towards Zakopane on foot and on skis. No diaries were kept to record the hours and days it took them to reach their destination while being buffeted by snow showers and fierce winds. Even in good weather it was an arduous journey. At that time of year the Tatra peaks, some as high as 2500 metres, were often beset by sudden blizzards which left treacherous snow drifts.

Christine had courage and determination in spades but she was not physically equipped for such a mission. After hiking for hours they were caught up in a ferocious snowstorm. Fortunately, Jan knew of a mountaineer's hut he'd once used and managed with great difficulty to get them there safely. Thoroughly exhausted, Christine fell into a deep sleep and later reported hearing voices crying for help in the severe weather sweeping across the mountain. In her fatigued state she feared she might have been hallucinating. What she heard were the shouts and pleas to be saved from a group of refugees fleeing Poland, many of whom perished that night.

Christine wasn't the only one, or one of the few, to make this hazardous journey. During the course of the war an untold number of couriers and refugees made similar crossings. This doesn't diminish in any way her accomplishments. To make this trip in late winter was extremely trying even for the most experienced mountaineer. Christine did not have access to the high-tech equipment available to contemporary climbers and had not spent any time preparing herself physically. Her achievement was the result of sheer determination.

She had displayed a certain naivete in thinking she could work her way up the Tatras and then enter Poland without much difficulty but that was Christine, supremely self-confident, assured of her own invincibility. Throughout her career as a British operative she seldom if ever laboured over detailed plans. She was both courageous and wilful, disdainful of the consequences of her actions. Only those who didn't know her well were surprised at her success in crossing the mountains under such conditions. This was exactly the sort of behaviour that prompted Owen O'Malley to remark that she had 'an almost pathological desire to take risks' and '. . would risk her life for what she believed in.'

Fortunately, members of the Polish Mountain Rescue Service had been very active around the border and helped prepare the ground for those entering the country as well as those fleeing it. Besides the Marusarz brothers other skiers had volunteered their services including their sister Helena. She was as courageous as her siblings but didn't live long enough to savour her exploits. In 1941 she was killed by German troops after a desperate pursuit across the mountains.2 Helena was not the only fatality suffered by a Mountain Rescue Service that assisted thousands of refugees in crossing the border. By the end of the war their own numbers had been severely decimated.

Once the Armia Krajowa GHQ structure had been established in Warsaw, it combined forces with another active resistance movement, the Union of Armed Struggle (*Zwiazek Walki Zbrojnej*) under General Kazimierz Sosnkowski, former ADC to Marshal Pilsudski. Together, these two organisations assumed control over all military and intelligence

---

*An estimated 40000 military, civilian and political figures escaped using these routes. See *Polish Resistance Movement in Poland and Abroad 1939-1945*. PWN-Polish Scientific Publishers. Warsaw 1987.

within the country. They mapped out major crossings in the mountains south into Czechoslovakia from Nowy Sacz, Zakopane and from villages near the border. To facilitate entry into Slovakia the AK-ZWZ ran contact points, provided couriers and sleeping places for them, supplied transport and guides. Local taxi drivers were recruited to help evacuate those who were leaving their battered country.

In her official report of this first journey Christine wrote that she had made the crossing alone. We now know that she did not. The Marusarz brothers and their colleagues remained active in the area long after she departed but she could not reveal their names, even to her British superiors, for fear that her report might fall into the wrong hands.

Christine and Jan went their separate ways once they reached Zakopane. She boarded a local train bound for Krakow then transferred to a second train which took her down to Warsaw. She had her first narrow escape from German authorities on the second leg of that journey. Instead of questioning her closely, the German conductor collecting tickets found himself charmed by this attractive self-effacing woman in need of assistance in placing her packages in the luggage rack. Men of all ranks found such brazen behaviour attractive but it was typical of Christine who early in life had developed the attitude that no harm would ever come to her.

The Warsaw that Christine remembered was almost unrecognisable. It had been heavily bombed in September and only desultory attempts had been made to remove the debris left by artillery shells and bombs dropped by the Luftwaffe. The Royal Castle, the nearby Old Town and the magnificent Cathedral of Saint John had been seriously damaged. The Prudential Insurance building, the tallest structure in the city, was without windows, its facade pockmarked with bullet and shell holes. Lovely pre-war squares such as the Saxon Gardens (*Plac Saski*) and Krasinski Square had been stripped of most of their foliage by the bombardment. Many of the city's streets were impassable because of the rubble that had toppled down. Dead horses lay in the streets. Weeks after the firing ceased work crews and individuals were still sifting through the remains of homes and office buildings, searching for survivors or for corpses.

The Nazi terror campaign against civilians was just unfolding and had not yet reached its crescendo when Christine arrived. After the shooting stopped German police began making summary arrests. Members of the intelligentsia - teachers, professors, authors and journalists, local and national politicians and leaders of the Jewish community - were the primary targets. The grim and efficient Gestapo had entered the country armed with lists of people to be arrested, many of whom were subsequently murdered. Rationing was instituted and a severe curfew put in place. To defy it sometimes meant death.

Besides violence the Germans tried various methods to break the Poles' collective will. In a clumsy attempt to soothe the Varsovians' anger they opened a casino for Poles only (*Cafe Klub*) on New World Avenue. It was not well attended and was eventually destroyed by the AK. The price of vodka was severely reduced hoping that the more gullible citizens would frequently be drunk and less likely to offer any resistance. German soldiers occasionally paid peasants for their grain with bottles of vodka to ensure their cooperation and good will. Whatever their approach they never found a Polish quisling [3] and were never able to obtain cooperation from the general public.

Though resistance groups had quickly formed once Poland was occupied acts of sabotage against German troops did not begin immediately. The Polish leadership, at least in the early days of the occupation, still held to the belief that British forces would launch a counterattack. As time passed without a response the peoples' morale began to sag but they never completely surrendered hope.

Christine, known by her code-name *Mucha* (the fly), delivered Harrison's subversive texts to her friend Teresa Lubienska.** Her flat on Salvation Place (*Plac Zbawiciela*), across from the magnificent Lazienki Park, had become the bustling headquarters for the Musketeers. Army officers being hunted by the Gestapo could find 'shelter, help, advice and a plateful of soup from Teresa's larder.'4 (*Mucha* was also the title of a popular Polish satirical magazine.)

The Musketeers had begun their subversive work within days of a cease-fire declaration. Their twin purposes were first, to acquire information about the German military that could be smuggled out of the country and delivered to the British. Secondly, to organise a campaign of anti-German propaganda that would undermine the morale of the enemy's troops. The Musketeers were not equipped to launch a campaign of sabotage or to harass the heavily armed Germans with hit-and-run attacks. But perhaps more to the point their leader Witkowski wasn't about to risk his position, or his life, by attacking German soldiers head-on. With Poland supine and leaderless he saw an opportunity to ultimately acquire more power for himself but decided to do it stealthily instead by plotting to undermine the Sikorski government.

The Musketeers' alliance with Christine and SOE lasted less then two years but proved to be more fruitful for the British than the mere distribution of propaganda. She had realised at once the potential of the Musketeers' efforts and volunteered to work with them, serving as a courier when possible and acting as the contact point in Budapest between them and Section D. They would in effect be by-passing both Polish intelligence agencies, the Deuxieme Bureau and the Seizieme Bureau. The *blitzkreig* of 1939 had severely disrupted their operations, leaving the Musketeers temporarily as the chief source for information coming out of Poland. It wasn't until later in 1940 that the two agencies took on more responsibility for intelligence matters. The Musketeers' valuable role in supplying the British with intelligence reports is confirmed in documents published by the Anglo-Polish Historical Committee : 'The first contacts between representatives of Polish resistance and British intelligence were established by the Musketeers [*Muszkietrze*] organization which in February 1940 had intelligence and counter-intelligence cells in 32 towns within the pre-war borders of Poland.'[5]

At Lubienska's flat Christine was reunited with Witkowski who had anointed himself with a number of cryptonyms such as Kapitan, Engineer, Teczynski and the more ornamental Baron von Tierbach. Amid the chaos in Warsaw he was in his element, according to General KS Rudnicki.*** He almost reveled in the tense atmosphere, roaming about the city making contacts, issuing orders and generally making himself important. Offering bribes, he established contacts within the Polish police force, or Blue Police, so-called because of the colour of their uniforms. He also managed to co-opt some lower ranking Germans from whom he could purchase weapons and supplies. The funds to pay bribes

***See *The Last of the War-Horses*, by KS Rudnicki DSO (London:Bachman & Turner 1974)

frequently came from Poles who had managed to hide large sums from the occupying German police forces and were frequently never re-paid.

Immediately after the invasion Witkowski had commandeered a room in Lubienska's flat which he converted into a darkroom. There, he and his colleagues set about creating bogus passports, postage stamps and visas which proved invaluable in helping scores of Poles evade the Gestapo and escape to other countries. The Musketeers' leader always seemed to have information to hand. He knew when the railways would be back in operation and he knew where to find a fleet of trucks that would, for a price, assist people in leaving Poland. Some of his co-conspirators feared that his enthusiasm for plotting had become so intense that he might expose them. That assessment was not far off the mark.

By early 1941 Witkowski had re-ordered his priorities. The accumulation of cash became his objective. It was an open secret that he and some of his colleagues received payment from the British in exchange for information provided. But as his appetite for money grew, it gave rise to tales of outright theft and even murder. In one notorious instance the sum of 40,000 dollars US, destined for the AK, went missing. The courier charged with bringing the money from Budapest was accused of having pocketed the funds and was subsequently murdered. Allegations have been made that Witkowski himself appropriated the money then shot the unfortunate man.6

It was also not unheard of for individuals within the Musketeers' organisation to sell to the British copies of intelligence reports that they had previously given to the Sikorski government. Stefan Witkowski was to remain the group's leader until his own assassination in 1942, allegedly ordered by the AK. But the true story of who actually killed him has been muddled by the revelation that the German authorities in Warsaw had tired of his complicated and fruitless plotting and had ordered him to be shot. A document in the pages of *Intelligence Cooperation between Poland and Great Britain* (2005) states that before the AK could act, the chief of the German police had him shot (18 Sept 1942) evidently to silence him because he was 'supposedly linked to criminal and bribery affairs.'[7]

Before leaving Poland, Christine concluded a working agreement with the Musketeers without the consent and knowledge of Section D. In correspondence discovered after the war her controllers expressed astonishment that she would have had the audacity to act so independently. It would not be the only instance of impetuous behaviour in which she suggested that she had the support of the British. Section D were nevertheless quite pleased to receive any intelligence smuggled out of Poland though the Sikorski government were vehemently annoyed at Witkowski's insistence on maintaining his independence.

Christine formalised this arrangement, as revealed in a 1943 memo to Major Peter Wilkinson from Captain Patrick Howarth who referred to '. . A document of purely historic interest which WILLING [Christine] asked me to copy for her, as the print was becoming illegible with the passage of time. It was the original charter for collaboration between her organisation and the British, and she herself brought the negative across the Hungarian border. One is amazed at the amount of verbiage for which she risked her life.' **** One is also surprised that this neophyte spy had the foresight to put into writing what she and the Musketeers had agreed.

Besides Howarth's comment there is this complaint in one SOE file about her

----

*****See* HS4/109 for correspondence between Howarth and Wilkinson.

unilateral decision, referring to it as 'a ghastly document pledging the British Govt to "Unreserved and exclusive support of W's [Witkowski] organisation." ' The author of this memo also complained about Christine's alleged influence on Minister O'Malley and George Taylor 'who seem to have fallen victim to Mme's well known persuasiveness.'

Once she had concluded her business with the Musketeers, Christine felt free to travel about the country without being suspect. Returning to familiar territory had given her a feeling of confidence, the conviction that on her own ground she was in command of her destiny. Though she had several narrow escapes neither German security nor their accomplices were able to apprehend her. While traveling on a train from Warsaw to Krakow a family friend recognised her and called to her by name. Christine defused the situation by stubbornly refusing to return the greeting

The Gestapo and the *Abwehr* (German military counter-intelligence) of course suspected that the British had operatives working in Poland but did not know specifically about Christine. Several *Volksdeutsch* (Germans born in Poland) in league with German security, tried to pass themselves off as British agents and spread the rumour that no one had come to Poland bringing news from Britain, a tactic they hoped would depress the Poles' collective morale. This stratagem almost succeeded. The AK initially distrusted Christine and might have killed her if friends had not vouched for her identity.

Before leaving Warsaw she visited the family home on Rozbrat street, close to the Vistula river. There, she found her mother alone but coping with her situation. She urged the countess to return with her to Budapest but the older woman steadfastly refused, insisting that she would remain in the city where her husband was buried. She naively believed that she would survive the war but even if she had decided to leave Warsaw, the odds of the elderly countess surviving the trek across the Tatras were slim. Christine's cousin Stanley Krystoforowicz (*aka* Stanley Christopher) provided an erroneous postscript to her futile attempt to convince her mother to leave Poland. He recalled that, shortly after she departed several plainclothes police arrived at the Skarbek home and took away her mother. She was never seen again, according to him. The Gestapo may have taken Stefania Skarbek in for questioning but the record of arrests and detainees held at Warsaw's infamous Pawiak prison, now a museum, gives more specific information about her disappearance. She was not not formally taken into custody and brought to the prison until January 30, 1942, almost two years after her daughter's final visit. Her name does not appear on any of the numerous lists of concentration camp victims or survivors, so it is almost certain that she perished in Pawiak along with thousands of other Poles. The Gestapo subsequently seized her home and converted it into an office. Ironically, Christine's great-great uncle, Fryderyk Florian Skarbek, Chopin's godfather, had initiated construction of Pawiak in the mid-nineteenth century. Christine's brother Andrzej was also arrested but survived the war, much of it as a German prisoner.

More precise details of why the Countess Skarbek was arrested and what happened to her afterwards are not known but of course the Gestapo did not need to present a list of grievances in order to arrest someone. They took whomever they pleased for real or for spurious reasons.

Christine received the news of her mother's arrest and presumed death with a dignified sorrow. She blamed herself for failing to get her mother out of harm's way but her determination to do her duty remained as strong as ever. She was realistic enough to know that there was little she could have done to save the countess who in the end turned out to be as obdurate as her daughter. After leaving her mother's home Christine travelled south to Krakow, the first leg of her exit from the country. She assumed she'd be returning to Poland again by which time her mother hopefully would have changed her mind. She was too optimistic while her mother's bravado was misplaced and proved to be ultimately fatal.

Displaying a mixture of disdain for the Germans with behaviour bordering on carelessness, Christine moved around Poland without much of an attempt to disguise herself. She really did not need to. She was after all a Polish woman traveling in her own country. Insofar as she was aware her name had not yet turned up on any Gestapo 'wanted' list. But the danger for her was compounded by the fact that, in addition to being a British operative, she was also the daughter of a Jew. That alone would have been enough to have her sent to a concentration camp had she been apprehended or worse.

In Krakow, Christine came perilously close to blowing her assignment. Once again, she made little attempt to disguise herself. When not wandering about the city gathering information she naively sought out relatives. In particular she attempted to find her young cousin Dzidzia+, [*dz, as in jail*], a nurse by training and another of the small army of couriers employed by the Musketeers. Besides crossing the Tatras, Dzidzia had travelled as far as France and Rome carrying messages to Polish operatives.

In spite of the petulant behaviour of the guide Johan, Christine had obtained the address of a Pani Jasinska,++ a resistance contact in Krakow. She made her way to Jasinska's flat and introduced herself as Andrzejewska but let it be known that this was a pseudonym. She described her hazardous crossing over the Tatras and the blizzard that had delayed her progress.8 'I arrived from Hungary . . . A terrible journey. I was hiking through the Tatras in a snowstorm when I heard cries for help, growing louder and then again quieter in the blizzard. We sheltered in the rocks of Dolina Cicha [Quiet Valley] [and] dared not go to the rescue. At dawn I came across the bodies of friends from Zakopane.'

She then asked for her cousin's address. Jasinska was startled by the stranger's candour and lack of guile. She asked who in Budapest had sent her and Christine replied by nonchalantly reeling off the names of Polish agents active in the Hungarian capital: Andrzej Kowerski (Andrew Kennedy), his cousin Adam Konopka and Wlodzimierz (Vladimir) Ledochowski also known as Jan Grodzicki. The last named, she claimed, was presently en route to France. Jasinska knew otherwise for she was well-acquainted with Vladimir and was startled when her visitor mentioned him so casually along with the news, incorrect as it were, about his journey to France. In fact, he was right there in Krakow.

Christine blithely went on to describe how she had been sent to Poland by 'an organisation working in parallel with that of General Sikorski.' In a larger sense the British were working in parallel with Sikorski. But if she was referring to any of the Polish cells in Budapest she was treading on shaky ground. Underground operatives could easily (and did) check her story. It was an unnecessary and potentially dangerous misrepresentation but she made it nevertheless, convinced of her own invincibility.

+Maria (Dzidzia) Krzeczunowicz was last seen in Belgrade in July 1945 in the company of Andrzej Sapieha. She was presumed by her family to have been captured and killed by the Germans.
++Polish term of respect, the equivalent of Madame or Mrs.

Christine's Polish ID card 1928. In response to the questions about languages she replied 'Polish French and German.' (lower right)   *Photo supplied by Jolanta Countess Mycielska*

The Elusive Madame G

FA (Freddy) Voigt, Guardian *diplomatic journalist and covert SIS agent.*   Wikipedia

Gustaf Getlich, Christine's first husband, skiing in Zakopane. c 1930.   *photo courtesy of Tomasz Getlich*

The Elusive Madame G

*Andrzej Kowerski, aka Andrew Kennedy. Virtuti Militari, MBE (Mil).
Christine's SOE colleague, lover and faithful friend.* Photo supplied by Slawka Wazacz

The Elusive Madame G

Captain Richard Truskowski, SOE
Photo supplied by Diana Hall

The Elusive Madame G

Christine in the Haute-Savoie beside a recently destroyed water duct near Embrun. August 1944
Photo with permission of the Special Forces Club

Chapter 6.
The Woman in the Tyrolean Hat

Jasinska was now genuinely alarmed and unsure of how to react. It occurred to her that the woman standing before her might be a Gestapo informer. Acting on impulse, Jasinska cut short the conversation by denying she knew Dzidzia's address. Furthermore, she denied ever having any contacts with any political organisation.

After her visitor had gone Jasinska contacted Vladimir Ledochowski and told her story. Vladimir, a handsome Polish artillery officer and Deuxieme Bureau agent under diplomatic cover, had already visited Budapest as a courier. Though he knew and had worked with Andrew he'd never met Christine. He also knew several of the men who were active in assisting Andrew with his exfiltration scheme for Polish prisoners. But he was not all work and no play. He had taken advantage of the best that the Hungarian capital had to offer and was frequently seen in the city's night spots, especially the popular Arizona Club.

Vladimir was perplexed that Christine had mentioned his name, for he was indeed active in the courier network in Budapest but he'd never come across her. That was due to an accident of chronology. He had arrived in December 1939 and left before she introduced herself to the refugee community in February. Acting on Jasinka's information he decided to warn his colleagues in Hungary. In the meantime, he said, 'It would be necessary to take care of her and discreetly find out more about her.'[1]

Before taking action he casually asked Jasinska to describe the new arrival. She gave the following response: 'Beautiful. She has fiery eyes and white teeth and very red lips. She is extremely pretty but I think she was once much prettier. She lacks the freshness of youth.' Ledochowski arranged a rendez-vous with the Krakow resistance leader to discuss this new development and, as they were talking, Dzidzia arrived unexpectedly. She told them that she'd just seen Christine on the street and, after giving the two men some background about her cousin, continued: 'She [Christine] had come to Poland with all kinds of papers, instructions, and propaganda materials. She was racking her brains about how to get these documents across the border when a Gestapo man entered the train compartment... In the course of the conversation with the officer she asked whether he could hide the large package of tea she was taking to her sick mother. The officer obliged with the readiness of a gentleman, not even suspecting that the package contained compromising materials.'[2]

Vladimir accepted Dzidzia's version of events without question. For the moment he had more important things on his mind. Once the snow on the mountain peaks had begun to melt in mid-March he began to make preparations for his return to Budapest. A meeting of AK leaders from the Krakow area was convened in the home of the doomed Dzidzia. There, he was given a comprehensive report on conditions in Poland to pass on to the AK's Romek operatives in Hungary, information about the number and disposition of German troops in Poland as well as plans for the beginning of a campaign of sabotage within the country. His group needed only the green light from the Sikorski government, still in France, to begin its own campaign of terror within Poland's borders.

Vladimir and a colleague carefully translated this material into a series of coded messages. In the evening he hurried to the Krakow rail station. While waiting in a queue to board the train the passengers were searched by German security police. As he awaited his turn he noticed an attractive woman wearing a Tyrolean hat loitering nearby. Suddenly the queue lurched forward and he eventually stumbled into a badly lighted second-class compartment. He had just settled in when the door flew open and the woman in the Tyrolean hat entered. He had just seen Christine Granville for the first time.

Before they could become acquainted the German conductor entered to collect the passengers' tickets. Christine held a third-class ticket and offered to pay for an upgrade. The flirtatious conductor, who smelled of drink, took the money from her then attempted to stuff it into the bosom of her coat, announcing that she could remain in the coach without paying for an upgraded ticket. Vladimir recalled that she seemed tired and yawned unashamedly. Both travelers eventually fell asleep. In the morning he awoke to find Christine gone. He assumed she had left the train at Tarnow, just north of his destination Nowy Sacz from where he would board a train bound for Slovakia.

He left the train at Nowy Sacz and stopped at a church to give thanks for a safe journey. He then made his way to a safe house whose location was known to only a select few. As he approached the building he noticed a horse-drawn carriage standing in front. Uncertain of what to make of it he lingered nearby until the driver emerged and drove off with his rig. He cautiously entered the house and, to his surprise, found Christine already there.

He introduced himself using his pseudonym 'Grodzicki.' Once the introductions were out of the way, they sat down to breakfast after which she repeated the tragic tale of the blizzard that had taken the lives of a group of Poles fleeing the country. Midway through her narrative Vladimir abruptly changed his friendly demeanour. He angrily revealed what he already knew about her - that she had visited Jasinska and other AK contacts, and that she had falsely claimed to know several top Polish agents including Vladimir himself.

Despite his scepticism about the nature of her business Vladimir could not take his eyes off her. He then disclosed his true identity, along with a bit of bragging about other female agents he had known. He later wrote in his memoir that she seemed impressed by his reputation. Christine must have found Vladimir quite appealing for she talked freely about herself and her lover Andrew Kennedy. She told Vladimir that she had been in Salisbury when the Germans invaded Poland, contradicting Gizycki's account that they had been in Addis Ababa. She was embarrassingly open about her relationships with her husband and with Andrew Kennedy. She confessed that she had tired of Gizycki and her comments about Andrew, if Vladimir is to be believed, were painfully frank. She told him that prior to any intimacy he had to repair to the bathroom, detach his artificial leg and then make his way back to the bedroom where Christine lay waiting for him.

After breakfast, and with Vladimir's suspicions allayed, he and Christine boarded a local train bound for the Polish-Slovak border, disembarking one stop before its destination of Piwniczna. They proceeded from there on foot. By then Vladimir had more on his mind than espionage. He claimed that she responded to his flirting and asked that he address her as Krystyna rather than the more formal *pani*.

At some point on their trek they picked up a local guide and a fourth, unnamed person, then continued their laborious journey. At the spot marking the border Christine stumbled and fell into Vladimir's arms. He kissed her and later wrote unabashedly that she returned the kiss with enthusiasm. He did not describe where his fellow travelers were at this juncture. (There are confusing accounts of who Christine's various companions were on her several attempts to enter Poland.) His description of her reaction is perhaps only slightly exaggerated. Following this passionate display of affection, she allegedly shouted in Polish, 'More! More! More!' (*Jeszcze! Jeszcze. Jescze!*)

Darkness had begun to fall as they continued on, now walking arm in arm, believing they had crossed into Slovakia. Their sudden affection for one another blinded them to the fact that they had been walking in a circle. The guide, as it turned out, was new to the job and was himself uncertain of the terrain. As they tried to retrace their steps they became disorientated. Vladimir tried to get his bearings from the stars but this attempt at navigation met with limited success and they soon found themselves at a familiar site on the Polish side of the border. Embarrassed by this turn of events, he humbly accepted the blame for the bungle.

They took shelter in a mountaineer's hut for the remainder of the night during which he seduced the eager Christine, according to the author. Out of discretion, and perhaps embarrassed, she never spoke of this liaison other than to admit to Andrew that it had happened. Her family were certainly not pleased with Vladimir's post-war revelations.

In the morning they resumed their journey, descending into a valley then climbing again. They were now in Slovakia. At the village of Lobowla, Christine and her new lover declared themselves to be exhausted and unable to continue. The guide was sent into town to fetch a taxi. The little group made its way across Slovakia by taxi and on foot, sometimes walking for hours without a break. At dusk they plunged down a wooded slope, a descent made all the more difficult by thickets of brambles and low-lying tree branches tearing at their clothes. While crossing a meadow Christine lost her shoes in the muddy field. Not wishing to pause to rest, Vladimir gallantly carried her on his back a short distance.

Eventually they happened onto the road to Kosice, Vladimir knew the location of a safe house where they managed several hours of sleep. In the morning another friendly taxi driver took them to the station where they caught a train to Budapest. As they drew nearer to the capital he asked Christine if she had someone waiting for her. She replied negatively. He was thinking of putting up at his usual stopping place, the Adasie Hotel, but Christine insisted, he wrote, that he come to her place. She warned him that the lovesick Radzyminski had a habit of dropping in unannounced. Despite his earlier mishap his obsession with her remained undiminished.

The journalist did turn up at the flat shortly after they arrived. She introduced the two men who eyed one another with suspicion. At length, Radzyminski excused himself, saying that he had to prepare for a journey to London.

Vladimir, blissfully unaware of her relationship with Andrew Kennedy, asked for his telephone number. She discouraged him from phoning, suggesting instead that they bathe and have dinner. They dined that night at the Kis Royal restaurant then returned to her flat where he spent the night. In the early hours of they were awakened by a very angry Kennedy. It seems that after leaving Christine's flat Razyminski had tracked him down and just couldn't wait to tell him about her new lover.

While there may be more than a bit of hyperbole in Ledochowski's tale, others, including Andrew, have acknowledged Christine's liaison with the Polish officer. He grudgingly forgave them, he said modestly. Kennedy maintained that the three gradually became friends and even gave his 'permission' for their new colleague to accompany Christine on her third mission to Poland, which turned out to be the most hazardous. A few years later they were reunited in Cairo though her passion for her gallant companion had cooled considerably by then.

Vladimir's is the only known account of his brief affair and is told in his untranslated memoir, published in Poland. His early draft of a proposed biography of Christine was severely criticised by friends because it allegedly included an explicit account of their fling. Kennedy in particular was said to be incensed at the intimate details revealed in the manuscript and angrily demanded that his rival re-write certain sections. The Countess Sophia Tarnowska* read the unedited version and thought that the author had agreed to comply with Andrew's wishes, writing a more sanitised account of their relationship. The original had contained material which had obviously upset and embarrassed him. It included accounts of Hungarian officers in crowded cafes putting their hands up Christine's skirt or attempting to feel her breasts. There are also frank and humiliating allegations in the dismissed lover's manuscript, to the effect that her enjoyment of intimacy with Kennedy was marred by his disability.

Though Vladimir has been accused of exaggerating the intensity of their brief relationship, no one doubted that it had happened. He insisted that the affair continued for almost three months and that he spent that time at Christine's Budapest flat. If so, she

*Interview with the Countess Sophia Tarnowska in London April 2002.

must have managed with the greatest difficulty to keep this relationship secret from Andrew. The affair came to an end when Christine decided to terminate it and asked Vladimir to leave. He complied with only the mildest protest and she promptly resumed her relationship with Andrew.

Vladimir also alleged that she pursued a similar strategy in Cairo with another man, again keeping Andrew in the dark until the affair was terminated at her insistence. If he was aware of this second betrayal he certainly maintained a stiff upper lip about it. Andrew was a brave man with physical courage in spades but emotionally vulnerable where she was concerned. He accepted her rumoured infidelities and flirtations because of his near-obsessive love for her and he suffered silently rather than risk a confrontation. Overlooked amid the emotional turmoil was the fact that she was still married to Jerzy Gizycki while the two of them carried on their affair.

Vladimir left for London on June 15 at the request of the Polish government, according to a report found in SOE's archive. But after the war he contradicted the contents of that document and insisted that, from Budapest, he had travelled directly to Belgrade where he remained for only a short while before moving on to Turkey. Eventually, he rejoined the Polish army in Palestine and was promoted to captain. He saw action against the Germans in North Africa, was wounded and sent to Egypt to recuperate. He did not see Christine again until 1943.

She had returned to Budapest in early April 1940 and delivered her report to Harrison who was about to leave for London. Christine was obviously elated by what was by any measure a successful mission and enthusiastically offered Section D a basket of suggestions for the widespread distribution of propaganda in Poland. She urged Harrison to produce more broadcast and print material, insisting that 'Poland is starving for real news - they are sick of German propaganda and they cannot get the news in Poland from England and other Allied radio stations owing to German interference.'

Section D had once promised Harrison a radio transmitter by which he could send bulletins to Poland at 'fixed hours on a fixed wave length.' He and Christine had envisioned an enterprise which would include stenographers to take down *verbatim* the content of the broadcasts. These would be reproduced by 'copying machines' and then distributed throughout Poland by couriers. Special newspapers with articles based on their bulletins would also be published and distributed.

She and Stanislaw Dubois, a socialist journalist, suggested that a secret weekly newspaper should be established with a press run of 10-15,000 copies. Dubois estimated he would need £100 a month to cover the cost of printing which presumably would be paid by the British. But the government never followed through on the suggestion and nothing more was heard of that plan.

Christine might have been positively brimming with enthusiasm but not all of her ideas were acceptable to Section D's leadership. Her proposal to involve a certain General S. Bulak-Balachowicz was immediately rejected. This general had once been involved with White Russians who had tried to raise a force to overthrow the Bolsheviks in the aftermath of the Russian revolution.

Bulak-Balachowicz now wanted to organise a force to attack Russian troops based in Poland. Mindful of its disastrous intervention against the Bolsheviks, the British quickly quashed the suggestion. The government even then, and certainly near war's end, would not countenance a fight with the Red Army on Polish soil even if it meant surrendering Poland to the Soviet Union. President Roosevelt and Prime Minister Churchill impressed upon Stalin their desire for cooperation with him when they met at Teheran in 1943. It was implicitly agreed that they would not attempt to wrest control of Poland from his armies. Stalin was quite pleased with that development, especially when the Allied leaders assured him that their forces would soon open a second front against the Germans, thereby taking the pressure off of Soviet troops. The lid on the Polish coffin was finally sealed at the Yalta Conference in 1945.

Christine's report gave some insight into the German regime in Poland. It was not widely known, for example, that the Gestapo and ordinary German soldiers despised one another, for the former were known to spy on their own forces as well as on the Poles. Ordinary soldiers scorned the Gestapo for their arrogant pose as an elite force but feared them at the same time, well-aware of their almost unbridled power.

As early as March 1941 the more militant Gestapo members and young troops were gradually withdrawn from Poland and replaced by older soldiers. The reason why became clear when Hitler's plans to attack the Soviet Union were discovered by the Musketeers.

Christine's marriage to Jerzy Gizycki played itself out against the turmoil and violent background of the war. Their enforced separation only hastened the demise of what in reality had been a fling on her part. She had been the main beneficiary of their union, for without him she might still have been in Poland when German troops poured across its border in 1939. Though their relationship was doomed from the beginning their parallel assignments, and Gizycki's abiding affection for his wife, meant that they still maintained contact with one another.

In early 1940, after Christine had left for Hungary, Gizycki himself was recruited by Section D. The date and the circumstances are unclear but by the spring he had established himself in France as one of their psychological warfare operatives. Thousands of Europeans, those who could get out, were fleeing westward. But safe havens were disappearing rapidly. In April 1940, Hitler's forces overran Denmark and Norway. The British received a small and temporary measure of satisfaction when a combined British, French and Polish force took the Norwegian port of Narvik in late May. It was an ill-conceived mission however and the Allied forces surrendered the port to the enemy on June 8.

True to his contrary nature, Gizycki went against the flow of traffic. He first stopped in Paris, a city whose collective nerves were stretched to the limit in anticipation of the arrival of the Germans. His assignment was to supply reports in the form of seemingly innocent articles and letters, describing conditions in Europe, especially in France.

While his wife was returning from her first journey into Poland, Gizycki left Paris and established himself in the Haute-Savoie in southeastern France. As he was legitimately a published writer there was no need to provide him with a cover story. Correspondence between Gizycki and Section D indicates that for all her husband's strength and experience, Christine was the more independent of the two. She grew into her role while he floundered. He was also painfully aware of the handicaps that limited his maneuverability. The British knew it too and used him sparingly. Unlike his wife, Gizycki occasionally gave some thought to the future and conjured up fantasies of a pastel-colored life of ease with her at his side. But she had other ideas. With the war in full flow Christine had found her *raison d'etre*. Until now she had drifted through life, worked sporadically, indulged in the occasional affair and enjoyed a certain amount of privilege as a member of the Polish gentry. She had not pursued a career heretofore and it is doubtful that she'd made any future plans beyond her marriage. Joining the fight for Poland's freedom gave meaning to her life even though, in reality, her role in the war was quite limited.

The nature of Christine's work of course precluded regular and open contact with Gizycki. He should have understood this but he allowed emotion to overcome reason. Her letters and notes to him were few and far between. In contrast, he wrote a stream of anxiety-ridden letters to his British controller, known only as *X.3*, asking, begging for news of her.[3] This confirms to some degree earlier observations about the parlous state of their marriage. While Gizycki had been establishing himself in France he completely lost touch with his wife. In a letter to Section D dated April 5, 1940, he wrote: 'Not having had any news from my wife for the last three weeks I am enormously worried. Kindly let me know if she is all right.'[4]

His letters to *X.3* were chatty and personal. In this communique he talked about his health and reported that he was recuperating from 'prolonged grippe.' He voiced concern that, at the moment, he had no 'useful work.' Gizycki was obviously lonely, cut off as he was from his country and from his family. Like Christine he had opted for a free-wheeling lifestyle that eschewed close and stable relationships. But he was less *blase* than she was and found the increased isolation difficult to deal with.

Before he could begin writing articles his London controller contacted him, informing him that Christine was in Poland 'visiting relatives.' In fact, she had already returned to Budapest from her first mission. Section D then asked Gizycki to 'compile a letter' which he should deliver to a Miss Eileen O'Hallaron on the Boulevard Raspail in Paris. The letter was to be written in the style of a traveler's musings as he wandered through France and those countries yet to be assaulted by the Germans.

At this juncture Arthur Goodwill suggested to George Taylor that Christine return to Britain. He believed that her talents were being wasted in Hungary, and that any problems she might have had were due to 'the weakness of A/H1 [Radziminsky].' Goodwill may have been referring to the fact that while Hubert Harrison was temporarily absent from Budapest, no one at the British legation had bothered to contact her, and she had not been paid. She was forced to rely upon Andrew with whom she now shared a flat. His income came from British military intelligence via the Polish government-in-exile. (Until they could retrieve the gold they had smuggled out of the country, the Poles were dependent upon loans from the American and the British governments to maintain their administration and their armed forces.)

Goodwill next suggested to Taylor that Christine might be sent to Paris to carry out a rather audacious project which she had proposed earlier, to be put in place in Budapest. She had naively suggested that a van be fitted out with a wireless transmitter and that she should be driven about the city in it, operating a kind of mobile communications center. (A driver would have to be provided as she had never learned to drive.) He may have been referring to the Signals Liaison Units, developed by Brigadier Sir Richard Gambier-Parry.**

These powerful transmitters emitted signals that could be picked up by receiving sets in Poland. They could be stationary or easily be converted into mobile units. The obvious advantage would be their mobility, thus reducing the likelihood of the Germans or Hungarians pinpointing the signals. (One of the stationary units was put in place on Whaddon Hall near Bletchley Park.)

Goodwill referred to these units as 'freedom stations.' But the plan would first have to be approved by the Polish Mission in France. In light of the imminent defeat of that nation, it was fortunate that Taylor ignored the suggestion. It was not a very practical suggestion in any event for such a set-up would have required the use of a large antenna, rendering her vehicle rather conspicuous. SOE operatives often made suggestions like this that turned out to be impractical if not impossible to carry out. A third and final proposal was made to send her, Andrew and one other agent to Belgrade. This suggestion was disregarded, allowing the couple to continue their valuable work in Hungary.

Before Gizycki could respond to their previous letter, Section D passed on to him a note from Christine. He replied on April 17 with obsequious thanks. She had told her husband the obvious - that she had been unable to contact him earlier for reasons that should have been apparent to him. Gizycki agreed (April 23) to write the Section's suggested report as soon as he could assemble the 'necessary staff.' In coded language he said he lacked the 'materials,' that is, the information, but he would nevertheless do what he could. He advised his controller that he could not make any promises regarding further reports and added that, as the high season had ended, he was the only person remaining in the

**Gambier-Parry was head of Section VIII (Communications) and RSS (Radio Security Service).

Haute Savoie hotel, aside from a couple who had been engaged as caretakers. He planned to stay on for a few more weeks, for his health, until he regained his 'form.'

X.3 replied at the end of April, thanking him for having sent 'two letters and a postcard,' indicating that Gizycki's report had been received. He was advised to write future articles in Polish, in triplicate, along with the English translation. This presented no problem for him because he was fluent in several languages and was quite up to the task.

Chapter 7.

Lost among the Magyars

With Vladimir Ledochowski out of the way Christine was able to smooth things over with Andrew and rejoined him in his exfiltration efforts. She had submitted a report about her mission to Poland to Harrison, assuming he would somehow get it to SOE London. But before he could read it he was asked to take on a brief assignment that would require him to travel to Belgrade and Athens. He would be absent from Budapest for only six weeks but promised that the British consulate would delegate someone to look after her. His optimism was not to be rewarded because, in his absence, the staff failed to keep in contact with her.

In late March 1940, MI5 had contacted the consulate, asking for Christine's current address. They had only a post office box number, Budapest 4, Postafiok 244, and were making a routine enquiry, most likely on behalf of the Home Office. It was only then that the consulate realised they had no idea where to find her. She had received no funding from them and to add insult to injury, they'd even forgotten her name. Consular officials also had to reluctantly admit that no one had passed on a vital message to Christine requesting that she return to London.

A frantic search for her was begun. Major Bickham Sweet-Escott, deputy to Taylor in Section D's Balkan operations bureau, became involved in this abbreviated mystery. In his memoir he wrote, 'Early in March she had disappeared in Budapest and we were afraid she had been arrested. One of my first jobs was to brief a Pole in London to go to Budapest and find her. He duly went off and tracked her down but he himself soon disappeared. He eventually turned up in hospital with a broken leg.'* He was speaking of course, of Radzyminski whose obsession with Christine had almost cost him his life.

The journalist had indeed succeeded in locating Christine. He again professed his love for her but she was more resolute than he, and emphatically rejected any suggestion of a relationship with him. Determined to revenge himself upon her once and for all, he had walked on to the Elizabeth Bridge one freezing cold night and leaped off into the dark waters of the Danube. Unfortunately, large sections of the river were still frozen and he broke his healthy leg in the fall. There are variations on the tales of Radzyminski's suicide attempts, depending on who is telling them.

In a report Christine hurriedly wrote after leaving Hungary in early 1941, she succinctly remarked that, 'There was also in Budapest a Pole called Radjiminsky (*sic*) who was also working with Taylor and who had been instructed to help me but he proved unsatisfactory and was dismissed by the British.'[1]

Sweet-Escott's comments confirm what she had hinted at earlier, namely that the lovesick journalist was also a Section D operative. As for the belated instructions for her to return to London, they could not have been acted upon as it turned out because the Italian government, about to declare war on Britain, had refused her application for a transit visa.

*See Sweet-Escott's book, *Baker Street Irregular* (Methuen 1965).

After leaving Hungary the following year Radzyminski turned up in France, in the company of Jerzy Gizycki. Both were attempting to flee the country before the rapidly advancing Germans. Gizycki was able to secure a berth on the last ship sailing from France to Britain but his traveling companion was not so lucky and perished in Europe.

Throughout her life Christine maintained a habit of picking up strays, dogs as well as men, in particular those without attachments. Radzyminski turned out to be one such person. It was a personality quirk of hers that would one day prove fatal.

Hubert Harrison meanwhile was unaware that Christine's whereabouts were soon to become a problem. When he left Budapest bound for Britain, he had carried her report with him but left Christine without access to her controller in London. Owen O'Malley strongly implied that Harrison had hurriedly left of his own accord, but it is highly unlikely that a key operative would leave his post without permission from his London handler unless his life was in grave danger. Nevertheless, O'Malley reported that, 'Hungary had got too hot for Harrison and I helped him get out through Italy.' O'Malley, who had previously taken great care to respect Hungary's neutrality, belatedly joined the struggle against the Germans.**

Harrison's departure was a blow for those opposed to the Horthy regime, for he was reportedly producing up to 100,000 propaganda pamphlets per week, had arranged financing for two political organisations and was attempting to mould a Catholic opposition to the Hungarian leader. His absence also affected Christine who'd been receiving forty

**See HS4/86 at The National Archives

pounds per month from Section D. These payments abruptly stopped without explanation but she continued her work as best she could, sending propaganda packets to Poland via other couriers.

In March the International Danube Commission imposed 'strict regulations' on the river to reduce the opportunities for sabotage to German shipping. This crackdown was in concert with German pressure on the Hungarian government for a more vigorous policing of its stretch of the Danube. As early as 1938 there had been discussions within the highest levels of the British government about how to disrupt the oil supply flowing from Romania to Germany in the event of war. The Danube then was one of the busiest interior shipping lanes in Europe and as such was an appetising and logical target for saboteurs. Several government departments including naval attaches were involved in concocting schemes to block the river. Among the proposals put forth was a suggestion to sink locomotives or barges laden with cement at the narrowest point of the river. The Section's operative Edward Howe claimed a small victory in response. He reported that an Hungarian operative named Lajos had blocked the river for two days by means of bribing the helmsman of a German lighter to run his ship aground. In the end, Prime Minister Neville Chamberlain and members of his cabinet decided to play it safe and ordered that there was not to be any British involvement in disrupting river traffic. Instead, they agreed to pressure the Romanian and Yugoslav governments to act.***

The Germans, until now apparently unaware of their vulnerability on the Danube, suddenly applied to the Hungarian government for permission to police its section of the river. Admiral Horthy responded by stepping up his own patrols on the Danube instead, a rare example of his refusal to cooperate with the Hitler government.

In between missions to Poland, Christine was asked to organise surveillance of shipping on the river. She asked Andrew for his assistance, mainly as her driver as she had never learned to drive a car. No report of their activities appears in SOE files but after the war Andrew claimed that he and his colleagues had succeeded in destroying at least one barge. He described to one writer how he and Christine had driven to a secluded point on the river bank where he detached his wooden leg before diving into the Danube. He fixed a 'limpet' mine to the underside of a barge while Christine kept watch nearby. As they hastily left the area he 'thought' he heard an explosion.

However heroic it might sound Andrew's account of this action is either exaggerated or cut from whole cloth. He would have carried out this act of sabotage in the winter of 1940-41 as he and Christine had made a rapid departure from Budapest in February. Limpet mines designed for 'underwater work', sometimes called Clams, were first manufactured in late 1940. They were made up by ES6 (Experimental Station 6). Unless Andrew was able to obtain one as early as January he could not have destroyed a barge using one of these devices. It would have been extremely difficult for him, or for anyone in Budapest, to obtain explosive materials so early on in the war that were both waterproof and that could be quickly attached to the bottom of a wooden barge. A Polish intelligence document, made public in 2005, confirms that at the time the barges in the Danube had wooden hulls.[2] There is no official account of this incident and Andrew never explained how he managed to work beneath the freezing waters without any diving gear.

***SOE agents blocked the Yugoslav section of the Danube for only two months in 1941.

In the late spring of 1940 all Czech organisations operating in Hungary were broken up by a combination of the Hungarian secret service and Gestapo officers working within the Ministry of the Interior. Horthy's government was gradually being undermined by German agents, reminiscent of the manner in which a previous administration had been infiltrated by Hungarian communists.

After the Czech resistance groups had been dispersed Horthy, under pressure from Berlin, began to crack down on known Polish organisations. Several Poles were arrested and their cache of weapons and explosives seized. Now under enormous pressure from the enemy Section D was forced to suspend its shipments of supplies and weapons destined for the Armia Krajowa via Hungary. Pressure on Polish refugees in Budapest had also been stepped up. Plainclothes police often prevented them from entering their Legation while others were allowed to enter the building only after submitting to a humiliating search. Addresses used by Poles, most quite innocently, were visited by local police searching for arms and explosives.

The Gestapo and the Hungarian Ministry of the Interior suspected, correctly, that Polish operatives were still active despite the harassment and the shut-down of Czech lines of communication. But they were unable to close the Polish links with Britain as long as their respective consulates remained open. Time, however, was on the German side and both consulates were forced to close early the following year.

Lacking a directive from London, Christine devoted herself to assisting her lover in his attempts to secure the release of more POW. Andrew had recently purchased a truck which he used to ferry groups of escapees from the Slovak border to safety in Budapest and points west. Irrespective of what was happening elsewhere, he threw himself with great vigour into his self-appointed task of rescuing British and Polish aircrews.

Musketeer couriers continued to arrive in Budapest, bringing information about conditions in Poland and about German troop movements. Not all the material was of great significance but when assembled together, the bits and pieces gave the British and the Polish governments a good idea of what they were up against.

Having had her attempts at cooperation with the fugitive Poles rebuffed, Christine enlisted Andrew in her own project, sending couriers to Poland and in turn receiving and translating reports they brought back to Budapest. These were passed on to Section D and SIS. In the absence of an organised intelligence-gathering effort by the Polish Deuxieme Bureau, the British had little choice but to rely on Christine and the Musketeers to provide whatever information they could get from inside Poland. They were joined in May by Kennedy's cousin Ludwig Popiel,**** lately of the Polish cavalry. He had brought with him an anti-tank rifle which he'd smuggled out of Poland and which Christine hid in her flat (Popiel was one of the last people to see her alive in 1952, just hours before her murder).

A Jesuit priest, Father Laski, became a welcomed addition to Christine's dwindling circle. His time with the Musketeers was short and he died in a concentration camp. The brother of one of Christine's school friends, Leon Gradowski (*aka* Michael Lis) joined the group and continued her work after she had been forced to leave Hungary. Gradowski

---

****Popiel held the rank of major in the Carpathian Lancers and later won an MC. He was also awarded two Virtuti Militari by the Polish government.

was an especially creative agent, at times flamboyant in his behaviour. He particularly enjoyed swanning around Budapest dressed as a German officer. After Christine and Andrew had escaped from a Hungarian prison and fled the city, Gradowski had his own incredible escape from the Gestapo while en route from Budapest to Istanbul carrying a batch of intelligence documents.

Those days in Budapest must have been exciting for Christine. She had finally found her *metier* and had become the center of attention largely through her own efforts. It was almost as if she had suddenly come of age. In Budapest she found herself surrounded by a coterie of admirers, not flirtatious young men, but men who were keenly aware of the importance of their mission. A single mis-step could lead to the collapse of their efforts, almost certain arrest and possible death. By late 1940 Hungarian authorities had begun closing in on them in earnest, urged on by the Gestapo.

The link-up with the Musketeers in Warsaw was proving to be a valuable asset for both the British and exiled Poles but the tiny circle of patriots began to shrink in late 1940. Two of Christine's closest associates, Marcin Lubomirski and Antoni Filipkiewicz, were arrested and sent to Mauthausen concentration camp. They both survived their imprisonment and were later awarded the King's Medal for Courage in the Cause of Freedom.

Christine's most important contact was someone she hadn't counted on, Owen O'Malley himself. Their initial meeting had concerned itself with introductions and perhaps an off-the-record briefing regarding her mission but the relationship gradually developed into a social one. Neither she nor O'Malley ever revealed what was said at their meetings but one can assume that, at some point, they discussed tactics and politics.

Christine and Andrew occasionally dined at the Legation of an evening where they also met Lady O'Malley and her eighteen-year-old daughter Kate. She had recently arrived in Hungary and was immediately smitten by Andrew while Christine appealed to Kate as an admired older sister. It was to be a friendship that survived the war, mostly because of Kate's efforts though Andrew came close to undermining it.[3]

Chapter 8.

The Fall of Paris and a Narrow Escape

After her return to Budapest in the spring of 1940, Christine divided her time between helping Andrew rescue downed aircrews and preparing for another mission to Poland. He registered no opposition this time, primarily because he knew the snow in the Tatras had already begun to melt, eliminating one of the hazards she would encounter while crossing the mountains. Besides, he knew that arguing with Christine would be fruitless. There are no existing details of this proposed second trip, a journey planned for either late May or early June. A document in the SOE archive tells us only that her second attempt to cross Slovakia and enter Poland was unsuccessful. She must have been turned back at the Hungary-Slovak border for if she had penetrated any deeper into Slovakia, closer to the Polish border, she surely would have been detained. A third attempt later in June also failed but this time with near-disastrous consequences.

There is a discrepancy in the chronology, and in other details, between her report, Vladimir's memoir and an earlier biography of Christine.* Vladimir wrote that they began an affair while returning to Budapest from Poland after escaping from a Slovak patrol. A second account, described in the biography for which Andrew supplied much of the detail,

---

Christine, a search for Christine Granville, by Madeleine Masson (Hamish Hamilton London 1975, revised and reprinted in 2005 by Virago).

does not disagree but adds that while crossing Slovakia they were nearly apprehended. To dramatise his account Andrew added that the pair had escaped into a forest with the sound of gun fire ringing in their ears and eventually returned safely to Budapest.1

Christine's report, dated February 1941, is at odds with both accounts. Her version of the third attempted entry into Poland, undertaken in mid-June 1940, made no mention whatever of Vladimir. She gave as few details as possible and may have inserted some misinformation in case the report fell into the wrong hands. She did mention a guide - she referred to him as 'a boy' - who travelled with her but did not name him. Patrick Howarth, who came to know Christine quite well in Cairo, supported her version of events, namely, that a Polish officer had accompanied her on that failed attempt to breach the Poland-Slovakia border.

Christine reported that she'd travelled alone because she '... was unable to find anybody to carry anything to Poland.' The package to be smuggled across the border was a bundle of cash to be handed over to the AK. Her reference to the boy detained along with her by the Slovak patrol was almost certainly Vladimir who fancied himself in love with her. His unpublished memoir, written some years after the war, leaves no doubt that he was her companion. On this third attempt to reach Warsaw they were stopped and questioned by a patrol at a rural train station in Slovakia. She reported that the soldiers searched them and discovered two bundles of cash in her backpack, one containing 145,000 Polish zlotys and seventy-five American dollars. Vladimir had been carrying 15,000 Danish kronen.

The Slovaks confiscated the money as well as their travel documents. Displaying their weapons menacingly, the soldiers forced Christine to stand against a wall while they interrogated her and shouted questions but she repeatedly denied being a British operative. She calmly pointed out that if she and her companion were taken prisoner senior officers were certain to appropriate the cash. The combination of her persuasiveness and the lure of hard currency, it seems, finally convinced the soldiers to release her and her companion, turning them back towards Hungary.

Vladimir painted a more melodramatic picture. He wrote that, after their documents and cash had been confiscated, the soldiers notified the Gestapo. The prisoners were then marched at gunpoint toward the patrol's base. While crossing a bridge he pretended to stumble, dropping a package of inflammatory photos he'd been carrying into the river below (one photo showed Britain's King George VI greeting General Sikorski). Meanwhile, Christine chatted with her captors, intimating that she was bored with her colleague even though he'd given her a diamond necklace (actually cut-glass), which she produced from her bag. One of the soldiers snatched the necklace, breaking the string and sending the 'gems' tumbling down the river bank. The soldiers (we are not told their numbers) abandoned their captives and plunged headlong down the embankment to retrieve the diamonds. Their prisoners seized the moment and fled to a nearby forest. They spent several days in hiding before making a difficult return trip to Budapest.

When Vladimir reported back to the Deuxieme Bureau he was strongly advised to cease working with Christine whom they saw as a liability. Some time after this episode the German authorities allegedly 'papered the walls of Polish rail stations with her photo.' That was presumably taken from her passport. The text offered a reward of 10,000

German marks for her capture. The only source for this tale is the minister Owen O'Malley and he never explained how he'd learned about those circulars. Whether or not they existed (no one else has ever reported seeing one) the fact remains that all elements of the German security police were now alerted to the presence of this British spy. They must have suspected that she was operating in Slovakia or in a nearby country but were not yet aware that Budapest was her base. The German authorities had her photo and knew her name. This could have caused trouble for her mother and brother, still living in Poland, but they apparently suffered no immediate reprisals. There can be no doubt though that, after her daring escape from the border guards, future crossings through Slovakia and travel in Poland had suddenly become more hazardous.

While Christine was down to her last few kopecks, her husband Jerzy Gizycki had been leading a comparatively comfortable life in Paris in his guise of travel writer. Ignoring the battles raging across the western front, he had left the relative safety of the Haute-Savoie and returned to the city despite France's own precarious position. He took rooms at the Hotel du Danube on the rue Jacob, recently vacated by General Sikorski, now safe in London. Gizycki was preparing an article for Section D but his wife's whereabouts were very much on his mind. She was otherwise occupied and did not seem as worried about her lack of contact with him. His situation suddenly changed for the worse. In May 1940 German forces unleashed full frontal assaults on Belgium, the Netherlands and Luxembourg. The Luftwaffe began air strikes on France on May 14. In four weeks' time divisions of the German army would be in Paris.

On May 21st Gizycki sent Section D a second article and noted that, 'In view of the situation in Norvay (*sic*), Holland, Belgium and, lately, in France - it was not easy to gather enough ' "optimistic" material.' He also wondered if in future schoolboys would think of him as an heroic figure, like the commandos who had recently stormed the German raider support ship *Altmark* to rescue British prisoners transferred from the doomed *Graf Spee*.2

Gizycki was chafing at the bit, wanting to do something more stimulating than merely writing psychological operations reports while Christine was obviously engaged in more serious work. He complained that aside from producing the articles he had no other duties. His own financial status now began to deteriorate and he needed cash. He agreed with Section D that, while he might provide more 'articles', the question of remuneration had not been settled. Rather than demand the payment due him he meekly asked that his handlers pay him whatever they considered to be right. Optimistically, he enclosed the address of his bank on Gray's Inn Road in London. He closed his signal on a glum note, writing that he had heard from Christine, still in Budapest and unable to leave. He expressed his regret that they would not be meeting due to 'complications', an oblique reference to belligerent Italy's refusal to grant her a transit visa on her proposed journey to Britain. 'Hard luck for me', he wrote.

Despite the *Luftwaffe's* attacks Gizycki remained at his post, writing his articles and delivering them to Miss O'Halloran whose true identity has yet to be revealed.

Dunkerque fell on June 4. A few days later Gizycki's London controller acknowledged receipt of his 'Polish News Letter' and agreed to pay him the princely sum of £25. Increasingly aware of his uncertain situation, Gizycki asked if he would be asked to provide more articles. Section D must have suspected that France would not survive the German onslaught and so replied that no promises could be made for the near future. He was told that the Section might pay for another article but would not need it for some time. He failed to take the hint that there would be no further assignments.

In a letter dated June 6th he repeated the news that he had heard from Christine. He spoke again of the failed rendez-vous and lamented the fact that she was unable to obtain travel documents from the Italian government. 'It does not look as if my desire to be with my wife or at least nearer to her, should be fulfilled soon.'$_3$ He casually mentioned that she had gone '. . . to see her people once more and should be back presently.' But $X.3$ would have known that. Gizycki was genuinely concerned for his wife's safety but he was completely in the dark about her affair with Andrew. It would be another year before he learned the truth.

The love-stricken journalist Radzyminski was about to make his final appearance in the story of Christine's life. Elements of the German army entered Paris on June 13th. As the French capital had been declared an open city, their occupation was easily completed the following day. Nevertheless, the *Luftwaffe* had dropped some bombs on the city causing fatalities. One bomb struck the Pont Mirabeau and another caused considerable damage in the Avenue de Versailles. A few days later General Charles de Gaulle broadcast to the French people from London, announced the formation of the Free French Committee and urged them not to give up hope.

The German advance on Paris finally made Gizycki's position untenable. He could no

The Elusive Madame G 113

longer provide Section D with any relevant information except at great risk to himself. Reluctantly, he joined the exodus from the capital, hoping to reach Angers some 280 kilometers southwest of Paris where the Polish government-in-exile had established its headquarters. The legendary bookseller Sylvia Beach poignantly described what Gizycki and others, observed:

'A lovely June in 1940. Sunny with blue skies. Only about 25,000 people were left in Paris. . . . through our tears, (we) watched the refugees moving through the city. They came in at the East Gate, crossed Paris by way of the Boulevard Saint Michel and the Luxembourg Gardens, then went out through the Orleans and Italie gates: cattle-drawn carts piled with household goods; on top of them children, old people and sick people, pregnant women and women with babies, poultry in coops, and dogs and cats. Sometimes they stopped at the Luxembourg Gardens to let the cows graze there.'[4]

Gizycki reached the Paris suburbs via the Metro where he paused at a bistro to have a drink. As luck would have it a Polish reporter whom he knew slightly wandered in. This was none other than Jozef Radzyminski, the same forlorn lover who had twice attempted suicide after Christine rejected him. Gizycki did not record whether Radzyminski confessed his love for Christine. But he was obviously unaware of the journalist's bizarre behaviour in Budapest, for he wrote to his controllers in London suggesting that they find some useful employment for him.

The two men struck up a conversation during which the journalist revealed that he had 'obtained' several Polish military passes and offered one to Gizycki. While they were finishing their drinks a truck-load of gendarmes arrived, fleeing the city like everyone else.

The two Poles boldly produced their passes and after a bit of haggling secured places on the truck bound for southern France. The roads leading out of Paris were clogged with both foot and vehicular traffic. Occasionally the sorry procession of refugees, bearing all manner of personal effects, would be strafed by German fighter planes.

Gizycki and his companion reached Orleans safely but remained only a short time. Gizycki was most anxious to reach Angers, optimistic that he could be of use to the new government. He approached the gendarmes' commander and demanded a car so that he and Radzyminski could continue on to Polish HQ. He convinced the officer that they were carrying documents which Sikorski desperately needed. Fortunately for him the French officer did not ask to see the non-existent papers and gave them one of his vehicles. The two men drove frantically to their destination. But their efforts were for nought for when they arrived, they found only a handful of Polish soldiers calmly loading furniture and boxes of documents onto trucks. The government itself, not trusting the French army to hold the line, had already decamped to London.

Gizycki and Radzyminski travelled with a group of Polish stragglers to Bayonne from where they hoped to escape into neutral Spain. They spent a restless night in Bayonne, thanks to a German air raid, where they heard rumours of a British transport ship docked at St Jean-de-Luz due to sail for Britain. The following morning they hurried to the dock side, arriving while the SS *Ettrick* was taking on passengers. Using his diplomatic credentials Gizycki secured a berth but Radzyminski lacked the appropriate papers and had to remain behind as his bogus documents did not pass inspection. The two never met again. An unconfirmed source added a lengthy postscript to Radzyminski's final days. The source reported that he had spent a short time in France guiding refugees to a location on the Spanish border where they could cross safely. He had obtained a Portugese passport but was aboard a train that crashed in Spain. He survived with minor injuries but the authorities detained him briefly before turning him over to the Germans who placed him on a train bound for Poland and a labour camp. The un-named source maintains that Radzyminski jumped from the train at some point and was never seen again.

The passengers aboard Gizycki's ship were a sorry melange of refugees from across Europe including some very well-known personalities. Chief among these were King Zog** of Albania along with his family, and allegedly, Alexander Kerensky, former prime minister of the revolutionary Russian Provisional Government. If Kerensky, and indeed Gizycki, were traveling on the same ship with King Zog then it must have been pseudonymously for their names do not appear on the ship's passenger manifest (available at Britain's National Archives). Either Gizycki's memory was faulty or else he was making a clumsy attempt to hide information which in the long run was unimportant. He returned safely to Britain and would soon be summoned back into service.

Christine remained in Budapest throughout the warm summer of 1940 but without an assignment from the newly formed Special Operations Executive and with only a tenuous link to London. The consulate's failure to look after her once Hubert Harrison departed is at least partially attributable to the organisational chaos that afflicted Section D and SOE throughout their existence, resulting in more than one major personnel shake-up.

** In his memoir Gizycki makes uncomplimentary remarks about Zog and implies that someone in the king's entourage stole his typewriter.

The *Luftwaffe* attacked the Straits of Dover in July in what were to be the opening shots of the Battle of Britain. By then much of Europe had been overrun by German forces. Christine and Andrew, aided by a small band of Poles and sometimes with O'Malley's assistance, continued their work, organising escapes from POW camps and sending the escapees on their way to Britain. The British were especially keen to have Allied aircrews exfiltrated, anticipating that they would be much needed in the very near future.

Andrew worked flat-out on this rescue mission. He sometimes drove from Budapest to the Yugoslav border, picked up exhausted prisoners then drove all the way back in a day without stopping for sleep. Christine watched with apprehension as his health was uppermost in her mind.

Winston Churchill had become prime Minister in May 1940, succeeding Neville Chamberlain. Shortly after taking office Churchill approved plans for a new intelligence organisation independent of MI5 and MI6. Lords Halifax and Hankey and Colonel Jo Holland were the main instigators of this scheme. After two months of haggling between the government and the Labour opposition, the plans became a reality.

The duties and many of the personnel of Section D, EH and MI(R) were folded into SOE which was itself divided initially into three sub-groups, SO1 for propaganda, SO2 for operations and sabotage, and SO3 for long-range planning. SOE files do not record Christine's assigned section but given the nature of her work in Poland it's most likely that she would have been drafted into SO2. Gwendoline Lees, an operative in Cairo, claimed that she had officially 'inducted' Christine into SOE in 1943.[5]

While the transition from Section D to SO2 was in progress Christine continued to receive and pass on intelligence reports from the Musketeers. She still managed to find the time and energy to assist Andrew in secretly transporting British and Polish escapees from Hungary to Britain. The Polish army in which Andrew had served no longer existed. It had been replaced by a re-organised military that consisted of the remnants of the units gathered in France under Sikorski's leadership plus the AK in Poland under the command of General Sosnkowski. There would soon be a large third component, composed of personnel taken captive by the Russians when they grabbed large parts of Poland after the German invasion, and held in Soviet forced labour camps. Though they would eventually fight alongside the Allies they would also become a force to be reckoned with in Polish politics. Their forthcoming release from internment, and their loyalty to General Wladyslaw Anders who had also endured captivity, would pose a serious threat to Sikorski's leadership if only temporarily.

Propaganda distribution and rescue efforts continued sporadically while MI6 grumbled about lack of cooperation from Owen O'Malley. An unsigned memo circulated in August 1940 complained that important work '. . . cannot be done unless the non-cooperative attitude adopted by the Minister in Budapest is reversed. We would be glad, therefore, if the necessary approach could be made to the Foreign Office so that pressure can be put upon Mr. O'Malley to revise his attitude.'***

Owen Saint Clair O'Malley (later Sir) as he was properly known, had been appointed British Minister to Hungary in May 1939. He was a colourful character, some would say eccentric, whose long career in the Foreign Office was pock-marked by disputes with his superiors and those with whom he worked. The son of a former attorney general and chief justice in several British colonies, he had been educated at Rugby and at Oxford where he studied for a career in the Foreign Office. There never seemed to have been any doubt about what his life's work would be.

Though O'Malley had a long history of distinguished service to the government, he was once involved in a scandal and had narrowly avoided disgrace. In the 1920s he had become involved with a group of FO staff who were speculating in French francs. When the insider dealing was discovered O'Malley did the honourable thing and offered his resignation. His career was saved by, among others, Robert Vansittart, who featured in Christine's early career and with whom O'Malley would later clash over the question of German expansion. He has been described as Vansittart's 'most outspoken and obstructive critic.' Instead of being sacked O'Malley was given a one-year suspension and deprived of five years' seniority. His father's position as attorney general was perhaps influential in saving his career.

Once war had been declared O'Malley voiced a very controversial opinion *vis a vis* Germany, namely that the British government should officially accept the Anschluss in direct opposition to Vansittart's attempts to secure Austrian and Italian cooperation. Though personally anti-Nazi, Vansittart advocated a non-interventionist position in Europe as Britain's official policy. O'Malley and his secretary, EH Carr, went even further by suggesting that Germany should be offered hegemony in central Europe in return for unchallenged British maritime supremacy.6

***See HS4/86 at The National Archives*

In his official capacity of British Minister to Hungary, O'Malley openly disapproved of SO2 operations, in particular, sabotage. Foreign Office policy then was to keep Hungary onside or at least neutral. But away from his duties O'Malley, always proud of his Irish ancestry, nevertheless decided to take a hand in subverting the Nazis. His attitude towards the policy of neutrality, which he personally supported, changed after the fall of France and he eagerly joined his two Polish friends in establishing safe routes to Britain for escaped Allied POW.

Despite his thinly disguised dislike for SOE 'projects' O'Malley did his part to promote the British cause. He put his own position in jeopardy by setting up a radio transmitter in the consulate bathroom which he and his wife Jane used on occasion to issue news bulletins to the local population, in the style of BBC broadcasts. He later proudly confessed to an American official, 'I had . . . the beginnings of a private organisation in my own hands for direct wireless communication between Budapest and Warsaw.'

O'Malley and Christine were singing from the same song sheet in respect of their efforts to spread propaganda though her target was Poland and his the Hungarians. Like many of the men who met Christine during her SOE career, he fell under her spell and was effusive in professing his admiration for her. In his memoir he described her as 'young, beautiful, gifted. . . She was the bravest person I ever knew, the only woman who had a positive *nostalgie* for danger. She could do anything with dynamite except eat it.'

Here, O'Malley was indulging in a bit of hyperbole for Christine was never directly involved in the use of explosives. The closest she came to dynamite was during the brief period when her flat was being used to hold weapons. She did not train in the use of explosives until 1944, prior to her mission in France and after O'Malley had left Hungary.

Jerzy Gizycki's penultimate letter to *X.3* was written in June after his narrow escape from France. It was a plaintive note stating that he had decided to move to Canada and 'to prepare there some sort of a home to which [Christine] would come when she gets out of her actual predicament.' Christine did not share her husband's desire and would rather have chewed nails than settle down. Moving to Canada either then or later would have been the furthest thing from her mind. She was absolutely single-minded about her work as an SOE operative and even her ongoing affair with Andrew failed to distract her from her chosen path. There is little doubt that she was a bit of a romantic as regards her status within British special operations. One wonders if she would have enjoyed the same level of elation had she merely been a Polish agent.

Hubert Harrison was finally replaced as Christine's Budapest contact in the autumn of 1940, precipitating a clash of personalities. The new man's name has been omitted from SOE files, perhaps accidentally, and Christine did not name him in summarising her activities while in Hungary. He did provide her with a bit of financial relief by putting her on a salary of 500 pengoes per month but otherwise gave her very little support. Whoever he was, he appeared to be timid and would only act on direct orders from Section D.

In October a Musketeer courier arrived from Poland with the news that another intelligence organisation had been formed (Christine did not disclose its name). Its remit was to carry out acts of sabotage in addition to providing information about enemy activity. This was probably Sikorski's recently formed umbrella organisation, Continental Action.

The courier informed Christine that CA had been established to coordinate attacks on the Germans in Poland well as keeping the occupiers under surveillance. That put it in direct conflict with the Musketeers who took pride in being regarded as the main source for information coming out of Poland.

In the aftermath of the German invasion the pre-war Polish government had been abolished and officials scattered across Europe. President Moscicki and his cabinet ministers had fled the country. Many of them, including the hawk-like foreign minister Beck had found a safe haven of sorts in neutral Romania which was under great pressure to turn the Poles over to the Germans. The two Polish intelligence bureaux+ were in disarray. Those officers who had evaded capture managed to reach France where they joined General Sikorski in forming a new government and a new army. A significant number went into hiding in Poland. In the almost complete absence of an official intelligence corps numerous independent groups like the Musketeers operated without supervision and with impunity, creating confusion and friction with SIS. Later, both SIS and the re-constituted Polish intelligence bureaux were united in bitter opposition to organisations like SOE and especially the Musketeers who were almost beyond their control.

+French was still the language of diplomacy in Europe. Beyond Poland's borders the two intelligence services, *Oddial drugi* and *Oddzial szosty*, preferred to be known as the Deuxieme Bureau and the Seizieme Bureau. In some British dispatches there were referred to as the 2nd Bureau and the 6th Bureau.

Chapter 9.
Last Mission to Poland

Whoever had compiled the most recent report delivered to Christine had done a fantastic job for it was literally bursting with news about developments in Poland. It identified the locations of German armament factories in the country plus plans to build more of the same using forced labour. It revealed the number of German regiments in Poland, their identifying insignia and their movements as well as plans to construct air fields on Polish soil, information on new-style torpedoes and mines and details of the U-boats which were hurriedly being built in the Gdansk shipyards. It was one of the most comprehensive intelligence reports that Section D/SOE was to receive from inside occupied territory.

Christine took on the task of translating this material from Polish into French. The information was then relayed by courier to Polish authorities in London who in turn handed it to the appropriate departments of the British government. Included in this treasure trove was a footnote to the effect that sixteen British pilots and crew had escaped from German detention in Poland and were in Warsaw, being sheltered in an institution for the aurally and orally disabled. German troops had already been ordered to enter such institutions, as well as those for the mentally ill and prisons, and kill all the inmates or else transfer them elsewhere for execution.

Christine volunteered to return to Warsaw to escort the aircrew back to Budapest.

But an entire month elapsed before Harrison's replacement finally decided to veto her proposed rescue mission, she complained. He pleaded lack of funds in his budget for such a mission and added that he would need special permission from London before dispensing any money to her or to anyone else. She was kept waiting for several more weeks by which time the airmen could well have been shot. She approached him a second time, offering to undertake the mission on her own if he was unwilling or unable to help. He relented but gave her only a fraction of the money she had requested.

Now that the Slovaks, and the Gestapo, had Christine's credentials in hand, crossing the Tatras to enter Poland became a much more dicey proposition. Military patrols began to appear more frequently in Slovakia, and the once-charming Zakopane and vicinity were declared *Sperrgebeit* (restricted areas). Despite allegedly having a price on her head Christine insisted on making one more trip to Poland, traveling on a forged Ukrainian visa. Accompanied by the courier Vladimir Szyc she left Budapest by train on November 8th and arrived at the familiar stop-over of Kosice on the 13th. One account names Father Laski as Christine's guide. But in her post-war interview with *Kurier Polski* Mrs Szyc claimed that she and her husband had once crossed the border with Christine. She succeeded in penetrating the Polish border only twice and it is well-documented that Jan Marusaz was her guide on the first crossing.

On this attempt in November she and her companion followed the usual route, crossing Slovakia and its border with Poland via train, then proceeding towards Zakopane on skis and on foot. They put up at the Kuehn villa in Poronin, just east of the resort, where they were looked after by Vincent Galica, a cadet officer of the 1st Regiment of the Podhale Riflemen.

Five days later Christine entered Warsaw only to learn that the British aircrew had fled after hearing a rumour, false, as it were, that the Hungarian government had joined the Axis. The airmen had made their way to Bialystok and from there took a train to Kiev. Christine reported that she'd seen this information on a postcard sent by one of the crew who wrote that they were now safe in Russia.

Though she had failed to contact the crewmen she was able to help another pair of British soldiers on this, her final mission to Poland and the last time she would see her homeland. The two soldiers, survivors of the defeated British Expeditionary Force (BEF), had managed to reach Poland but in a weakened condition. Instinctively she sought to get them out of the country as soon as possible. However, the Musketeers had given her more microfilmed documents, revealing the extent of the German military build-up, to be delivered to London. She couldn't wait for the soldiers to recover and had to leave them in the hands of Witkowski's people while she prepared to return to Budapest.

More trouble loomed when Szyc failed to appear at the appointed time for the return trip. Another courier was pressed into service and together they made an uneventful crossing over the mountains, arriving in Budapest tired but safe. It was only later that she learned of Szyc's death, allegedly murdered by none other than the Musketeers' leader Witkowski. The group had begun to come apart, largely because Witkowski had developed other interests, namely the accumulation of cash and amenities denied to his fellow Poles. The cause of his dispute with Szyc has been obscured in a fog of accusations and counter-claims but it is almost certain that the unexplained loss of a large sum of money which Szyc was to deliver to the AK precipitated their lethal falling-out.

Witkowski however was not the only one playing fast and loose with money. Individual Musketeers occasionally siphoned off funds destined for the AK and used the money to support their own activities. Some Polish officers were still running private cells even though a new government was in place in France. Colonel Swietochowski, for one, allegedly used his own funds to pay his men and gave them orders that sometimes ran contrary to what SIS and the Polish intelligence bureaux were planning. Romek, the AK's cell in Budapest, was reported to have been compromised and some of its members were accused of running rogue missions that had little to do with gathering military intelligence. Orders then came from Warsaw that all intelligence reports being passed from the Polish Underground to London via Budapest were not to be interpreted or even read by Romek but were to be sent directly to SIS without delay.

In the midst of all this unrestrained activity was one of the most effective cells, that being run by Christine and Andrew. Nevertheless, Colonel Stanislaw Rostworowski fearing that they would compromise Romek by embarking upon their own missions, was most unhappy about their presence. He was said to have breathed a sigh of relief when the pair finally departed Budapest in early 1941.

In 1975 Kazimierza Lewanska-Szyc, the murdered man's widow, told a Polish newspaper that she and her husband had once accompanied Christine on a round-trip journey from Warsaw to Budapest. Her husband had become somewhat of a local hero, having made a daring escape from the dreaded Palace, the former tuberculosis sanatorium in

Zakopane converted by the Gestapo into an interrogation center. It was rumoured that he killed a guard while breaking away from his German captors.

Szyc however did not live long enough to savour his freedom. Two Polish authors, writing after the war, differed on how he met his fate. In his book Alfons Filars reported that Szyc had been stopped at a German vehicle checkpoint between Radom and Warsaw, and had been shot dead when he attempted to flee.1 Roman Buczek sensationally claimed that Szyc was murdered by Witkowski.2 He alleged that the Musketeers' leader shot the courier as the two men sat talking in a car, an assassination approved by the AK.

After the war, Mrs. Lewanska-Szyc said of Christine: 'She was an incredibly brave woman. Beautiful and brave. . . She was a great conspirator and was a gifted story-teller, she had many friends and acquaintances.'* The courier's widow was not the first, and would not be the last, to describe Christine as 'a story-teller.'

The BEF men that Christine had left behind in Warsaw eventually regained their health and finally met with her in Belgrade in the spring of 1941. The information she brought back from that final mission included alarming details about new types of gases the Germans were preparing to use. This intelligence had been copied onto 35 mm microfilm which she hid in her gloves. Her report also provided details of subversive radio activities about to be launched by the AK who planned to provide a regular information service from Poland, and from inside Germany to Britain. The Poles' optimism seemed boundless in contrast to the mood of their colleagues in Budapest, alarmed that the Poland-Hungary-Britain connection was becoming increasingly difficult to maintain.

*Interview given to *Kurier Polska* in 1975.

Separately, the Musketeers' had smuggled a letter into Budapest claiming that the German military had press-ganged a large number of Polish workers and had sent them to Berlin. Alerted in advance of this move, AK leaders seized the opportunity to embed some of their own engineers into the work force and were thus able to receive reports from inside the Reich. These engineers were now providing details of rail movements within Germany, including brief descriptions of their freight, possibly from reading the waybills attached to each car as it was loaded. Radio frequencies and the call-signs to be used by the Poles were also contained in the letter, encoded for security in an English-Russian dictionary which Christine had brought back from an earlier mission.

Section D lost track of Christine again in the autumn of 1940. Fryday replied to their query with the ominous news that no one had heard from her since the late summer. This was not quite true because she continued to assist Andrew Kennedy with his exfiltration scheme and the Musketeers certainly knew how to find her. It appears that Harrison's rapid departure from Budapest, along with the incompetence of his replacement, was at the root of the confusion. Her new section chief was aware that she'd embarked on another journey to Poland to attempt to rescue the downed airmen. This information should have been conveyed to Section D. Even though Christine was a rank amateur in the hazardous business of espionage they placed an enormous amount of faith in what she had to say about conditions in Poland. Though she had been a British agent for less than a year Section officials accepted without question her reports. Their reliance on her word alone underlines how desperate the government were for information from inside occupied Poland.

Their only other source, prior to the autumn of 1941, was the untested Musketeers.

In late November, Phillip Leake (symbol D/HJ)** dispatched a note to the still pseudonymous Fryday asking for news of Christine. Fryday replied that no one had heard from her since the late summer. (It is not clear why Leake wanted to get in contact with her and who had instructed him to.) Leake quoted from Harrison's report on her valuable work in Budapest to date, saying that she was 'a person of remarkable courage and intelligence whose qualities and good will are at present being wasted in idleness.' He suggested to Fryday that Hubert Harrison, who had returned to England months ago and was then working for the *Daily Express*, might know where she was. Fryday must have passed the query to Freddy Voigt (unless Fryday and Voigt were one in the same person), for Lieutenant Colonel Harold Perkins, head of SOE's Polish section, received a memo two days later signed *X.3* asking him to contact Harrison at the *Express*. Perkins was reminded that, 'This woman was doing excellent work in Poland for us, and merits any help we can give her.' It was a bit of clutching at straws. Harrison had left Hungary the previous spring so it was unlikely that he would have known where to find Christine six months later.

Jerzy Gizycki had reached England safely in June after his escape from occupied France and he too contacted Perkins asking for information about his apparently missing wife. A number of people now joined the search. Telegrams and signals flew back and forth from London to Budapest demanding to know the whereabouts of the newly formed SOE's most important agent. Consular staff were dispatched to Christine's last known address in

---

**Leake was caught up in a German bombing raid and killed while on a mission in Romania in 1944.

the Hungarian capital where the population had become increasingly concerned for its own safety, never mind that of a British agent. SOE's worries were finally allayed when she returned from Poland after her failed attempt to rescue the British aircrew.

Thoroughly exhausted, Christine re-appeared in Budapest on November 25th and submitted a lengthy report to her section chief. She ostentatiously turned over to him a small amount of money remaining from the funds that he'd given her earlier to point up his tight-fisted attitude. But she had not forgotten or forgiven what she saw as his lack of cooperation. In summing up her activities in Budapest some months later Christine noted that he had not acted promptly on the information she and the Musketeers had provided. She accused her own section chief of sitting on that intelligence report for two months which seems incredibly irresponsible. Her charge against him was supported, and the length of time extended, in a memo written by Major Peter Wilkinson, Royal Fusiliers, who reported to Lieutenant Colonel Perkins. He alleged that this lapse was due to gross carelessness and maintained that the man had ignored her report for as much as four months, not two (Wilkinson would shortly re-appear in less supportive circumstances).

Whatever their differences, Christine was able to persuade her section chief to send another courier from an unnamed military group to Poland. He eventually returned with two British airmen in tow. They'd been traveling on false papers which she urged should be returned to Poland immediately to be used by couriers. The Musketeer who rescued the RAF men also brought out more microfilm which he gave to Christine's new leader. He in turn refused to allow her to read this latest report. She was indignant but as station head he was under no obligation to share its contents with his operatives. She however believed herself to be central to this operation and thus entitled to see it. As far as SOE were concerned the report was to be read on a 'need-to-know' basis only.

When Christine continued to badger her section chief for information about the latest news from Poland, she was told that the microfilm had been sent on to Colonel WTC Lethbridge (Mil AA), the Passport Control Officer in Belgrade. She must have felt terribly frustrated when she met Lethbridge a few months later and he denied having received the films. Obviously the creation of SOE during the summer of 1940, and its absorption of Section D and MI(R), had not resulted in a more disciplined organisation. Christine's final charge against Harrison's replacement was that he'd lost the forged Ukrainian travel documents that she had used to facilitate her safe passage through Slovakia. He never recovered them and Minister O'Malley had to hastily create new visas for her before she could make her escape from Hungary the following year.

Several weeks after returning from Poland she received a final communique from her contact in Warsaw who had heard nothing from the British in reply to the two long reports he had sent. He was discouraged by this lack of response and told Christine that, '... the British seemed very queer people and were acting very strangely.'[3]

Events were about to overtake Christine and some of her colleagues. Gizycki had recovered quickly from his melancholy mood and returned to London, eager to take on another assignment. He had temporarily discarded his fantasy of life in Canada with Christine at his side, and was to spend the next two years hurrying from one SOE mission to another. After arriving safely in London in late June he contacted Section D, suggesting that perhaps they could find work for his erstwhile traveling companion Radzyminski whom he believed to be still in France. In fact, after the two men separated the Polish journalist had been arrested in Spain. Whether he was killed while leaping from a train bound for a concentration camp has never been confirmed. The *Dictionary of Polish Journalists* noted only that he was killed by the Germans in 'unknown circumstances.'

Gizycki's last, hurried communique in his exchange with *X.3* is undated. He curtly announced that he would be going away 'on official mission.' He closed with the melodramatic statement, 'If should not be back, kindly take care of my wife.'[4]

In the dreary weeks of the winter of 1940-41, Christine fell ill with a bad case of flu. At one point her persistent cough caused her to spit blood. For the next few weeks Christine and Andrew remained inactive, aware that they were being watched. The Polish Legation was finally closed on January 15th at the insistence of the German government. In the early hours of the 24th the pair were arrested at their flat by Hungarian Ministry of Interior officers and taken to police headquarters on Hortemiklos Ucca.

In a later, unadorned account of that episode Christine wrote that they had been released within twenty-four hours after questioning. She made no reference to the manner in which their release had been secured other than to say that she had repeatedly denied any relationship with the British. Much has been made however of an alleged tongue-biting episode. The details of this apocryphal tale could only have come from Andrew for there is no indication that she ever mentioned it to anyone else. When asked what he knew of this episode, Patrick Howarth replied that he could not say with certainty if she had indeed lacerated her own tongue but that 'it was something she would have done!'[5]

Andrew's account is the only version of what happened next. The lovers were separated once they arrived at the prison. Christine was placed in a cell while he was interrogated and roughed up by his captors. The search of his person included the dismantling of his artificial limb. His face was bruised when he was finally returned to his cell, having refused to give his interrogators any information whatever. Christine was then brought in to be questioned. The police charged that she was a British agent and as proof offered the identity document that had been taken from her by the Slovak border guards. She denied it was hers and the accusation that she'd been seen visiting the British Embassy. She couldn't resist flippantly adding that at least she'd been invited, a courtesy that the German ambassador had not extended to her.

Christine bit her tongue hard enough to cause bleeding either while in her cell or during a lull in the interrogation She blotted the blood with her handkerchief but allowed some of it to dribble from her mouth. Seeing the blood and Christine's disheveled appearance an officer summoned the prison doctor who enquired about the source of the bleeding. She innocently replied that she had had tuberculosis some years ago. Alarmed, the doctor examined her and had her chest x-rayed. Her lungs still bore the scars of the prewar respiratory illness she had contracted while employed by the Fiat auto firm. The doctor reported his findings to the prison commander along with the urgent suggestion that she should be released immediately. Tuberculosis was still highly prevalent in eastern Europe and the doctor was keen not to have the disease spread throughout the prison.

Aside from the threat of a virulent disease, it hardly needed pointing out that neutral Hungary could ill-afford to have the death of a British agent on its hands. Christine and her 'husband' were released forthwith. Andrew later recalled that she really was not at all well though her condition was not life-threatening. Looking back at this episode he speculated that the Hungarian doctor was unusually enthusiastic in his demand for their release, an unexpected ally as it turned out.[6]

There are unconfirmed reports that Gestapo agents were present during these interrogations. Admiral Horthy was under enormous pressure to maintain Hungary's neutrality but a request from the Nazi regime could not be denied. There is no truth however to the speculation that Christine was released on Horthy's orders because of her family's tie to him. This is stretching the point a bit. A distant relative of hers, from the Galicia branch of the Skarbeks, had married one of Horthy's female relatives years before. In some accounts of her life the unnamed woman is referred to as her 'aunt.' She could hardly have been more than a cousin to Christine, several times removed.

Lieutenant Colonel Francis Cammaerts, Christine's future section chief in France, recalled that Allied operatives occasionally used the same tongue-biting ruse that Christine had employed to obtain her release. 'The Germans were very frightened of TB and if you spat blood they tended to tell you to go on your way.' Cammaerts used that tactic when being questioned by German police in Avignon.[7] SOE, and presumably all British intelligence operatives, were taught a number of simple survival stratagems for survival that appeared in a British propaganda booklet titled 'First Aid.' To fake tuberculosis, the anonymous author recommends among other ploys that an operative in danger of arrest or imprisonment should cut his/her finger and 'suck out some blood which you mix in your mouth with the mucus. People whose gums bleed easily will find this even simpler.'[8] This antiwar, anti-Hitler publication could have been from smuggled into Germany by an SOE operative or even written by one of its agents somewhere inside the country.

The booklet contains neither author name nor date though the year 1944 is mentioned. Reading the text, it becomes apparent that it was being circulated in the final stages of the war when many, perhaps most Germans, had lost their enthusiasm for Hitler and were desperately seeking ways to avoid working in armaments factories, a favourite target of Allied bombing. Another of the methods recommended for acquiring a doctor's certificate attesting to his patient's illness was to swallow a small portion of cordite. It would turn the patient's skin grey and cause nausea. Its effects would last for approximately forty-eight hours and the 'patient' then would be restored to health. The author Frederick Forsyth included this ruse in his novel and film, *The Day of the Jackal*.[9]

Andrew knew full well that they were not yet out of danger after they left the prison. He was certain - and he was proved to be correct - that their flat would be kept under surveillance. To resume their work would endanger their entire network. They would have to seek safe haven elsewhere but first they would have to outwit the plainclothes police who had made themselves conspicuous in a car parked across from their building. He hatched a plan to divert the attention of the vigilant detectives and escape. He had always been an auto enthusiast and owned two cars in the year that he lived in Budapest. A colleague was invited round to the flat and was asked to move Andrew's Chevrolet into the street, leaving the garage doors ajar. In the meantime he and Christine quickly loaded their luggage into his second car, the two-seater Opel. Once the garage doors had been flung open Andrew drove out at speed and headed for the British consulate.[10]

Chapter 10.
Breakout from Budapest

Christine and Andrew arrived at their destination well ahead of their pursuers. Owen O'Malley offered them asylum with no questions asked and without regard for his own safety. He was well aware though that the Gestapo had the consulate under surveillance and that his two guests could not remain in the country for long. In fact they were no longer safe in Europe. A plan was contrived to smuggle them out of Budapest and across the Yugoslav border.*

Andrew speculated that they had about three days before being forced to move on or be captured. But their situation was not as bad as feared. They were after all on British territory and it is unlikely that Admiral Horthy would have risked damaging relations with Britain by barging into their consulate. O'Malley was in a much better position to judge the safe length of their stay. He believed that best place for the two operatives was Cairo where they would be taken under the protective wing of the local SOE head of mission. In his memoir he recalled, 'Some months before this [the escape] I had realised that the German police net, working through disloyal members of the Hungarian police or in the Hungarian General Staff, was closing around Christine. I begged her, implored her to leave

*A fictitious account of this episode can be found in the Ann Bridge novel *op.cit.*

the country while there was still time but she was obstinate and refused.

'Finally, at the eleventh hour she agreed. It was a Saturday afternoon. Now, the Gestapo had many curious habits, and among them was a great attachment to a weekend without engagements. We therefore felt confident that we had till the early hours of Monday to put a planned escape into operation, and accordingly, I told a junior member of my staff to drive to Belgrade on the following Sunday with a Legation car and Christine rolled up in the boot.'[1]

But she would need a new passport and transit visas as she had already lost two sets of papers, one to the Slovak border guards and another to the Section D head in Budapest. O'Malley ordered new documents to be quickly drawn up. The actual names of the Polish operatives could no longer be used for they were wanted by both the Hungarian secret police and the Gestapo. O'Malley convened a meeting withe the fugitive Poles and several of the consulate staff. O'Malley's daughter Kate was also invited to join the gathering. Some years after the war Andrew recalled that it was she who had suggested the surnames 'Granville' and 'Kennedy.' Perhaps Kate had some knowledge of Lady Harriet Granville, wife of the British ambassador to France in the 1840s, whose popular Paris salon had been graced by the presence of Chopin. Krystyna's name was easily translated into Christine and now her new surname would have the same initial letter as her married name Gizycki.

'Andrew' is the common English translation of Andrzej. A surname beginning with the same initial letter as his family name was suggested. That brought to mind a relative of his who had married an Irishman named Kennedy. In a matter of minutes the two had changed their identities. O'Malley, his personal assistant and Kate had all contributed to this hurried conference.

To complete her disguise Christine suggested 1915 as her birth year. She maintained this fiction for the remainder of her life, subtracting seven years from her actual age. With her slender figure and attractive features, she could easily pass for a younger woman. Thus, Krystyna Skarbek and Andrzej Kowerski became universally known as Christine Granville and Andrew Kennedy. He was delighted with his new Irish name and she now felt more English than ever before. Several of her colleagues have commented, or have written, that she had developed a deep affection for English culture though few ever gave any examples of how she expressed that feeling.**

While new travel documents were being produced work continued on plans to get the pair safely out of Budapest. O'Malley had run this escape gauntlet once before and was familiar with the routine. After the fall of France in June two British officers who'd been captured and imprisoned in Poland escaped and made their way to Budapest, thanks to the underground routes already established by Andrew. O'Malley had given the officers temporary shelter at the Legation while bogus visas were produced identifying them as staff then ferried them across the border to Belgrade without any questions being asked.

On a Sunday morning in February 1941, O'Malley and his staff began making final preparations for their guests' departure. None of the cars allotted to the Legation was large enough for the intended purpose so O'Malley volunteered the use of his own Chrysler. This car and several other vehicles including a four-ton lorry had been donated to the

---

***See* Madeleine Masson's account of this meeting in her book, *Christine, SOE agent & Churchill's favourite spy* (London: Virago 2005)

legation by the Shell Oil Company. Spare tires and other equipment were removed from the Chrysler's boot and a comfortable space was created for the newly anointed Christine.

Andrew was loathe to part with his beloved Opel so it was agreed that he would take the car across the Yugoslav border on his own. But first they had to negotiate their way past the Hungarian policemen who patrolled in front of the building. A lone policeman on duty that day observed unusual activities in the courtyard but seemed unaware of what the staff were up to. According to O'Malley, 'The policeman . . . stared somberly at the proceedings but they were nice men accustomed to get hot cocoa on snowy nights in the porter's lodge. So Christine went off, sitting demurely beside the driver.'[2] Andrew followed behind in the Opel. O'Malley wrote in his memoirs that he thought this method of escape was 'sufficiently risky and bloodthirsty to appeal to her. 'I did not embarrass the Foreign Office by reporting to them Christine's escape which, like my transactions with the POW, were not part of a Minister's duties.'[3]

Before they approached Lenti on the Yugoslav border the driver pulled off to the side of the road and Christine crawled into the boot, covering herself with blankets..' A legation chauffeur drove the minister's car across the border without being challenged. O'Malley obviously had a special affection for Christine for in a summing-up report written after leaving Hungary he wrote, 'She is a rare and peculiar character and for all her attractiveness not everybody's cup of tea.' Despite his grumbling about SOE, O'Malley had his own private spirit of adventure. Within a few months he and his family would also be fleeing Budapest assisted by none other than Jerzy Gizycki.

The legation driver and his passengers separated once they arrived in Belgrade.

Mindful that Nazi agents were now everywhere, The couple took rooms at a small nondescript hotel. O'Malley joined them for a brief reunion. 'We had a fine party at the Serbski Kral and went to see the stomach (*sic*) dancers in some low haunt afterwards.' Tom Masterson, under the cover of First Secretary at the legation, was the SOE station head in Belgrade assisted by press attache Julian Amery. Masterson was one of the older operatives in the field, still active in the field at the age of sixty.

Shortly after Christine and Andrew arrived in Belgrade, George Taylor appeared on the scene to make an inspection tour of SOE's Balkan operations. Before returning to Britain he formally recruited Andrew into SO2 (operations and sabotage) The earlier agreement Christine had concluded with Taylor was still considered to be in force and there was no need to alter her status. For all intents and purposes she too became an SO2 operative

The threat of a German invasion to each country they passed through as the couple headed east seemed to heighten their sense of excitement. One journalist-cum-SOE operative wrote, 'It was impossible to over-emphasise the hectic gaiety of most of the Balkan capitals as war or occupation drew nearer.'[4]

According to one estimate, there were more than 150 major restaurants in full swing in central Belgrade in early 1941. Ordinary citizens seemed reluctant to choose sides. The majority tried to be both pro-British and pro-Soviet Union but Union Jacks were more in evidence than hammer-and-sickle banners. The Yugoslav government however were leaning toward cooperation with the Germans. Spontaneous student-led anti-German demonstrations were anxiously watched by foreign journalists sipping coffee from the

the safety of crowded cafes.

The Yugoslavs, unlike the Hungarians, still retained a royal family. After the assassination of King Alexander in 1934, Prince Paul ruled as senior Regent as Alexander's son, Peter II, was only eleven years old in 1941. Like all their neighbours the Yugoslavs were being pressured by both the Germans and the British to declare their hand. Prince Paul tried to walk a thin line between the two opposing powers but Section D and SOE suspected that at heart he was really pro-German. The government were very unpopular with their own people but at that early stage of the war the British were in no position to encourage a *coup*. They made a tepid attempt to sway the Yugoslavs in January by sending the MP and diarist Chips Channon to Belgrade in an unsuccessful effort to persuade Paul to join the allied cause.

When it came time to continue their journey Christine realised that she would have some difficulty leaving Yugoslavia. Because of the unorthodox manner in which she had entered the country she'd missed the opportunity to have an entry visa stamped in her passport. Fortunately, John Bennett, a young English lawyer, was on hand. Bennett, a tall, thin prematurely balding man whose behaviour was occasionally described as wild, was an effective officer who later did good work in Albania and Istanbul. He was also the British Passport Control Officer in Belgrade (as well as the local SIS operative), and he knew how to go about having her papers fixed.

Christine and Andrew were now ready to continue their journey but there remained the question of who would replace her in Budapest. It was extremely important for the Musketeers, and for the AK, to have an open line into Hungary. As if SOE needed reminding, Professor Kot nevertheless emphasised the country's strategic importance. 'This is our most important base for communications with Poland which becomes thus in imminent danger. If this communication will [be] cut off, we shall not have many other opportunities to establish a contact with Poland.'

The few clandestine Polish organisations remaining in Hungary were now coming under intense pressure from increased numbers of Gestapo agents using Hungarian Interior Ministry agents as their proxies. In September, the Military Attache and Deuxieme Bureau man in Budapest, Lieutenant-Colonel Jan Emisarski, had to flee to avoid capture. Early the following year virtually all Polish intelligence cells in Budapest were rolled up.

After Christine's departure the Budapest-Poland connection disintegrated. Much to Andrew's surprise she nominated her husband Jerzy Gizycki as her replacement. Andrew wasn't the only one perplexed by her decision. Major Wilkinson, with whom she was about to clash, questioned her selection in a lengthy report written in late May. He was critical of the decision to appoint Gizycki as Owen O'Malley's assistant military attache (once he had reached Budapest). Ordinarily such appointments were subject to the approval of the Foreign Office and the War Office.

In a memo to Brigadier Gubbins, Wilkinson wrote: 'I cannot understand why G. [Gizycki] was chosen to go to Budapest. To begin with he is a man of only moderate ability, he is not liked or trusted by the Hecka organisation [deputy head of the Deuxieme Bureau] nor do I think he represents any interests but his own.'[5]

More puzzling is why Wilkinson had previously asked Taylor to have Gizycki 'released from Polish service.' Unless of course he wanted to use him in an operation of his own. Taylor found his man in Dakar. Gizycki's story was that he'd been sent by the Sikorski government to retrieve from the French the gold from that they had smuggled out of the Polish treasury at the Poles' request shortly before the German invasion. In this he was only partially successful. Most of the gold remained in French hands until the end of the war. Before Gizycki could begin work on another book Taylor had a mission for him to carry out, one that would mean his return to Europe. By nominating him as her replacement in Budapest, Christine had unintentionally scuppered whatever plans Wilkinson may have had for her husband.

Shortly before Christine was to leave Belgrade a Musketeer courier arrived from Poland and presented her with a role of microfilm to be delivered to SOE station in Istanbul. There was no time to read it then as events in Yugoslavia were fast overtaking them. With the microfilm hidden in a hollowed-out space in Andrew's artificial leg the intrepid couple prepared to leave Belgrade. He packed the small car to the gunwales with as much as he could cram into it and still leave space for the two of them. They hadn't left Belgrade a moment too soon. Several weeks later Prince Paul caved in to German pressure and signed the anti-Soviet Tripartite Agreement.6 The Serb population, with close cultural and linguistic ties to Russia, were furious. Popular dissent spread like wildfire throughout the country, fed in no small way by SOE operatives. Two days after he signed the pact Paul was overthrown by a coalition of military officers and members of the Communist Party in a *coup* organised with the help of SOE.

The drive to Bulgaria was uneventful. Andrew has commented elsewhere that his companion was not a musical person and objected to having the car radio playing as they drove along.7 At every stop en route to Cairo, British agents, alerted to their arrival, were on hand to greet them. In Sofia accommodation had already been booked for them. Despite the bungling in Budapest and the temporary disconnection with Christine SOE placed a high value on keeping her and her companion safe. They entered the Bulgarian capital on the night of February 23-24 and the following day Christine went to the British Legation. She took along the microfilm and presented it to Aidan Crawley, the Air Attache,*** unaware of its startling revelations.

Crawley remembered well that first meeting. 'In early February we had two unusual visitors. A beautiful young Polish woman called Christine Gyjiska [sic] and a round-faced, jolly ex-Polish officer called Andrew Kowerski walked into my office and said they had just driven from Budapest. Both had been working with the Polish underground but had been arrested in Budapest and interrogated under the muzzles of sub-machine guns. Fortunately the interrogators, Magyar officers who hated the Germans, had released them.

'They had brought with them several rolls of microfilm which showed that large-scale preparations were being made by the Germans in Poland for a campaign against the Russians. This was the first positive evidence of its kind, and having sent a report both to Cairo and to London, I arranged for Christine and Andrew to take their films via Istanbul to Egypt. I was soon to learn that she was already a legendary Polish heroine.'8

The contents of the Musketeers' microfilm proved more explosive than anyone had suspected. Witkowski's organisation, which has never been properly credited with

---

***Aidan Merivale Crawley, MBE. Shot down in 1941, held prisoner until 1945. Later served as both a Labour and a Conservative MP. He also worked as both a print and television journalist. Married to the author Virgina Cowles.

exposing the Germans' treacherous plans, provided documented evidence that proved beyond doubt that the *Wehrmacht* were moving masses of troops and materiel to Poland's eastern border. Their detailed report even contained a list of the quantities of petrol the German vehicles would need to launch this massive assault on the Soviet Union. Churchill did not act immediately upon receipt of this information. He and his inner circle had to study the film carefully before passing it on to Stalin. But the prime minister did contact him about ten days prior to the German invasion.

Christine's admirers, especially Kennedy, have given her sole credit for alerting Churchill to the Germans' plans. But during the winter of 1940-41 Stalin had received several such warnings and chose to ignore all of them including Churchill's. His own spy Richard Sorge had alerted the Soviet leader in the early spring of 1940 from his position inside the Japanese Embassy.9 A Polish woman, Halina Szymanska, reported that the *Abwehr* chief Admiral Canaris was plotting to overthrow Hitler and then sue for peace.10 . The Czechs wanted a share of glory too and claimed that they had 'turned' an *Abwehr* officer who leaked details of Operation Barbarossa. Stalin dismissed all this as so much Allied propaganda. In 2013 the obituary of Mildred Fish Harnack, an American journalist who had once lived in Germany, revealed that the anti-Nazi resistance dubbed the Red Orchestra had been providing Stalin with intelligence reports about Operation Barbarossa for about nine months prior to June 1941. Obviously he had no need of Churchill's warning. Though much has been made of Christine's news it turned out to be an exercise in futility.

Some of the details in Crawley's recollection do not square with archival accounts. His visitors had not been threatened by sub-machine guns by Hungarian police who did not simply release their prisoners. That had been effected by Christine's more than credible tongue-biting act. Crawley's statement also gave rise to the rumour that he was secretly employing her on behalf of the Air Ministry. Her reputation had begun to spread but her most courageous actions of the war were yet to be played out.

She and Andrew spent some leisure time with Crawley, filling him in on the details of their operation in Hungary. They also met with Andrew Tarnowski, the Polish minister to Bulgaria and nephew of Countess Sophia Tarnowska. He had once been lauded by Professor Kot as 'a most accomplished plotter,' appointed by General Sikorski to oversee the remnants of Witkowski's Musketeers once they had been incorporated into the government's intelligence bureaux. Christine however was not impressed and referred to him as 'an old fogey.' She paused in her travels long enough to write a report to be sent to London, beginning with the details of her recruitment, her forays into Poland, her arrest in Hungary (but not the manner of her escape) and the journey to Sofia.

Bulgaria provided only temporary respite for her. For the time being it was safe but the window of opportunity was slowly being drawn down. The country would soon be overtaken by war but which army would enter Sofia first had not yet been decided. Ordinary Bulgarians were no great friends of the Germans and historically the population had always preferred the company of the Russians. Prime Minister Filov and his Foreign Minister were thought, rightly as it turned out, to be pro-German, leaving little doubt whose side they would be on in the struggle for European domination.

SOE had already been at work attempting to undermine the Bulgarian government and to prevent, or at least delay, any alliance with the Germans. But funds alloted for propaganda were minuscule and only the Peasant Party, led by Georgi Dimitrov, was willing to launch a campaign of violence. Half-hearted attempts at sabotage urged on by SO2 produced just one success, the derailment of a goods train carrying supplies of oil. Apparently, this was accomplished by one of Dimitrov's men using a crowbar. The saboteurs were rounded up shortly afterwards and there were no further attempts on the government either by Dimitrov or by SO2.

Journalist and sometime SOE agent David Walker described the feverish scene in Sofia when he arrived from Romania. 'In this lunatic circus roundabout, here we were all again: journalists, agents, the strangely mobile blondes who often contrived to move faster than the correspondents, scurrying diplomats, the anonymous shadowy faces, frequently unshaven, that seemed to lower over every Balkan bar, and pale, drawn, overworked security police whose task it was to follow us.'[11]

Christine and Andrew could not linger in Sofia, however exotic and exciting it might have been. Crawley warned them that German forces were advancing swiftly throughout Europe and would be arriving in Bulgaria imminently. He also revealed that the British were about to sever their ties with the Bulgarians and that he would be unable to intervene should they be taken prisoner. In late February 1941, Britain did break off diplomatic relations with Bulgaria. Agents, journalists and their hangers-on decamped for Istanbul, the only remaining safe haven outside the dubious security of the Soviet Union. Christine and Andrew departed just a few days before German troops entered Sofia on the 1st of March. Crawley had to await his opportunity to escape until mid-month.

Crossing the Bulgarian-Turkish turned out to be somewhat difficult. A border guard mistook Andrew's registration plates for German because of the similarity between theirs and those of the Poles. The German-speaking guard challenged him and fortunately Andrew knew enough of the language to reply in kind. For a brief moment the situation seemed to be under control.[12] When the guard examined their passports and found them to be British his demeanor changed. He curtly informed them that the border was closed. Andrew was about to protest but Christine intervened before he could start a row.

The Bulgarians became even more suspicious when Andrew casually mentioned that they were en route to Istanbul. They were ordered to remove all their belongings from the Opel so that it might be searched. After a fruitless examination of the vehicle the guards insisted that he remove the tires. This he did only with the greatest difficulty, hampered by his artificial limb. Having found nothing suspicious in the car, the officious guards then informed the exhausted couple that the border crossing into Turkey would not be opened until the following morning. In the meantime, they would be expected to sleep in the car which meant spending the night in a cramped, upright position.

Christine looked unwell enough to elicit pity from at least one of the Bulgarian patrol. He invited the exhausted couple to sleep on the floor of an empty room in the soldiers' barracks. The shelter improved their situation only marginally as it had neither a proper bed nor mattress. In the morning they were offered some relief by a thoughtful guard who brought them hot coffee. There were further delays while the officer-in-charge made a call to Sofia to get permission to allow the now fed-up travelers to continue on their way. It was mid-day before they reached the Turkish border.

Part III. 1941-1943
Chapter 11. The Flight Into Egypt

After his escape from France on the last ship to leave that country, Gizycki left an ungrammatical message with SOE asking them to take care of Christine 'if should not be heard from.' No one knows if he had embarked upon a top-secret mission or why he sent that cryptic note. But he was heard from again, turning up in the Gambia in February 1941. Gizycki never explained why he was there but his stay was brief. He was summoned to Lagos by George Taylor several weeks after arriving and was told that his services were now required in Budapest, a move suggested by Christine. Taylor asked him to travel on SOE's behalf to Istanbul via Egypt where he would receive details of an important mission. He neglected however to inform Gizycki that Christine and Andrew Kennedy were already en route to the Turkish capital through which he would shortly have to pass. In Istanbul he would have the penultimate meeting with his wife.

Diplomatic ties had been snapping right across Europe as Christine and Andrew made their way east. In March the Hungarian government finally broke off diplomatic relations with Britain, forcing them to close their consulate and leaving Owen O'Malley with no option but to quit Budapest.

Despite Hungary's new and reluctant adversarial position, Premier Admiral Horthy was not unfriendly toward the British minister. Even at this late date he was trying to play both ends against the middle. He advised O'Malley that travel through Europe was no longer safe and that perhaps the minister should leave his daughter Kate behind. Horthy offered to vouch for her safety. To no one's surprise O'Malley politely rejected the offer.

Travel through western Europe was obviously out of the question even for a British diplomat. To the south Yugoslavia was in turmoil, leaving O'Malley and his entourage of about fifty with the only option of proceeding to Russia via Romania, not a very comfortable alternative. The Romanian government too was under continuous pressure from the Hitler regime, not least of all because the former Polish president and his ministers were still being held under house arrest. The Romanians were loathe to release the Polish party, partly because it would infuriate the Germans and partly because the Sikorski government were paying them to provide President Moscicki and his ministers with decent room and board.

O'Malley was not keen to attempt passage through the Soviet Union but help was due to arrive shortly in the form of Jerzy Gizycki.

The intrepid Christine and her companion were briefly detained at the Turkish border by a group of soldiers intent on seizing the Opel. Using French, English and gestures, Christine resolved the crisis only to have the Turks insist that one of their number had to accompany them to Istanbul. The situation would have been comical if the Polish couple had not been so drained of energy. To argue further with the soldiers seemed useless. After much haggling a compromise was agreed upon. One of the soldiers would somehow wedge himself into the tiny Opel and in this manner they set off for the capital.

At the Turkish border the car had to be deposited with Customs until they were ready to leave the city. They took a room at the Park Hotel, one of Istanbul's most modern hostelries, courtesy of the British government. They soon discovered that the Park was not the exclusive preserve of the British but that agents from other countries, both friend and foe, had also booked into the hotel. At times the lobby resembled a convention of spies. To add to the tension Christine discovered that both the German and the Soviet Union embassies were cheek-by-jowl with their hotel. Lieutenant Colonel Bickham Sweet-Escott had visited Istanbul in 1941 and had found it 'pullulating with his own side's staff and agents, let alone the enemy's; not to speak of journalists from both sides and from the neutrals.'[1]

In early 1941 operatives from across Europe had converged on Istanbul, driven eastward by the irresistible tide of German conquests. Though it had lost its status as capital to Ankara, it was by far the city of choice for government operatives and others less legitimate seeking to make their fortunes dealing in the black arts. On a practical level Istanbul was closer to Europe than Ankara and much more cosmopolitan. Thus, officials from all sides and their agents found it a more agreeable place in which to conduct their secretive business. It had 'a long tradition as a centre of international intrigue and double-dealing ,' observed Professor MRD Foot, SOE historian.

Word of their successes in Hungary had preceded the Polish couple and there were congratulations all around as they were received by British officials like minor celebrities. But Christine was not totally relieved to be free of Hungary. She was desperately concerned that the connections she had arranged between Warsaw and Budapest remain intact.

A Musketeer courier arrived as if by pre-arranged signal and assured her that the system she helped create was still active even though its numbers had been severely reduced. As proof, he passed on to her more microfilmed reports to be delivered to SOE Cairo. Despite the presence of so many of the enemy Christine felt secure enough to tour the city guided by another of her many friends from Poland. Accompanied by Andrew, she visited the fabled Topkapi Palace, the Grand Mosque and inspected the boisterous markets on walks through the crowded streets.

Just as they were beginning to relax, a message came through that Gizycki was en route to Istanbul. Andrew expressed his apprehension about her husband's reaction should he learn about the relationship between himself and Christine. She however was more sanguine about meeting Gizycki and remained focused on her mission, dismissing any talk about their personal lives. Though she was no longer in love with Gizycki, she acknowledged his courage and had vouched for his willingness to replace her in Budapest. Other SOE operatives who knew Gizycki were not certain that he was the right choice for the job. But all agreed that, though he might be difficult to work with, he would throw himself with abandon into whatever task had been set for him.

Christine's brief respite from hurried travel was not duty-free. First, there was a debriefing at the British Legation where she met with Gardyne de Chastelain, SOE section chief in Istanbul who was to direct sabotage operations. He had been recruited from his job in the oil industry where he'd been a highly paid executive. Before being assigned by SOE to work in Turkey he had lived and worked for years in Romania. His knowledge of that country, its language and its oil fields made him a valuable addition to the Executive's roster.2 After the collapse of the Romanian government in 1941 it was felt that he would be safer in Istanbul where he could continue his covert operations. There, he enhanced his reputation as man of great competence with a strong personality to match.

Istanbul was a hive of undercover activity throughout the war. In addition to de Chastelaine's cell Britain had three other agencies quietly at work in Turkey: SIS for intelligence gathering; the Naval Intelligence Division (NID) to monitor enemy shipping; and Secret Intelligence Middle East (SIME). Though they all flew the Union Jack, figuratively speaking, the agencies were rivals, loathe to share their secrets. SIS in particular had always looked upon SOE with condescension and gave it little support.

The governments of Germany, the USSR, France and Czechoslovakia also had operatives at work in the city as did the exiled governments of Greece and Bulgaria. The British however had shown the most imagination. When the consulate staff withdrew from Sofia they took along the putative saboteur Georgi Dimitrov, smuggling him across the Turkish border hidden in a packing case, a less elegant method of transport than O'Malley had provided for Christine.

A variety of accusations had been leveled against SOE in its short life, many of them from anonymous sources. These were often tales of large sums of money being squandered, of inexperienced operatives bungling their missions. At times its rivalry with SIS became quite vicious. SIS deputy Claude Dansey absolutely hated the idea of these amateur spies encroaching on his territory. When the passenger ship *Normandie* burned in New York harbour (1942), he allegedly phoned SOE London to congratulate them on another job well done.3

Because of its lack of a solid track record SOE were under tremendous pressure to produce results. Thus far it had few major successes. Christine's link-up with the Musketeers must be considered one of them, though at this stage of the war there was little the British government could do with the intelligence they had thus far received from Poland. But contacts in Greece had been established against overwhelming odds and SOE could take credit for assisting in the overthrow in Yugoslavia of the pro-German Regent, Prince Paul.

The presence in Istanbul of so many British operatives resulted in few major embarrassing incidents and the Foreign Office were able to maintain their posture of neutrality with Turkey. The FO continued to pursue a policy of caution when dealing with the Turks as it had thus far with all neutral countries. This did not sit well with SOE whose brief included sabotage and who were anxious to stir things up against German interests. It had yet to 'set Europe afire' as Churchill had challenged them to do. Indeed, SOE's major successes were few and far between. They did establish a framework for covert operations in several European countries but in the end FO policy prevailed as it had in Hungary. The cautious stance favoured by the FO notwithstanding, SOE operatives did make one attempt at sabotage. Limpet mines were attached to two Italian oil tankers docked in Istanbul harbour but they failed to explode. Thus, Britain's neutral position *vis a vis* Turkey was accidentally if precariously maintained.

The Musketeers were active here too despite pleas from the Sikorski government to SOE to cease working with them. Warsaw was rife with rumours that Witkowski and his organisation had been compromised by Gestapo informants, causing Sikorski and the Seizieme Bureau to pressure the Turkish government to stop allowing 'bags of mail' to be delivered to Christine. She was obviously under surveillance by one of the Polish intelligence agencies.

The terminology is a colourful exaggeration. It's highly unlikely that a covert agent in Istanbul would be receiving 'bags' of documents delivered by the Turkish postal service. The Musketeers preferred method of smuggling their reports out of the country was to copy them on to microfilm and deliver them by hand. Regardless of the form in which reports were delivered to Christine, the Turks were not duly alarmed. They did not respond immediately to the Polish request but did eventually halt deliveries of any sort to her. But only after she had received at least another half-dozen 'packages.'

The Sikorski government's persistent interventions eventually disrupted Christine's contacts with the Musketeers. There was little she could accomplish in Istanbul, especially now that the British had come to rely more heavily on the Deuxieme Bureau for its reports from Poland. In Warsaw, Witkowski's behaviour had become more erratic, diluting the Musketeers' effectiveness. Before Christine left Istanbul to continue the journey to Palestine, she received one final report from a courier but such contacts were now few and far between. Her lines of communication between Warsaw and Budapest had also been severed as a result of the termination of British-Hungarian diplomatic ties. The frightening and relentless advance of the *Wehrmacht* made her position even more precarious. There was to be one more surprise for her before she left Turkey.

Jerzy Gizycki was now nearing the end of his twin careers as British courier and jack-of-all trades for the Polish government but he had one last mission to carry out before retiring. At his meeting with Taylor he had been ordered to report to Istanbul to meet with de Chastelain. At the conclusion of that meeting he was given an address in the city and told to proceed there at once. According to Gizycki, when he arrived at the specified address he was surprised to have his wife open the door to him (Christine seemed to possess an uncanny ability to sniff out safe houses). Though her greeting was warm enough he suspected that something was amiss. She however remained calm and tight-lipped. There would be no discussion of her relationship with Andrew.

Andrew's recollection of their meeting is much less melodramatic. He recalled driving Christine to the harbour to meet Gizycki's ship. Though they had met briefly years ago in Zakopane, he was still impressed by Gizycki's powerful physique, and Kennedy was not a small man himself. He dropped Christine and her husband at the Pera Palace Hotel and spent the remainder of the day otherwise occupied.4

At the hotel she deflected any questions about her lover and instead told Gizycki about her work in Hungary, her incursions into Poland and how she had escaped from Budapest. She also related in detail about how, while returning to Hungary, a German fighter plane had spotted her and her guide and strafed them near the Polish-Slovak border. With such exciting news being thrust at him Gizycki hardly had time to voice his suspicions about her relationship with Andrew. Their primary concern was the work still to be done in Budapest. Christine passed on the names of her contacts, hoping that at least a few of them were still active, and assured him that Owen O'Malley would give him whatever assistance he required to maintain communications with Warsaw. All in all it turned out to be a congenial meeting but Andrew breathed a sigh of relief when Gizycki finally departed.

Lacking an assignment, and with none in the offing, Christine and Andrew remained in their hotel for some days. But he became increasingly restless and wanted to move on. He was prepared to continue the journey to what was then Palestine via Syria, still a French protectorate, and now in the hands of the pro-German Vichy government. The couple's chances of obtaining Syrian transit visas seemed slim. At the last minute Christine decided to accompany Andrew and went alone to the French consulate where, using her fluency in French and irresistible powers of persuasion, she secured the necessary travel documents.

Evidently, the German 'wanted' posters bearing her photo as described by O'Malley, had not been circulated among Vichy officials. If so, the fault could be ascribed to the weak and ineffective Austrian Otto Steinhausl who had become temporary president of Interpol before the Nazis took total control of the organisation in 1939.5

There was a spot of bother at Turkish Customs when Andrew tried to reclaim his Opel. An official refused to release the car and announced his intention to sell it off. In despair Gizycki retreated to the British consulate where he was told quite frankly that he would have to pay a bribe if he wanted the vehicle returned. With his reluctant agreement a member of the consulate staff quietly arranged for a go-between to handle the transaction.

Once the couple had crossed the Bosphorus and arrived on the Asian side of Turkey,

Andrew retrieved his Opel (it had been shipped on a separate ferry) and the travelers pushed on. They spent one night at a bug-infested hotel on the Syrian-Turkish border before continuing on towards Palestine.

They paused for a night in Beirut where there seemed to be an unsettling friendliness between French and German officers in the hotel lobby. They departed the next morning and drove on to Palestine where they were relieved to find British officials on hand to meet them. The staff provided them with documents needed to secure petrol and other necessities, and arrangements were made for a hotel room in Haifa.

Christine and her lover had left behind a job well done in Europe and, for the time being, were out of reach of German police agencies. Hundreds of British and Polish personnel had been rescued from behind enemy lines as a result of their unselfish efforts. Equally important, she had established an invaluable intelligence link between SIS and Witkowski's Musketeers.

Signals from SOE London to other sections gave the Polish pair high marks for their work. They were now looking forward to their next assignment after a bit of rest and relaxation. Most of all they were longing to stretch their legs after the cramped ride across southeastern Europe. They managed a few relaxing weeks in Palestine, unaware of events about to unfold in Cairo.

The trouble came not from the Nazis but from within the Polish intelligence community. While Christine and Andrew had been making their dash across southern Europe, SOE chiefs in Cairo and London had begun to receive disturbing reports about them and the Musketeers. It was strongly hinted that she in particular might have been turned by the Nazis. Questions were being asked about her quick release from a Hungarian prison. Doubts were expressed within Polish government circles about how she and Andrew managed to cross Europe without being apprehended by the Gestapo and its collaborators.

There was no secret about the source of the accusations. They had come from one *Pulkownik* (Colonel) Jozef Matecki, deputy head of the Seizieme Bureau in Cairo. His signals to Wilkinson and to other SOE officers were signed with the cryptonym Jakub Alek, the generic name for whoever held the post of deputy at the time. Matecki had had at one time a promising military career. At the conclusion of the first world war he had been named ADC to Marshal Pilsudski though he was not greatly enamoured of the Polish leader. He was closer in temperament to General Kazimierz Sosnkowski, commander of the Polish Secret Army since the beginning of the occupation. His abilities as an officer had never been in doubt but, like Christine, he was obstinate, unwilling to compromise his principles and followed his instructions to the letter. He was also a great friend of General Stanislaw Kopanski, commander of the Polish Carpathian Brigade, yet another of her friends in the tangled web of Polish relationships. Within the Seizieme Bureau, Matecki held the key to all arrangements for sending government couriers into Europe. His behaviour towards Christine may have resulted from what he saw as a threat to his own position, competition from someone as free-wheeling and as successful as she had been in Hungary. There was also a hint of envy, ignited perhaps by the praise being heaped upon her by British intelligence officers.

The Elusive Madame G

Christine and Lady Livia (Pussi) Deakin at the Gezira Club c 1943.

Photo supplied by Slawka Wazacz

Lt Col Francis Cammaerts ('Roger'), leader of Jockey Circuit in France.   *Cammaerts*

Andrew, Christine and an unidentified officer in Egypt. c 1943. Permission from the British Library

The Elusive Madame G

Christine and Muriel Bankes in front of their hotel on Boissy d'Anglais, Paris. c 1946
From the film 'No Ordinary Countess' by Slawka Wazacz

The Elusive Madame G

Kate O'Malley and Lord Tweedsmuir in the House of Commons at the launch party for his autobiography, 'The Rags of Time.' 1990. *Photo loaned by Lord Tweedsmuir*

Lt (Count) Vladimir Ledochowski, Polish Carpathian Brigade.   Photo courtesy of Jan Ledochowski

Chapter 12.
Honourable People

Matecki was certainly justified in suspecting that the Musketeers had been infiltrated by Nazi sympathisers for the Gestapo had attempted in various ways to compromise Witkowski's organisation. But Matecki 1 could only speculate and offered no hard evidence to prove Christine's alleged duplicity. He had made derogatory remarks about Andrew and Gizycki as well, on more than one occasion. He had also gone so far as to assert that Christine had inadvertently caused the death of one of his operatives on the Polish-Slovak border. Matecki did not support this accusation with substantive details and no one at SOE London bothered to enquire. Her reports, and those of others, do not mention any fatalities resulting from her missions to Poland. Nevertheless, frantic messages flew back and forth from Cairo to London to Istanbul urging that none of the trio be given any further assignments.

In late May 1941, SOE Cairo instructed its operatives to approach Matecki and ask what evidence he had against Christine and the others. A week later another memo from SIS was circulated among top SOE officers (Brigadier Gubbins, Major Wilkinson and Lieutenant Colonel Guy Tamplin) to the effect that an unnamed operative had spoken with Matecki who had repeated his allegations but without giving specifics. He again questioned the ease with which the couple had been released from prison in Hungary, and wondered how they had managed to elude the Gestapo and their sympathisers in their dash from Budapest to Palestine.

The Polish officer poisoned the well further by alleging that she was in touch with officials in Vichy France, another charge which he could not substantiate. That apparently was a reference to the relative ease with which she had secured transit visas from the pro-Vichy Syrian government.

Though Matecki had provided only a thin tissue of unproven charges against her, it was left to Major Wilkinson to take definitive action. It was standard SIS procedure to refrain from using personnel who had been in enemy hands and had been released or who had escaped in questionable circumstances. Despite these allegations and a spate of rumours about Christine's loyalty, she and Andrew Kennedy appeared to be fully functioning SOE operatives. A telegram to Wilkinson from London dated June 5th changed all that. The wire stated tersely: 'We must lay off O [Witkowski] organization as detrimental to official work. Therefore we must not employ X, Y and Z for this purpose nor encourage them to continue.'[2]

SOE passed on its suspicions about Christine to the Polish government-in-exile. Sikorski, who at the time held the offices of prime minister and commander-in-chief of the Polish armed forces, quickly decided that all support for her and the Musketeers had to be terminated.

Christine's life of leisure in the Holy Land was disrupted in early June by an urgent summons to report to SOE Cairo. Initially, she hoped another assignment might be in the offing. But Andrew recalled that toward the end of their stay in Palestine, Polish acquaintances had begun to distance themselves from the couple, a premonition that something unpleasant was about to occur. They were totally unprepared for what happened next.

Major Peter Wilkinson greeted the couple upon their arrival in Cairo but once introductions were out of the way, he bluntly informed the pair that they were to be dismissed immediately, citing Jakub Alek's allegations as the basis for his action. The Polish pair angrily denied the charge of disloyalty and pleaded their case for remaining on the job. They felt certain their lines into Poland could be reconstituted using Istanbul as their base. Wilkinson had just made a hurried inspection tour of SOE operations in Crete, Cairo and Jerusalem before returning to the Egyptian capital and was in no mood to argue. Supported by London SOE, he was adamant that they were to be dismissed but whether or not intentionally, he 'neglected to have them struck off the SOE pay-roll '. . . While they had no employment they at least had income.' (This was reportedly due to George Taylor's intervention on their behalf.)

They were not interviewed by other British intelligence agencies and were not arrested but were left to fend for themselves. Considering the gravity of the charges against them, unofficial though they were, it would have seemed logical for Wilkinson or someone in authority to have removed them from Cairo and returned to London for further questioning.

Before any such action could be contemplated their position was clarified by Colonel Stanislaw Hemel, *aka* Heczka of the Seizieme Bureau. They could still be employed by

SOE, he opined, if a well-defined assignment in the Balkans were to become available. But under no circumstances were they to be directly involved in Polish affairs and were not to be given assignments that would require working in Poland or in Germany (This is not as improbable as it sounds. The Musketeers had operatives in place within the Third Reich as early as 1940).

Many years later Wilkinson admitted that he had handled the affair badly and regretted it. He wrote: 'They were a glamorous couple who deserved better of their fellow countrymen.' Exactly who he was referring to is not clear, for both the Poles and the British treated the pair - especially Christine - with a certain amount of disdain and suspicion.[3]

Wilkinson was however being a bit disingenuous. In his role as M's deputy he already knew her by reputation and had formed a rather sceptical opinion of her. His decision to sack the couple was not without his own prejudice. He had betrayed his feelings in an earlier memo, written to M on May 28, in which he lightly dismissed the pair and seemed to give credence to prevailing rumours: 'This couple (the Gizyckis) and their colleague Andre Koversky [sic], promise to be rather a problem. You remember the story. Madame G. was introduced by Sir Robert Vansittart to D [Lt Col Lawrence Grand] who took a fancy to her. She was despatched to Budapest towards the end of 1939 to work on communication with Poland. . . . His [Kennedy] only claim to fame is that he used to run a clandestine lorry service for evacuating Poles from Hungary to Yugoslavia. In this he was fairly successful,' Wilkinson grudgingly concluded.[4]

It should not have been difficult for an officer of his position and rank to discover that Andrew had been awarded the Virtuti Militari for his heroism in Poland. As for

Christine he wrote: '... J.A. [Alek] tells me that to his certain knowledge she was in touch with British, French and the less reputable Polish organisations while in Budapest.' Alek never validated any of these charges. Nevertheless, after he had been replaced Wilkinson expressed some regret, saying that he thought Alek 'a capable and charming fellow.'

Weeks after he had dismissed Christine, Wilkinson continued to make sarcastic remarks about her and Gizycki too. 'Incidentally, Z [Gizycki] has arrived here and I have here his report in which I, not unnaturally, feature as the principal villain. I am extremely sorry that all his trouble should be so attributable to us and now that his wife has gone off with her boyfriend I do not know quite what amends we can make; although I gather that their marriage had never looked very permanent and that he had, up till the war, been living in Africa by mutual consent.'[5]

The last item is completely false. Christine and her husband had been together in Africa - they were after all on the last days of their honeymoon before Gizycki was to have settled in as Polish consul - and had sailed for England together once war had been declared in Europe. Having censored one of her letters from which he extracted bits of information, Wilkinson had to admit that the material '... which, if it is accurate seems rather good stuff.' As if it were needed this was indeed confirmation of her value as an SOE operative.

Wilkinson remarked upon a document, seen also by Patrick Howarth, that promised unlimited support for her projects. 'There were also [in the same censored letter] some photographs of documents committing the British government to unreserved support! These latter rather alarming. We mustn't make this sort of mistake again.'[6] Photographs of that document, signed by an official whose name has been deleted from the original, prove conclusively that Section D had agreed to give Christine unconditional support for her projects in Budapest. She carried the negative of this document with her for many months until it began to deteriorate.

Dejected and angry at being dismissed, Christine and Andrew left Wilkinson's office not quite sure what their next move would be. They were to remain inactive for more than two years.

Not content with suspending Christine, British intelligence officials began to suspect everyone who had had any contact with her. The Musketeers had lately come under suspicion for their insistence on working independently of government strictures. Though SOE had become thoroughly sceptical about the Musketeers' loyalty, they hedged their bets by adding that the group should continue to receive assistance in its evacuation of British personnel from Poland and elsewhere in Europe.

Major Wilkinson also asked General Sikorski to check on Andrew's military status. The general promised he would look into the matter though it was his opinion that Andrew was now a civilian and should be reporting to the Polish Consul-General. What he didn't know was that Andrew had avoided reporting to Kopanski's Motorised Brigade on instructions from SOE London. Together with Christine he had been directed to contact 'useful organisations' only through SO2.

Kopanski now appeared to be questioning Andrew's loyalty to the brigade. The situation was finally salvaged by the suggestion that Sikorski explain Andrew's mission directly to the general, thus lifting the burden of suspicion from Andrew's shoulders. Later,

Kopanski offered him a commission in his brigade. As a condition of their suspension from active duty the suspect couple were not permitted to leave Palestine though they were not confined to quarters. Until the matter of their loyalty was settled the pair would be kept under light surveillance. Colonel Harry Blake-Tyler, former AMA in Budapest and now in Istanbul, was asked to keep a watchful eye on Gizycki. Major Wilkinson signaled that he would deal with Christine and Andrew.

In May, Wilkinson alerted M (Brigadier Colin Gubbins) to Christine's questionable behaviour. After outlining how certain Polish operatives would be monitored he remarked, '... There is in addition Norton [Gizycki] and the elusive Madame Gysicka [sic]. These two appear to have established further communication with 38-Land [Poland], and 22,500 [Lieutenant Colonel H. Gibson], the Navy and the RAF are listening-in at Istanbul...'[7]

SOE's investigation into Matecki's charges uncovered some support for Andrew, much to Wilkinson's surprise. He had been quite prepared to write a negative report about Christine's colleague but instead had to write to M that Jan Emisarski, the Deuxieme Bureau chief who had been forced to flee Budapest, '... gives Y. [Kennedy] an excellent character reference and understands that 38-Landers [Poles] in 15-Land [Hungary] were most appreciative of his work.' George Taylor and Colonel SW Bailey also made statements in support of both Christine and her lover.

After carefully and surreptitiously examining Christine's correspondence Wilkinson allowed that the investigation had found much to her credit and nothing to her detriment. 'J.A. [Jakub Alek] possibly mistaken about his suspicions,' he wrote.

Documents released years after the war reveal that Wilkinson had a high regard for Matecki but remained suspicious of Christine and her motives. Doubts about her loyalty were exacerbated by a complaint received from Heczka of the Seizieme Bureau and Matecki's superior officer, to the effect that the Musketeers were interfering with the work of his own operatives inside Poland. Heczka belittled their efforts, maintaining that they were a 'minority affair' and, 'although it [the Musketeers] makes a lot of noise and professes to be able to do a lot even the little it can do definitely hinders the official organisation and certainly endangers it.'

Heczka was also perturbed because, since Christine's hurried departure and the crackdown on Poles in Budapest, w/t connections between Hungary and Poland were not running smoothly. He failed to recognise that her line of communication into Warsaw had been independent of Heczka's so she was hardly to blame. The credit for disrupting the Budapest-Warsaw connection must go to the Hungarian secret police, aided and abetted by the Gestapo. Both Hezcka and Matecki revealed themselves to be deeply resentful of the success registered thus far by Christine and the Musketeers. They firmly believed that the situation in Poland required intelligence-gathering to be performed by professionals, not by those they considered to be amateurs. The MI6 deputy Claude Dansey and many others in the service of British intelligence shared this same attitude.

Heczka in particular sought to undermine the Musketeers by convincing Sikorski that the organisation had been infiltrated by Nazi stooges. That in turn bolstered the general's decision to sever all ties with the Musketeers and their operatives, including Christine, Andrew and Gizycki. The rumours put about by Matecki* also led to a directive freezing SOE recruitment of Czechs or Poles for the time being, unless their individual cases had been properly vetted. Those already employed by the government were now to have their backgrounds investigated too.

This alarm led to questions being raised about Polish operatives, such as Gizycki, who had already completed hazardous missions for SOE. A perplexed officer wrote to his section chief, 'I know that he is in Istanbul where he was previously but do not know for whom he is now working. Is it directly for us, for D/H2 [Colonel Bailey], or for whom? He seems to be a case in point.'

Christine's suspension from SOE was followed by a long lull of unemployment that lasted nearly three years. Except for a surveillance trip into Syria in the autumn of 1941 1941, she and Andrew were at loose ends for much of the time though they remained on SOE's payroll.

The bitter rivalry among the Polish political factions, and the influx of Czech and Polish operatives into the Middle East, was now proving to be a serious problem for Cairo SOE and for the British government. The Poles especially were a puzzle, for though they were Britain's loyal ally they always seemed to be holding something back. Their arms-length stance toward the British had been evident since they had first arrived in Budapest in 1940. Once the AK had established itself there it had begun demanding its own codes and radio frequencies.

*Matecki was later carpeted by Brigadier Shearer for having sent a synopsis of the Middle East situation to Warsaw, first by radio, then in writing to his Istanbul contact. The latter message was intercepted by British intelligence and Matecki was threatened with severe penalties if he breached security again.

After their Budapest consulate had been closed down in 1941 those Poles who hadn't been arrested made their way to Palestine and Cairo. Soon afterwards reports began to filter back to London about unofficial activities being undertaken by rival Polish freelance cells in Turkey as well as in the Middle East.

With most of their networks on mainland Europe destroyed or seriously disrupted, officers of the Polish government's own intelligent bureaux had also made their way to Cairo along with an untold number of pesky freelancers attempting to sell information, much of it of dubious value, to the British. These informants needed to be vetted, a job that was delegated to Colonel Guy Tamplin, Director of Special Operations for the Balkans, who was to become Christine's devoted friend. After having met her and Andrew for the first time he expressed the belief that they were honourable people. Satisfied of their innocence, he did not expend a great deal of effort investigating their backgrounds despite Matecki's complaints.

Matecki was finally replaced as 'Jakub Alek' by Walerian Mercik (cryptonym SUN) in the summer of 1941. Heczka departed the following year thus relieving Christine of both her antagonists. But an aura of mystery hovered over the newly arrived Mercik whose wife had been murdered in Cyprus and whose killer was never found.

Chapter 13.
Breaking Hearts at the Gezira Club

Cairo during the war was a city of great contrasts - huge palaces, squalid slums, exiled European rulers and wealthy Cairenes living in the midst of an army of beggars. The most imposing parts of the city were King Farouk's enormous Royal Palace of Abdin and the nearby Parliament buildings. The wealthiest of Cairo's citizens lived here and in Garden City, a neighbourhood comprised mainly of Egyptian and British families. The majority of Cairo's population however were working-class and poor Egyptians, many of them Muslims. Contact between rich Cairenes and the British on one side, and the ordinary people of Cairo on the other was at best minimal.[1] The British had their own clubs but also colonised the best hotels like Shepheard's. In the better restaurants they mingled with wealthy and educated Egyptians or with Europeans of a similar class. Groppi's was perhaps one of the few popular restaurants where officers and enlisted men could mix though its prices put it out of bounds for most ordinary soldiers.[2]

Concealed - sometimes not too well - in the dense population was a large contingent of operatives from opposing sides in the war. They too preferred the westernised bars and hotels to the less hygienic quarters of the city.

The war in Europe imposed itself on the Middle East in the autumn of 1940. Benito Mussolini was the first to bring the chaos of war across the Mediterranean. Though Hitler's willing but wary ally, he was put off by the Nazi dictator's habit of launching attacks on other nations without first consulting him. He decided to demonstrate that he too could be equally brutal and cunning. Determined to exert control over the Balkans he launched three divisions against Greece in October 1941. But the resistance offered by the Greeks turned out to be much stronger than anticipated and the Italian campaign there, and in neighbouring Albania, was over within three weeks.

Anxious to avenge his humiliation Mussolini ordered a reluctant General Graziani to commence an attack against British positions in Egypt. But the British military were more than a match for the Italians. In December, General Archibald Wavell launched a counter-offensive that took him from Sidi Barani in Egypt to Tobruk and to Benghazi in Libya within two months. These victories proved to be a terrific morale booster for the British (General Erwin Rommel would recapture Benghazi in March.) But before long the Germans, who had come to the aid of the hapless Italians, penetrated the Egyptian border and also counter-attacked Tobruk though they were unable to overcome the fierce resistance put up by a combined force of Poles, Australians and New Zealanders.

Rommel's troops remained on Egypt's borders until December, posing a continuous threat to British positions as well as to Egypt itself and caused widespread anxiety in Cairo.

Ever since the fall of France the British government had been concerned that Germany, with Vichy France under its thumbs, might attempt to invade the Middle East not to advance their policy *Lebensraum* but to seize control of valuable oil fields. There was also serious concern over whether the Turks would permit German forces to cross their sovereign territory and mount an invasion of the Middle East. To prevent this from happening British and Free French forces decided to launch a preemptive assault against Syria.

Prior to any assault on Syria, Allied forces would need to have surveillance conducted on that country's borders as well as on the approaches to the bridges over the Tigris and Euphrates rivers in the event that it became necessary to blow them. Major Wilkinson did a *volte-face* and decided that Christine might be just the person to carry out such a mission. He did not however formally reinstate her and Andrew. He did contact Guy Tamplin with the news that the Seizieme Bureau had given the green light for them to undertake the assignment. But it was Tamplin who had first suggested to M in August 1941 that Christine, with Andrew as her driver, might be sent to Syria and remain there '. . . waiting to see what happens politically further north. In the meantime X. [Christine] could be usefully employed supplying us [with intelligence] which I should imagine she would find quite easy to get.'

Since being sacked by Wilkinson in June, Christine had been at loose ends and needed to find work. The payments she received from SOE were barely enough to sustain her. Fortunately there were plenty of officers about willing to wine and dine her. Prior to being tapped for the Syria job she had briefly been employed in the offices of a Colonel Zazulinski. M described him as a 'large, florid and very shifty-looking Jew' who was one of Professor Kot's men. Zazulinski denied ever having met him and once again SOE were left wondering who was telling the truth. Zazulinski's unspecified dissatisfaction with

Christine's work seemed a minor matter by comparison. Her employment at his office had been abruptly terminated, according to a cryptic note in SOE files, 'because she was not suitable.' No further explanation was given. She next found a position with a British government office in Cairo before being asked to go to Syria.

For this mission, a seemingly rather pleasant duty, Christine would be controlled by 'Edmund', the code-name for Felix Carver, an executive at an Egyptian cotton firm. She and Andrew crossed the Egyptian-Syrian border without any difficulty, posing as tourists. They had official transit visas in hand and with Christine's command of French, they were unlikely to arouse suspicion. They moved freely about the country with Andrew in his customary role as chauffeur. It seems that, despite being dismissed by Wilkinson, SOE were quite willing to use the pair when it served their purpose.

They spent much of their time touring the country in a leisurely manner. In Aleppo they stayed at a first-class hotel in that ancient city, paid for by the British government. It was here that she met El Effendi Durani, the son of the former Emperor of Afghanistan. He reportedly became very attracted to her but she saw to it that they remained just friends. Durani was most likely to have been the 'splendid-looking Afghan major' described by Lady Deakin as the officer who was sometimes seen with Christine. In a rare display of girlish indiscretion, she once said to Deakin, 'he would die for me.'[3]

That she was still in Aleppo as late as November is confirmed in a message from Colonel de Chastelain to Major Perkins suggesting that intelligence brought out of the Balkans by the Polish operative Majewski be sent to her for evaluation. De Chastelain reminded Perkins that she also knew the operatives in Budapest now working for Gizycki.

One British writer has claimed that Christine somehow assisted the British 8th Army in gaining victory in Syria but did not provide any details. In fact, no explanation of her role in this episode has ever been offered to describe, even in general terms, exactly how she achieved that *coup*. The chronology of events does not support this assertion. Christine did cross Syria with Andrew en route to Palestine in the spring of 1941 but spent only one night in Damascus. The 8th Army launched its forces against Syria just five days after she and Andrew had been dismissed by Major Wilkinson (on or about June 12). The Vichy French commander signed surrender terms on July 12. It is difficult to understand how in such a short time frame she, acting either alone or with Andrew in unfamiliar territory, could have travelled from Cairo into Syria, gathered whatever intelligence the 8th Army required then passed it back to them in time to gather, brief and equip a force that could overwhelm combined Syrian-French forces, admittedly not a powerful enemy

The fact is, the 8th Army had gone into action against Syria within days of Christine's confrontation with Wilkinson. Its War Diary entries for the 16th and 17th of June 1941, written less than a week after Christine's suspension, reveals that '74 engineers [were] now operating behind French lines around Damascus cutting telephone lines and making explosions.'[4] Aside from the absence of validation of Christine's contribution to the British triumph, historians have also cast doubt on SOE's role in depriving Vichy France of its Syrian colony. One SOE historian described it as 'a little fire behind the rich smoke of claims.'[5] In the shake-up of SOE Cairo personnel in the summer of 1941, the reliability of SO2's claims of successful sabotage in Syria was among the items questioned.

Shortly after their victory in Syria, British forces went on to take Lebanon and, with

Stalin's tacit support, seized control of Iran.

If Christine did take on a reconnaissance mission to Syria what information she could glean remains in files not available to the public. Whatever she may have discovered was not of immediate importance however for events elsewhere lessened the British need for surveillance of Syria's borders. In the autumn of 1941 German forces had become stalled in Russia when subjected to ferocious counterattacks by the Red Army. Hitler's focus necessarily shifted from the Middle East where for the moment Rommel seemed to be holding his own. But any plans Hitler might have had for further action there had to be shelved.

It has been suggested that suspending Christine had merely been a smoke screen to distract the enemy's attention from her forthcoming mission. But in light of the fact that she remained inactive for nearly three years, it seems more likely that her mission, after Syria had surrendered, was a one-off action authorised by Wilkinson. Surveillance of Syrian borders had seemed a necessary precaution at the time but one that could be carried out by an agent whose services were not required urgently elsewhere. Thus, contrary to what her admirers have claimed, Christine did not 'fight the Nazis across Europe for five years.' She carried out only this one mission between November 1940 and the spring of 1944.

Though she had been officially suspended there was nothing to prevent Christine from maintaining contact with the Musketeers. Whatever information she received from Poland was duly passed on to Cairo SOE who were unabashedly grateful to have it. That in turn irked Polish government officials when they learned of Christine's continuing relationship with British intelligence. They requested in the strongest terms that SIS either cut off all contact with her or establish a formal link. But privately the London Poles secretly hoped that whatever intelligence reports the British received from their beleaguered country would eventually be shared with them.

Guy Tamplin was sincere in his efforts to find a useful assignment for his two Polish friends. He suggested that perhaps Andrew should be given a course in handling explosives '. . . so that he could be in a position to deal with railways if and when necessary.' Andrew never did have the opportunity to demolish rail lines but he did spend an afternoon with explosives' expert Captain T. Bruce Mitford who was about to test a newly manufactured device. He accompanied Mitford to a nearby river and watched curiously as Mitford hurled the explosive into the water, hoping to observe its results. The two men were rewarded not only with the anticipated detonation but with a number of fish thrown up by the force of the blast, thus providing them with the catch of the day. Whether this was another of Andrew's Hemingway-esque tales was never verified by Captain Mitford.

When Christine and Andrew finally returned to Cairo, still officially unemployed, she began to frequent the legendary Gezira Club and soon became one of its regulars, taking full advantage of the comforts it had to offer. But while she sunned herself and generally relaxed, SOE leadership had worked itself into a lather over her future. Having already sacked her and her lover on orders from London, Major Wilkinson disclaimed any further responsibility for them as well as for Gizycki, suggesting 'that their future should be decided by A/D [George Taylor].' This must have confused and angered the couple who had eagerly carried out a mission at Wilkinson's request only to return to Cairo to be treated like pariahs.

Taylor's initial response in the matter was surprisingly tepid, given his previous support for Christine. He wrote that he felt 'most benevolently inclined' towards her and her partner. He believed them to be good people but avoided the question of their status, adding that 'he did not feel in a position to issue any instructions as to their future.'

With rumours of treachery and loose-living swirling around her, and fighting continuing on Egypt's borders, Christine remained unperturbed. She turned up frequently at the Gezira Club where she assumed a feline pose (as described by Andrew), content to spend hours lying in the sun. Because she had never learned to swim she could not avail herself of the club's pool. Though she seemed to be at the club almost daily the author Artemis Cooper claimed that those she interviewed for her splendid book *Cairo in the war 1939-1945* never mentioned Christine Granville. It seems an odd omission given that so many of the characters in the book - Countess Tarnowska, Bickham Sweet-Escott, Guy Tamplin, to name but a few - were well-acquainted with Christine.

The Gezira Sporting Club, to give it its proper name, was a huge island complex in the Nile with manicured lawns, a golf course, polo pitch, cricket grounds, a race course and facilities for squash, tennis, croquet and a swimming pool. It had been developed and presented to the British by the Khedive Tewfik.* Most of its members were British businessmen, high-ranking civil servants, military officers and their wives, along with a with a small contingent of wealthy Egyptians.

Evenings were spent with Andrew at local cafes or dining with friends from the Polish exile community. Christine was certainly aware of the back-and-forth desert battles being fought between British and German forces but there was little she could do to directly involve herself. She adapted quickly to the agreeable way of life at the club and became a familiar figure, visiting on a daily basis even though she was not a member. But she knew the right people who provided her access. She spent so much time at the Gezira that her post was directed there. She had always loved the combination of sun and warm weather in great contrast to her native Poland where such conditions were available for only two to three months of the year. In Cairo she had found her near-perfect setting with heat and sunshine frequently on offer.

After the contretemps with Major Wilkinson the Gezira Club provided Christine with welcome relief. Though Andrew remained her constant companion she quickly acquired a coterie of followers and that in turn inspired a steady stream of rumours about her private life. In such a hot-house atmosphere there were flirtations, some more serious than others.

Despite the lack of action and offers of return to London she seemed reluctant to travel, ostensibly because the louche life of Cairo offered some compensation for her forced inactivity. But in the back of her mind she must have realised that her best opportunity for re-joining the war effort in some capacity was to remain within close proximity to British forces in the Middle East. As the threat from the Germans began to recede the Cairene rumour mill hummed with gossip about a probable Allied invasion of Europe.

*An uncle to King Farouk and leader of the upper-class nationalist movement.

Surely there would be an assignment for Christine, perhaps another covert entry into Poland. For the time being however a return to Europe where the Gestapo were hunting for her was out of the question.

Her fondness for this new and comfortable life notwithstanding, she was quite willing to expose herself to danger whenever called upon. There was never any question that she would reject an assignment because it might cause her discomfort. Though Christine could at times be described as enigmatic she was no prima dona.

The tension between Christine and the Polish intelligence bureaux continued for much of the time that she was in Egypt. It was prolonged by occasional sniping from the Poles even though they lacked any hard evidence of treachery against her. In October 1941 Heczka complained to Major Wilkinson that she and Andrew were still exfiltrating Allied personnel from occupied territory at the behest of the British even after it had been agreed that their services would be terminated.

Wilkinson denied the charge which was absurd on the face of it. Given their distance from Europe - they were in Syria at the time - and their sporadic communication with Polish couriers, it is highly unlikely that they were able to do much hands-on exfiltrating. As deputy head of the Seizieme Bureau, Heczka should have known that travel in and out of Poland had become extremely difficult and more hazardous as the Germans tightened their grip on the country. Wilkinson had what he called 'a show-down' with Heczka and his bureau after which he was replaced.

After his penultimate meeting with Christine, Jerzy Gyzycki had set out for Budapest traveling under the surname Gordon (in coded messages he was usually known as G.N.

Norton). He delivered a diplomatic pouch to the British Legation in Belgrade then made his way to Budapest where Owen O'Malley had begun the process of closing down the consulate. Gizycki arrived on the April the 1st while his wife was en route to Palestine. Their respective missions had them traveling on parallel tracks as they crossed Europe except that they were moving in opposite directions. She had innocently assumed that a new assignment awaited her in Cairo. If she had any concerns about her husband she did not confide them to anyone. Meanwhile Gizycki set to work in an attempt to rebuild the Warsaw-Budapest connection. A reunion with Christine was much on his mind and he had a very definite idea about what the future held for them once the war was over.

In his memoir Owen O'Malley recalled that he was unsure of what to do with Gizycki but he must have been writing under the strictures of the Official Secrets Act for Gizycki's mission had been clearly defined and O'Malley would have known that. He was to jump-start the courier lines left dangling after his wife's hasty departure. O'Malley claims to have appointed Gizycki as his AMA even though he was not a British citizen. An SOE document however confirms that he had been ordered to do this by a higher authority. At that stage of the war it didn't much matter.

Once he'd done what was necessary to re-establish communications with Warsaw, Gizycki was charged with helping O'Malley close down the consulate and accompany the minister and his family on their escape route to the Soviet Union. SOE had never intended for Gizycki to remain in Budapest for long as it was obvious by late 1940 that the consulate's days were numbered. But his posting was not a mere coincidence. He knew his way around eastern Europe and spoke Russian fluently, a decided advantage as the Soviet

Union remained the only safe haven, albeit an unsettled one, for British officials fleeing central Europe. To make for Turkey, already bulging with British diplomats and military personnel, would have involved attempting to cross the now hostile borders of Bulgaria.

While O'Malley packed up his family and destroyed as many documents as he could, Gizycki worked frantically in the short time available to put the Budapest-Warsaw link in proper order. In the days remaining before they were to leave Hungary he made contact with a reliable Polish source, a remnant of Christine's old band. This unnamed man was to remain behind and maintain contact with the Musketeers, a most hazardous mission considering that the Hungarian police and the Gestapo had combined to eliminate almost all the Czech and Polish undercover cells. Before leaving Hungary Gizycki arranged for Christine's colleague, referred to only as 'A' in SOE files, to have sufficient funds to last several months. A large portion of the money was eventually turned over to the Musketeers. The courier who carried it to Warsaw had narrowly avoided capture by the Nazis who were still in the midst of their violent repression of the Poles. He'd been confronted by Gestapo agents while crossing Poland by train but managed to destroy a message he was carrying and escaped.

'A' also reported that the Hungarian secret police were on to him and that he fully expected to be arrested. In anticipation of being detained he destroyed a 532-page cypher but the versatile Musketeers promptly created a new code, enabling them to contact their opposite numbers in Belgrade and Istanbul as well as with those few still in Budapest. In his report on this adventure, Gizycki criticised the British lack of response to overtures made by Christine's source in Poland in November 1940. Writing in fractured English he stated that this absence of cooperation forced the Poles to contact 'Polish organisms abroad.'

While Gizycki was fully engaged in re-establishing connections with Warsaw, O'Malley had abruptly decided to bring forward their departure date forcing him to hurriedly wrap up his work. Gizycki recorded in detail their furtive trip to the Soviet Union. While his account deals mainly with the particulars of travel arrangements his recollections of Lady O'Malley in particular are unflattering. Against advice she had brought with her an enormous steamer trunk and needed help in loading it onto the train. He wrote frankly that, 'Mrs O'Malley was a writer and a nut. Well, perhaps only half-mad. Anyway, there was definitely something not quite right with her noodle.'[6]

Lord Tweedsmuir (aka William Buchan) knew the OMalley family well and concurred with Gizycki's description of Lady O'Malley.[7] He found her 'rather tiresome.' But 'her own autobiography shows her as brave, determined and decidedly what the French call a *maitresse femme*. Those characteristics were much in evidence. A good writer, though, especially, as usual in her earliest work.'

O'Malley, Gizycki and their entourage arrived in Moscow without incident. After a pause to catch their collective breath the minister, his family and first secretary travelled by train across Siberia then sailed to Japan from where they took a second ship to America. They remained in Washington, DC, for several weeks during which time O'Malley provided the American government with a lengthy report about conditions in Hungary, calling attention to the intense rivalry between Polish factions.[8]

Once he had seen off the minister and his family, the doughty Gizycki left the Soviet

Union, crossed the Caspian Sea into Iran and travelled to Istanbul where he hoped to be reunited with his wife. He later claimed that he'd sent a cypher to Istanbul SOE asking that they contact Christine and inform her that he was en route. The cypher's contents somehow had become garbled. Instead of asking that she remain in Istanbul to await her husband, the opposite instruction was delivered. When Gizycki arrived and found her gone - and the phrasing of the cypher altered - he was livid, insisting that someone within SOE had either had changed the message deliberately or had copied it incorrectly.

Christine would have gone ahead in any event for she had her own agenda. But that was not the end of Gizycki's dispute with SOE. He reported that he had sent three sealed packets of documents, mostly reports from the Musketeers, via diplomatic pouch but found that only one had turned up in Istanbul. Major Wilkinson had been the recipient of that pouch and he insisted that only two packets of documents had been received which he combined into one package before handing them on to Christine. The matter was never settled conclusively, leaving Gizycki in a funk.

He had for some time been quietly stewing over the allegation against him and his wife, that they were 'suspect' because the Musketeers had allegedly become tainted. Wilkinson contended that the organisation had been penetrated 'because it was mainly composed of amateurs' and, like many of his fellow officers, he was sceptical about their competence in intelligence operations though he continued to cooperate with them.

Gizycki had by now accumulated a catalogue of complaints to lodge against SOE before he finally decided to resign. Like his marriage his relationship with SOE was approaching its climax. His mission in Budapest accomplished, he hurried to Istanbul anticipating a romantic interlude with Christine only to find that she'd already left. He went on to Cairo where by chance he met Colonel SW Bailey who informed him that she'd gone to Jerusalem on private business. Bailey offered to take Gizycki with him to the Holy City, unaware of what was about to happen.

When Gizycki finally caught up with Christine she told him first about the acrimonious meeting with Wilkinson. He immediately assumed her innocence and rallied to her defence. She did not have to convince him for he was already in a black mood over the mishandled cypher and the unresolved dispute over the number of packets he'd sent from Budapest. He cursed Wilkinson and the British for the off-handed manner in which they had treated her. Finishing off his tirade while she listened apprehensively, he grandly announced that henceforth he would have nothing to do with SOE. But worse was to come, for him.

Christine then admitted her affair with Andrew, signaling that their marriage was over. Gizycki was furious over her deception but after some angry words regained his composure and reluctantly accepted the situation. In a melancholy mood he later recalled, 'They were lovers and we had to part.' But he could not resist making this catty remark: 'Knowing my wife, I was sure that sex played a very small part in her decision, or even, no part at all.'[9]

The obvious implication was that he himself had performed more than satisfactorily in the bedroom and therefore she had left him for other reasons. None of her other lovers ever complained about the physical side of their relationships either (or perhaps they were more discreet than he, with the exception of the ebullient Ledochowski).

Nevertheless he was full of admiration for his wife and for Andrew. '... they had done together some crazy things, both were fearless and eager for more danger and excitement, and their common experiences made Krystyna feel that, now, she was closer to Kowerski [Kennedy] than to me.' As for Andrew himself, Gizycki commented: 'One thing was fortunate about it [the affair] - Kowerski was an upright, fine man. I could see that he felt rotten about the whole mess, so I told him not to take it hard, that it was not his fault but the war's and that I understood how it all happened.'

Though he had lost his wife to another man Gizycki determinedly stood by her. He composed an emotional final report to SOE, a lengthy harangue against the British government then literally left the field of battle. His service to the British and Polish governments had now come to an end. But for all his bluster Gizycki had at least achieved something of value in Budapest. Guy Tamplin came across him soon after this episode and reported that he seemed extremely upset. 'I gather his personal life has gone wrong as XY. [Christine and Andrew] is now own firm and for this we are to blame !'

An SOE memorandum dated November 22nd (HS4/286) acknowledged Gizycki's service to the British war effort but contained the admission that SOE had no further employment for him.10 He retired to Canada and took up the less glamorous position as manager of a hostel for immigrant Poles. He continued to write, publishing articles in Polish newspapers in Canada and in London. He travelled frequently but had little or no contact with Christine and did not attend her funeral. He died in May 1970, in unknown circumstances, in Oxaca, Mexico.

Despite the increased difficulty in entering and leaving Poland one of Christine's most active, and most interesting, female couriers, Klementyna Mankowska who claimed the title of countess, managed to make her way to Cairo where she was interviewed by Wilkinson. Afterwards he remarked that he was inclined to believe that she 'was quite innocent,' of charges that she too was a double agent. She had brought with her rolls of microfilm containing intelligence reports and most valuable of all, the dictionary cypher used by Christine in Budapest.

Mankowska had joined the Musketeers early on in the war and worked for the German army on instructions from Witkowski. She was soon arrested but released. She was taken into custody a second time and given the choice of working for the Germans or imprisonment in a concentration camp. She eagerly took the first option but immediately upon arriving in Britain as a 'German spy,' turned herself into the authorities.

With their surveillance of Syria's borders concluded, Christine and Andrew returned to Cairo in the late autumn of 1941 to find their employment status unaltered. The uncertainty over their future lingered into 1942 with no one willing to make a final decision regarding their predicament. They were unemployed and for the time being remained unemployable. Responding to a rumour that the Deuxieme Bureau might take her on, Christine made it clear to Tamplin that she would not work for them unless she could retain her British passport. This document was of course bogus, bearing a fictitious name and a false date of birth. Krystyna had not yet officially become Christine Granville though everyone on the British side knew her by that name. The more courteous officers addressed her in dispatches as Madame Gizycka.

Six months had elapsed since Wilkinson had sacked Christine and he had yet to receive further instructions from London regarding her disposition. He contacted SOE HQ to urge that somebody make a decision about her fate, offering to 'carry the can' himself if necessary. His own thinking was that SOE should wash its hands of this pair of operatives as gently as possible. They should be permitted to remain in Cairo, paid 'a considerable sum of money as a reward for their services, receive an official letter of thanks and then be handed over to join the Poles here.'[11]

Christine would have bridled at the thought of being delivered to another organisation as if she were a prize mare awarded to a peasant. If this had been allowed to happen the government-in-exile surely would have removed her from active duty and relegated her to menial work in London. But Wilkinson thought it pointless to leave her floundering in Cairo where she might become 'a source of disgruntlement.' In a telegram to London he described her as a 'menace' and was apprehensive that perhaps she 'knew too much.'

He was being more cautious than was necessary, not to mention unfair to Christine. Despite her reputation as a 'spy', she ranked rather low in the pecking order of intelligence operatives. Her sphere of activity thus far had been limited to the structure of the courier system between Poland and Hungary, now almost defunct, and the names of the British section chiefs with whom she had contact. While her work was certainly important and the information she had accumulated could cost lives in the wrong hands, it was not so important that it would have disrupted plans for the D-Day landings or other major undertaking.

The ambivalence and confusion surrounding the dilemma of Christine's future amply demonstrate SOE's recognition of her courage and talents. Yet they could not take the chance that she and the Musketeers might be working for the Nazis however reluctantly.

There was simply too much at stake. SOE were already under tremendous pressure to produce results while at the same time fending off rumours of sloth on the part of some its operatives. Cairo SOE did seem to have an inordinate number of employees on hand (many were not there by choice) and it required a substantial budget to sustain such a large staff. By the spring of 1942 SOE had trained 1600 operatives and had a budget of £2.5 million, a considerable sum in those days.

Back in Whitehall the size of that budget was being questioned, especially since the organisation's activities in Europe had yielded only a few noteworthy successes. Lady Ranfurly* was partly responsible for instigating an investigation into the activities of the Cairo office, complaining to the visiting Foreign Secretary Anthony Eden that there were too many 'good-time Charlies' hanging about with not much to do. Ranfurly's anxieties over the condition of her prisoner-of-war husband played no small part in her decision to go to Eden.[12]

The first of two purges of SOE Cairo personnel had already taken place before Christine arrived in Egypt. These were carried out in the hope of making SOE more efficient. To date, it had not 'set Europe ablaze' as Churchill had so exuberantly wished. Acting on persistent rumours, including Ranfurly's complaint of over-spending and non-stop parties, Sir Frank Nelson, Operational Head of SOE (CD), was sent to Cairo to investigate in the spring of 1941. On the ground the situation turned out not to be as bad as advertised. Nevertheless the Cairo section chief George Pollock was sent back to England and a

---

*Lady Ranfurly, *nee* Hermione Llewellyn, formerly personal assistant to Lord and Lady Wakehurst, Governor of New South Wales. *See* her autobiographical *To War with Whitaker* (Wm Heinemann 1994).

number of his staff were reassigned or relieved of duties

The number of personnel was reduced and both sections of SOE - propaganda (SO1) and sabotage (SO2) - were now brought together in one office block known as Rustem Buildings with Colonel Terence Maxwell in charge. Neither the address nor the purpose of the buildings were meant to be known to the general public yet every taxi driver in Cairo apparently knew about this so-called secret location referred to as 'Hush-Hush House.' It was here on the roof that Christine began her training as a wireless radio operator.

Amid the turmoil within SOE, Wilkinson and others continued to grapple with the problem of suitable employment for Christine. One officer suggested that the situation should be resolved at a meeting between the heads of SOE and the Polish intelligence bureaux. No such meeting was convened and the issue continued to be bounced from one pair of hands to another. No one was willing to make a final decision, partly out of fear of offending Christine whom they all respected. Considering the effort required to maintain their numerous operatives and various missions, SOE country section officers seemed to expend an inordinate amount of time and paperwork discussing the future of one operative among the nearly two thousand on its roster.

Wilkinson had already performed the unpleasant task of dismissing Christine and Andrew but it remained for a higher authority to decide their final disposition. In late January 1942 Wilkinson received a signal from the head of the ME ops desk in London, Lieutenant Colonel JSA Pearson (symbol D/HV), informing him that he could send the couple to England if their presence continued 'to cause embarrassment. They might be returned,' it was suggested, 'via the Cape [a nice long journey] but they could not be promised employment in England.'

The desert war was raging not far from Egyptian territory and there was a very noticeable level of anxiety discernible especially among the educated and merchant classes, as well as among the European exiles who had sought refuge in Cairo. America's forced entry into the war in December 1941 did not allay their fears for it would be at least a year before they could assemble a force large enough to fight on two fronts.

The German capture of Benghazi in January 1942 caused panic in some quarters of Cairo. Student-led riots flared in the streets, anti-British in tenor. It wasn't so much that the Cairenes longed for Nazi domination. Rather, they saw Britain in a moment of weakness and sought to take advantage of the situation to overthrow their colonial masters. British Commonwealth forces were far from defeated however. While Benghazi was under assault the 8th Army attacked and captured Tripoli.

In early February 1942, London SOE sent a second telegram to Wilkinson advising him that 'Polish authorities here remain adamant regarding X and Y and we have no option but to recommend you send them to London where we will have to cope.'

In March, Andrew had to have his prosthetic limb replaced because an infection had developed in the stump of his leg. Christine told Guy Tamplin that the operation had been very painful and it would be several weeks before he could walk properly. Andrew could deal with the pain but he was more frustrated at having his return to action delayed. Tamplin reported this news to M, along with something more sinister. Count Wiktor Rozwadowski of the Deuxieme Bureau and a childhood friend of Christine's, had enquired after another Polish agent known as 'L' (Richard Maczynski), someone known to Tamplin.

After a brief conversation Christine said to Tamplin, *sotto voce*, that a contact in the Polish community had warned he would 'soon crash over L.'

Maczynski had long been suspected of being a double agent by both the British and the Poles. Fearing that the latter would 'bump him off' before they could interrogate him, British operatives quietly took Maczynski into custody and moved him across the Syrian border where they questioned him. He willingly gave up details of German organisations in the Balkans, in Turkey and in the Middle East.

Tamplin was taken aback by Christine's warning for he had a close relationship with the Poles and was respected by them as one of the few SOE officers who could speak their language. Before the war he had been a banker in Poland and was quite familiar with the Baltic states where he had met and married a Latvian woman. In a memo to M, Tamplin returned to the subject of employment for Christine. His opinion, accurate as it turned out, was that she and Andrew were reluctant to return to England. She had been offered jobs in Cairo by unnamed British organisations but had rejected the offers because, '. . . the work seems rather distasteful to her, as it is local security.'[13] No attempts were made on Tamplin's life but he did die suddenly the following year.

In the meantime Christine's inexplicably glowing reputation continued to grow despite her inactivity. A British soldier with the Sudan Defence Force met her at a party and noted in his diary for March 18, 1942, 'Met Christine Granville very altogether sinewy strong spy & very Polish (although half Irish). I think she spies for us. Quite good company."**

In her desperation to find meaningful employment Christine contacted Lieutenant

General Wladyslaw Anders, commander of the newly formed Polish II Corps, recently arrived in Cairo.14 Tamplin had previously had a private interview with Anders and reported to Wilkinson that, 'He [Anders] is anxious to use them [Christine and Andrew] and has obtained a statement from the 38-Land [Polish] headquarters to say that they have nothing against them.'15

When Tamplin emerged from Anders' office he found the couple waiting to see the general. Afterwards Anders confided to Tamplin that he had no doubts whatsoever about their loyalty to the Allied cause. Armed with this assurance Tamplin wrote, 'I think and hope that they will get a job and be taken off our hands.'16 Vera Atkins supported Anders' statement with this post-war comment about Christine: 'She was utterly loyal and dedicated to the Allies, and nothing would have made her betray her trust.'

Tamplin's optimism was not matched by any action on the part of SOE. By April no decision had been taken on Christine's status. She had now been in Cairo for nearly a year, idled by baseless rumours. The issue of her re-instatement was not something that ranked high on SOE's list of priorities. The SOE high command continued to avoid a decision, preferring to pass the problem along from hand to hand. They were more concerned with maintaining lines of communication inside occupied Europe while fending off the bureaucratic embrace of the British military whose Middle East GHQ were determined to rein in this seemingly autonomous organisation.

**These comments were found in the diary of a British soldier (rank unknown) with the surname Castrades of the 60th Rifles, Ninth Army, MEE. 1942. They were written in a Scribbling Diary purchased at the price of one shilling & sixpence.

General Sir Archibald Wavell had written to SOE chief Dr Hugh Dalton (also a Labour Party MP) in May 1941, pointing out that some of the Executive's operations were incompatible with military projects. He reminded Dalton that in the beginning he'd been prepared to be open-minded about SOE activities but they had now developed their own agenda and seldom bothered coordinating their activities with Army HQ. Dalton rejected Wavell's views of his organisation's functions and reiterated that these were political subversion, spreading political propaganda and committing acts of sabotage.

Anthony Eden however took sides with the military. He wrote several memoranda to Churchill in April 1942 expressing the view that SOE should be under the control of the chiefs of staff, that it was incongruous for a minister for Economic Warfare (Dalton) to be responsible for an espionage bureau. He complained too that SOE often went against policy in neutral countries such as Portugal,Turkey and Greece where SOE operatives had been accused of attempting to undermine the elected governments.

That SOE had its own codes independent of those of SIS also seemed to rankle Eden who, as foreign secretary, claimed final authority over SIS. He was even more irritated, and embarrassed no doubt, when the Turkish ambassador advised him that SOE operatives seemed to have an abundance of money and some of its men were out of control. If these complaints reached Churchill's ears he didn't appeared to be at all perturbed. He preferred to let SOE continue independently of the service chiefs. In February 1942 Lord Selborne replaced Dalton. Though Eden and Wavell had lost the battle for control of SOE, the organisation had been sternly reminded that in neutral countries FO policy would prevail. General Wavell was re-assured that SOE would not undertake any overt activities, especially sabotage, in any country where military operations were in progress without coordinating with Army GHQ, Middle East Forces.

Still at a loss about what to do with Christine, Wilkinson signaled London suggesting that, 'Gisycka and Co. be employed in the local censorship.' Lieutenant Colonel Pearson replied that this would be acceptable to him. At this juncture Colonel AD Seddon, head of SOE Russian section, weighed in with a cryptic message. He wrote that his contact in Moscow had been given the names of Christine and her partner, and that this person would notify the NKVD (later KGB). Why the Russian security services had to be notified of these events was never spelt out. Certainly nothing came of it. But contact between opposing intelligence agencies was not unheard of though the public were generally unaware of it. This was perhaps an SIS offering to the NVKD by way of letting them know that the Polish couple would not be interfering in eastern Europe, soon to become a Russian sphere of influence.

Part IV. 1944

Chapter 14. Mixed Doubles

In May 1942 Christine asked for permission to join the WAAS (South African Women's Auxiliary Service) in some capacity - anything that did not require being confined to an office. But the women of WAAS were recruited precisely for that purpose, to relieve men from desk-jobs and make them available for front-line duty. WAAS had nothing else to offer her.

She briefly considered joining the ATS (Auxiliary Territorial Service) whose assignments took them closer to the actual fighting. They provided radar and radio operators, aircraft spotters, drivers and whatever was needed short of engaging in combat. It was perhaps a passing fancy for Christine never applied to ATS. At Patrick Howarth's suggestion she did begin a training course in wireless radio telegraphy.

Rommel launched an offensive against British positions in May. The Germans took Tobruk in June and had reached El Alamein by the 1st of July. This precipitated panic in Cairo, not only among the general population but within SOE as well. Thousands of documents were hurriedly destroyed and the SOE leadership prepared to abandon the city for Palestine.(The destruction of these files has left a huge gap in the annals of the service.)

The panic was short lived however and afterwards Colonel Maxwell was replaced at Rustem Buildings in August 1942 by Lord Glenconner * who had previously been head of

SOE's Balkan and Middle East section. Control of its Russian mission was also added to his portfolio. His promotion was to be part of a major shake-up of the leadership. In addition to naming Lord Selborne** as head of SOE, the banker Sir Charles Hambro succeeded Sir Frank Nelson as CD.

In June, General Stanislaw Kopanski arrived in Cairo. Christine and Andrew met with him, each claiming the general as another of their myriad old friends. Andrew had served with him in 1939 but she could not have known him nearly as well. In any event, Kopanski offered no immediate solution to their employment problem. He could not employ either of them without first consulting SOE who had already placed severe restrictions upon their activities.

Christine's predicament dragged on into the summer without resolution. In July she took a job as a waitress which she must have loathed. She wrote to Owen O'Malley, saying that she was '. . . on the rocks.' Throughout the war and afterwards the O'Malleys maintained contact with her thanks mainly to the efforts of young Kate who wrote to Christine as often as she could. Some of Christine's letters to Kate survived the war. As for her lover, Howarth noted that he was now working for SOE 'as a kind of transport officer.'

The responsibility for Christine was next passed to the sympathetic Colonel Tamplin who had always been concerned for her fate because he believed that SOE and the British

*C.G. Tennant (1899-1983), 2nd Lord Glenconner. SOE Balkan desk 1940-41, head of SOE Cairo 1942-43.
**Roundell Cecil Palmer, 3rd Earl of Selborne 1887-1971.

government owed her a great deal. He felt that it had a duty to repatriate her if that was what she wanted. He suggested to Lord Selborne, and to George Taylor, that she and Andrew might be employed by General Anders at a salary of £42 (Egyptian) per month.

Colonel Taylor, who had previously begged off responsibility for her, abruptly changed his tune and signaled Tamplin saying that the British were 'under the strongest possible obligation to X [Christine].' He went on to say that he had given his word that she would not again be as badly let down as she had been in Budapest when the staff at the consulate had completely lost sight of her.

Between her small SOE salary and her work as a waitress she was able to make ends meet. In July she was again offered passage to England but declined, saying that she preferred to remain in Cairo perhaps because there had been a hint that she might be officially re-employed by SOE. Tamplin reported to Taylor that she was currently being provided for financially and that she lacked nothing except employment. 'We are trying to remedy this.' During the years 1942 and 1943 several missions were proposed which which might have made use of her talents. Taylor suggested to Colonel HN Sporborg, principal private secretary to Lord Selborne, that Christine might be 'employed' in France. With her expertise in the language, and in appearance, she could easily pass for a French woman. Andrew's French however was rudimentary at best. That, plus his obvious handicap, might arouse the suspicions of Vichy counter-intelligence, and quite likely the Gestapo. Virtually all such proposals envisioned him working alongside his lover but he was becoming restless and would soon resolve his own predicament.

A suggestion that the pair might be sent to Istanbul was rejected when someone pointed out that she was too well known there. The possibility of an assignment in Russia was raised but then neither of them spoke Russian. In that respect they were like many SOE operatives who were frequently posted to countries lacking any knowledge of the host nation's culture or language. SOE officers were, almost without exception, men and women of 'energy and initiative, and quite a number of them were intellectually outstanding and possessed an excellent political flair.' But these qualities were rendered useless if the operative could not communicate with officials or ordinary citizens.

Major Wilkinson was posted back to England in July 1942, to be replaced by Captain Patrick Howarth. Before leaving the UK, Howarth had received a report from Major Richard Truszkowski*** on a number of intelligence matters including an account of the exploits of the dashing Polish couple. Truscoe, as he was known (and as he would become legally known post-war), wrote to Wilkinson that, 'Inactivity is driving these subjects desperate. They are now trying to get a job with some US Mission here [Cairo].'

He reported derogatory comments made by Christine about the Seizieme Bureau, to the effect that they, along with the Deuxieme Bureau and the Kot organisation, were 'nincompoops, jacks-in-office, and scoundrels.' She was of the opinion that Professor Kot was 'universally execrated' in the Middle East. Her feelings were no doubt reciprocated by the personnel of those reviled (by her) organisations. Truszkowski added that she was regarded by the above-mentioned groups 'with the utmost suspicion, partly because of what

---

***Truszkowski, later promoted to colonel, was an Englishman of Polish parentage. He had been a member of the British Mission to Poland at the time of the German invasion. He and his family made a dramatic escape from the country in borrowed cars in the chaotic aftermath of the fighting.

she knows (and says), and partly as an English spy, paid to ferret out Two-Land [Poland] secrets for our benefit.'[1]

A report in the Polish Minorities Section**** supports Christine's comments about the two Polish intelligence agencies. 'These people [the two Polish intelligence agencies] were either "warring" in the same office or from separate offices but the bulk of their energy was wasted in throwing dirt at one another. Right up until 1944 these various bureaux were suspect and were a curse to all concerned. They constantly accused each other of being "double agents" and these accusations often taken up and fostered by well-meaning but ignorant British officers who spent a good deal of their time chasing hares which never existed."

The report drew two conclusions, first, that with the exception of Truszkowski, Tamplin and Wilkinson, 'there were never any SOE officers in the Middle East with an intimate knowledge of Polish problems,' and more damning, 'The only useful activities carried out by these [Polish] bureaux which extended from Istanbul to Cairo was the passing of couriers and correspondence from Poland to the UK and vice versa.'

Christine's role as 'an English spy' has not been much discussed in articles or books about her which inevitably focus on her heroics or her affairs. But Truszkowski's description of her is supported by comments in SOE reports as well as by Howarth and by Wilkinson. She was not a spy in the conventional sense. She never worked under deep cover and much of the information she passed on to SOE, supplied by contacts within the Polish

****See HS7/184 at The National Archives.

community, was not of grave importance. Often, she merely provided background information on certain Polish government officials and intelligence operatives.

There may be material of more significance buried in SIS archives but there is no evidence that SOE ever asked her officially to eavesdrop on Cairo's Polish community. They certainly would not have given her written instructions to do so (if they did those instructions have long since vanished). It is more likely that she was asked, off-the-record, to report conversations to her section chief that she considered to be of value. However she was approached, the correspondence of Wilkinson, Howarth and Truszkowski leaves no doubt that she was keeping them informed on what was being said in Polish intelligence circles.

A former civil servant, curator of the SOE files post-war, replied to a query asking if there was more proof of her eavesdropping. He wrote, '. . . several of the early papers refer to work done by Christine and the others for Section D before SOE came into existence may require some excisions. . . . There are also a number of post-war papers which will probably not be released.'

This information-gathering was not done out of any sense of vindictiveness towards the Poles but because Christine felt it her duty as a British agent. Still, she probably had not forgotten the rude response to her offer of cooperation with Polish agents when she first arrived in Budapest. If she did provide SOE with any deeply held Polish secrets they are not on offer at The National Archives. Much of what is available to the public is mostly gossip. Those bits of information that were of a serious nature did not measurably aid the British because they had already decided not to contest Soviet domination of Poland.

Christine and SOE developed a symbiotic relationship while she was in Cairo. Though she had been absent from Budapest for more than two years SOE still sought information from her on matters Hungarian. But by 1943 her contacts in Budapest had either fled or else had been arrested. Nevertheless she was always ready to give advice or offer an opinion. Similarly, she was often asked if the Poles would sign a treaty of cooperation with the Russians or what their post-war plans might be. But she'd been away from Poland for a lengthy spell and, with the demise of the Musketeers, her contacts there were few and far between.

Once Witkowski had been murdered Christine's pipeline of information had been virtually severed. The two Polish intelligence agencies suspected her and made it clear to SOE that they would not approve her involvement with any mission that had anything remotely to do with Polish affairs. (The Seizieme Bureau later relented and approved her participation in the aborted Operation Kris.) The Armia Krajowa would have nothing to do with her either. Criticism of Christine from these quarters was met by her with contempt. She was quite flattered to wear the uniform of a British officer and she had more than fulfilled her first assignment of infiltrating Poland, bringing out intelligence documents and establishing a courier route between Budapest and Warsaw. She had much to be proud of. Polish agents, by contrast, and whatever achievements they may have had, were unknown in the world at large whereas between the two world wars British agents had been glamourised in films and novels. She was obviously happy to be among their numbers.

SOE, lacking any direct contact from inside Hungary or Poland, convinced itself that she was a reliable source of information from within those two countries. Patrick Howarth, in a report to Wilkinson, wrote, 'The information contained [in] my [previous report] and subsequent signals on the same subject comes of course from WILLING [Christine], but I must stress again that her name in no circumstances be mentioned in connection with this subject, as this would only increase her established reputation as a spy employed by the British to watch the I-landers [Poles], and I should also lose a good deal of valuable information which I at present obtain from her.'[2]

It is curious that Christine's file folder for 1943 at TNA is completely empty while other folders contain vast amounts of documentation. Yet statements like Howarth's in his PF and in the files of his correspondents, confirm that she was passing information to them gleaned from Polish sources during that year.

Howarth had arrived in Cairo at the beginning of August 1942. His first encounter with Christine was, as might be expected, at the Gezira Club. Guy Tamplin was there with her on that occasion. The talk turned to a position available with Codes and Cyphers but she implied that she was not interested. Howarth seemed mildly annoyed by her attitude, he admitted, because he believed that everyone should contribute to the war effort in any way possible. When he asked for an explanation she replied in French that while she had great physical endurance, her intellectual ability was limited. This was not true at all but was simply her way of saying that a desk-job was not for her.

Howarth already knew about her involvement with Witkowski's Musketeers and the antagonism harboured towards her by virtually all Polish exile groups. Oddly enough Andrew never aroused the ire of the Poles as much as she did. This is attributable to several factors: first, he was respected for having won the Virtuti Militari for his heroism during the German invasion of Poland; second, he was not as attached to the British as she seemed to be; and third, he was, frankly, less abrasive than she could be. Howarth became close to both of them but it was with the latter that he enjoyed his off-duty hours at some of Cairo's best watering holes.

Howarth recalled that, 'They were living in a house at the Zamalek, a fashionable suburb of Cairo [in close proximity to the Gezira Club]. Andrew spent most of his time with Polish officers while Christine seemed to have a different set of friends, including Edward (Ted) Howe whom she had previously met in Budapest.'3

On her advice Howarth took a room at the same boarding house. He drew information from her that proved to be a combination of substance and tittle-tattle. Among the more solid bits of intelligence she passed on to him included the news that the Germans were drafting Polish workers into the Balkans to be used as forced labour, indicating that those Poles would be 'employed' either in arms-producing factories or on farms.

She also introduced Howarth to the colourful and audacious Leon Gradowski, *aka* Michael Lis or the Baltic Baron, one of the Musketeers whom she had known from her tour of duty in Budapest. An early prisoner-of-war, Lis had escaped from a train bound for a German concentration camp and returned to Warsaw. There, he joined the Musketeers and made covert trips into Hungary carrying microfilmed documents. On one occasion he was called upon to deliver a package of films to Istanbul but was again captured by the Germans, this time in Yugoslavia. He was put on another train destined for another camp but leaped from this one too, badly damaging his leg in the process. Fortunately he was discovered by a friendly local priest who gave him first aid and helped him return to

Budapest. Eventually he wormed his way into the good graces of a German officer, thanks to a woman known to both of them. To his utter amazement the officer unwittingly offered him a seat on a flight to Istanbul.

Howarth hoped to lure at least some of the Polish labourers onto the Allied side by using operatives who spoke their language. Besides having Polish officers parachuted into Greece and Yugoslavia, he wanted to insert an SOE operative into Albania. Lis was selected for this mission at Christine's recommendation. Ultimately he was not able to contact any of the labourers but instead was caught up in a fire-fight with German troops. For his heroism in this action he was awarded the Military Cross.

Lis was only one of a crowd of Christine's odd assortment of friends. The Countess Sophie Tarnowska shared a Cairo villa with a group of SOE officers, including her future husband Captain William (Billy) Moss.+ He and a fellow officer had coaxed Tarnowska and two other women into sharing the spacious villa with them but the two women withdrew from this arrangement. Undaunted, Tarnowska moved into the villa but for her own protection kept a pet mongoose tethered to her bed and hid a ceremonial sword under her pillow. A former officer who visited the villa recalled that the sword hung in its scabbard on the wall behind her bed.

The villa, known locally as Tara, became the scene of frequent wild parties during which all manner of objects, including a burning sofa, were hurled from the windows. Gunshots were occasionally heard ringing through the building but there were no reported

---

+Author of *Ill Met By Moonlight* (Harrap 1950), an account of how he and Patrick Leigh Fermor kidnapped the German General Major Kreipe from Crete.

casualties.4 Among those sharing Tara were the future author, Captain Patrick Leigh Fermor and Major Xan Fielding who would later be rescued from a firing squad by Christine's quick thinking. Tarnowska, who helped organise the Cairo chapter of the International Red Cross, somehow survived this menage.5

For the remainder of her stay in Cairo, Christine continued to provide Howarth and Truszkowski with information on the Musketeers, the Polish community in Cairo and on the ZWZ (Union of Armed Struggle) in Poland.

At the end of August, Field Marshal Rommel's attempt to reach the Nile was thwarted by the tactics of British Commonwealth troops led by General Bernard Montgomery who had replaced Auchinleck as commander of the British Eighth Army in the Middle East. Allied superiority in the air and on the Mediterranean decimated Rommel's supply lines from Europe. The end was now in sight for Germany's Middle East forces though they maintained a toe-hold by seizing Tunisia. The British triumphed at the second battle of El Alamein in October and in November Operation Torch6 became a reality as American forces landed in Algeria and Morocco. Hitler's frenzied reaction was to pour more troops into North Africa. The Germans and Italians doggedly fought on until March 1943 when they were at last overwhelmed by the Allies. Before his battered forces surrendered Rommel, who had fought heroically, was recalled to France where he was charged with reinforcing the Atlantic Wall in Normandy.

Returning to the simmering problem of how to best employ Christine and Andrew, Major Truszkowski suggested that the latter should be employed 'as a sort of transport officer' because of his knowledge of cars while she might be engaged as his secretary. Truszkowski suspected, correctly as it turned out, that she would not be pleased with such an arrangement. 'She is browned off, but more because of inactivity than anything else.'

While SOE brass continued to procrastinate Christine kept Howarth abreast of the goings-on among the Cairo Poles. She reported that Witkowski and the Musketeers had lost their independent status and were now taking orders directly from General Sikorski. Her suspicion was that 'two old fogies' under the general's command were now leading the group. One of the 'fogies' was Andrew Tarnowski whom she had met in Sofia. They were being financed by the Sikorski government whereas previously they had relied on loans and SOE funds smuggled in by couriers. The obvious reason for this change in allegiance was that Witkowski had been assassinated in September 1942 and those Musketeers who had avoided capture by the German police had willingly joined Sikorski. Considering Christine's sources in Poland, though they might be dwindling in numbers, it is puzzling that she wasn't informed of Witkowski's death until much later after the event. Nevertheless, she was able to report to Howarth that the alliance between ZWZ and the AK had fractured and they had split into as many as twenty factions. This was no exaggeration but a prime example of how badly fragmented the Poles were. But what they lacked in cohesion they made up for in spirit.

Christine had known Captain Truszkowski before Howarth arrived in Cairo and occasionally passed on bits of information to him as well but much of what remains is merely hearsay. She had recently discovered that an operative named Bader (cryptonym LEG) '...

was of Jewish origin, with a wife, now in I-land [Poland] with children. He is thought to be ready to do anything for financial advantage, and to be financially acquisitive. He was rather in love with a French (Levantine?) girl in Beirut. He was known to have maintained a correspondence with Vichy French in N-land [Turkey] by their diplomatic bag, and this, among other things was viewed dimly by our security.'

Her own experience should have taught her the dangers of any sort of dealing with Vichy. Her brief encounter with their officials in Syria had been enough for Jakub Alek to accuse of her truckling with the enemy. Truszkowski confirmed her story using other sources and found that Bader was considered by those close to Sikorski to be 'pretty useless'.

When Walerian Mercik (cryptonym SUN) became the new Jakub Alek, replacing Christine's earlier tormentor Colonel Matecki, she supplied this titbit: 'Of the man himself ... he was a post office official in a village belonging to ACE [Sikorski].' Another morsel of gossip passed on to Truszkowski concerned her childhood friend Count Wiktor Rozwadowski (cryptonym SMART). Rozwadowski had connections with some of Poland's wealthiest families though his link to the aristocracy was tenuous. She reported that Wiktor was in love with an Hungarian 'Jewess' who was on the staff of GSI (K)++ in Cairo. However, she had recently been sent to England along with other personnel in the aftermath of Lord Selborne's re-organisation of Cairo SOE. The woman in question was alleged to have extracted a considerable sum of money from the Count 'without, annoyingly enough, delivering any equivalent services in return. SMART also gave her letters of

++ General Staff Intelligence (K) dealt with censorship.

introduction to I's [Poles] in London, including ACE [General Sikorski], representing her to be a person of the utmost trustworthiness.'7

Christine challenged her friend's loyalty by recalling that his abilities had been questioned by those who had worked with him in Budapest. They suspected that his aristocratic contacts were really Nazi sympathisers. This comment got back to Wiktor and he indignantly signaled Sikorski, complaining that someone within Polish SOE had accused him of being a Nazi informer. Sikorski replied in the strongest terms that the accusers would be seriously dealt with. Wiktor was quite pleased with the general's response and triumphantly showed the letter to Andrew Kennedy as an example of his own importance.

Christine was not quite finished with Wiktor however. She sarcastically remarked to Truszkowski that Wiktor's brother was in an asylum and that he himself deserved to be similarly confined. Wiktor was eventually posted to Beirut to take up a position with the Red Cross after which Howarth commented: 'I am rather sorry, as I like him personally, and we have had some excellent mixed doubles.

After having had lengthy meetings Christine and Andrew separately Truszkowski gave a frank assessment of their respective personalities in December 1942. He began by stating that the 'problem' of Christine *et al* had been reactivated - exacerbated, really - by Colonel Taylor's recent visit to Cairo during which he had attempted to intervene on her behalf to resolve the problem of her unemployment.

Truszkowski found the situation complicated not only by the personalities involved (especially hers), but also because of the violent dislike of her by virtually all Polish organisations outside the home country. This in turn fed her reluctance to return to

England for fear that the Deuxieme Bureau would put her in the 'cooler' at the first opportunity. Re-deploying her in Europe was out of the question because the Gestapo were still looking for her. She and Andrew had naively hoped that they would be able to operate again in occupied countries without being noticed but Gardyne de Chastelaine, writing from Istanbul, let Truszkowski know how wrong they were.

During these interviews Truszkowski had elicited conflicting, tender and sometimes humorous statements. For her part Christine was adamant about not being separated from her colleague and lover because she believed he could not look after himself. In a separate interview Andrew voiced exactly the same fears about her. He had suggested marriage on more than one occasion but she wasn't having it despite her obvious love for him. (She had also turned down a proposal from a Captain Cookham whose identity remains obscure. This, according to Andrew). Even if she had been inclined to marry, there remained the small obstacle of her ongoing marriage to Jerzy Gizycki.

The subject of an office position had been bandied about again but Christine dis - played emotions bordering on the hysterical at the thought of being relegated to doing administrative or secretarial work. Truszkowski concurred with Howarth that she was 'a most delightful person.' But he added: ' . . . I have no doubt that she believes very much of what she says.'[8] He observed that her opposition to office work was in no small part '. . . due partly to a feeling of incompetence on her part, and partly due to a general inferiority complex.' His remarks will come as a surprise to those familiar with stories of her heroics.

Though she had been employed in an office in Warsaw Christine obviously felt ill at ease in such confined environments where she would be required to conform to the routines of the business world. But whether she suffered from an inferiority complex is arguable. Had she put her mind to it she could have easily mastered the routine tasks of filing and typing. The truth is she simply did not have the patience to perform such repetitive chores on a daily basis. The thought of being relegated to an office for any length of time must have filled her with loathing.

Howarth characterised her negative reaction to office work as 'pathological.' He believed that the real reason for her rejection of such employment was due to her determination never to accept the second-rate. For her, a job as a clerk or secretary was too prosaic to contemplate. Truszkowski's report includes what is probably the most brutal assessment of Christine by anyone who knew her. This did not prevent them from becoming friends, a relationship that continued into the post-war years. Some of what he had to say contradicts the image of the courageous, have-a-go heroism for which she was noted. Latter-day amateur psychologists might conclude that she was an overachiever perhaps making up for a lack of confidence.

It was Truszkowski's observation that if she were to be criticised, and she was seldom criticised openly by SOE officers, 'she would probably burst into tears and drop the job forthwith.' He may have known her better than anyone except Andrew but this contention seems a bit far-fetched.

He concluded his character analysis by charging that she was diffident and timid in meeting new contacts and, 'tends to give the worst possible impression of herself.' What seems more accurate is his assertion that she could be extremely obstinate and that once she had made a decision, no amount of arguing would cause her to change her mind.

Andrew, by contrast, was seen as a less complex character, very straightforward. While he could be more susceptible to persuasion than his lover he was nevertheless fiercely independent. Despite Andrew's obvious courage and strength Truszkowski reported that Christine believed him to have a weak character, a man most likely to spend his money on 'riotous living.' Andrew was amused by her assessment but pretended not to notice. Truszkowski thought his judgment the more accurate of the two.

On a more serious note Truszkowski was certain that none of the active Polish organisations would have anything to do with either of them. For their part the Polish government-in-exile would insist, he said, that both of them resume their Polish nationalities. That was a curious remark to make as there is no evidence that they ever renounced their citizenship, something they would have been unlikely to do. Their applications to become naturalised British subjects were not made until 1946 by Christine and in the following year by Andrew.[9]

Though the couple were later to receive accolades from both the British and French governments, Truszkowski was of the opinion that they did not have any special talents for conspiratorial work. He believed they would function best in situations where courage and determination were required, situations which did not demand absolute discretion. On the basis of this assessment one might think that she would have been better suited for combat.

Christine had more than amply demonstrated her courage and determination by completing demanding journeys across the Tatra mountains, and during her perilous breakout from Budapest to Palestine. Her later actions in southern France would have supported Truszkowski's assertions about these personal characteristics. But he was right about her lack of discretion. That had more to do with her impatience, her haste to accomplish a mission, rather than an ignorance of the dangers around her.

Throughout her life she had encountered very few obstacles to whatever it was she had wished to do. Supervision in her childhood had been almost non-existent. When she tired of a marriage she simply moved on. She had been accepted into Section D without the barriers of formal training or testing, and it was not until the end of the campaign in southern France that someone actually said 'no' to her, with the authority to back it up.

In at least two instances she had moved about in occupied territory with the bare minimum of disguises. In Poland she had openly walked the streets of Krakow and Warsaw, almost daring the Germans to discover her. Later, in France, she would demonstrate the same reckless abandon for her own safety. Owen O'Malley had got it right when he remarked earlier that she had a pathological desire to take risks.

During her interview with him Christine casually informed Truszkowski that she would happily become a nurse, particularly if she could be assigned to a war zone. It was as if she were defying death, a challenge that would be met soon enough. In the event that she could not become a nurse her other preferences were to train as a radio wireless operator or work with POW. Despite the references to personal courage and the desire to be set down in dangerous territory, Christine disliked firearms and never learned to use a pistol properly. Howarth observed her firearms instruction and recalled that, when firing a pistol, she closed her eyes and turned her head to one side.+++ Though she unabashedly enjoyed the comfortable life of Cairo and the Gezira Club where she had a circle of admirers, she was sensitive to her predicament. She made it abundantly clear to Truszkowski that she felt 'rather humiliated at receiving pay without giving equivalent services in return.'

Truszkowski recommended to Major Wilkinson that she be offered work in one of the aforementioned roles. Andrew, it was generally agreed, could be most gainfully employed as a mechanic, working on military vehicles. But he had something more adventurous in mind. None of SOE's commanders seemed confident that he could again resume a behind-the-lines role. Despite his knowledge of central Europe and the heroic work he had performed in Hungary, they were quite content to see him sidelined and at work in the military car pool.

Alerted to Andrew's predicament, General Kopanski contacted Truszkowski, saying he would be pleased to give Andrew an assignment in his Brigade. Christine objected, fearing that in desert conditions sand would insinuate itself between the stump of his leg and the prosthesis, exposing him to unnecessary pain and possibly serious infection. They were now beginning to act like an old married couple, each afraid to let go of the other. Truszkowski concluded his lengthy analysis by recommending against repatriating them to England. He suggested instead that Taylor be asked to 'pull the necessary strings in Cairo' and find roles for them locally.

Not surprisingly Wilkinson bounced the ball back to Truszkowski. He agreed that they should not be returned to England, that Andrew should be given a job as an auto

+++Christine was issued a Polish-made 9 mm Baretta which has been displayed at London's Imperial War Museum. Its ownership is unknown.

mechanic and that Christine should be employed in one of the three categories mentioned in Truszkowski's report. But yet, infuriatingly, no one was willing to make a firm decision about the fate of these two complex personalities. The matter might have been resolved swiftly if Wilkinson had only appealed for a decision from his immediate superior, Brigadier Mockler-Ferryman, or to SOE's Deputy CD Brigadier Gubbins.

While in London in 1943 to have his prosthetic leg adjusted Andrew paid the first of several visits to the Truszkowski home in Hampstead. After Christine returned from France in 1944 she accompanied him on another occasion. There seemed to be a peculiar bond of affection between her and Truszkowski. Perhaps she saw in him a more dependable and stronger father-figure than Count Skarbek had been. Truszkowski's daughter Diana recalled how Christine had ignored her and her younger sister and spent the afternoon in her father's study.

The two sisters remembered Andrew as being the more congenial of their two visitors. They wickedly enjoyed kicking his wooden leg under the table until a badly aimed kick hit the wrong limb. Another man had come to Hampstead with the couple but declined to enter the house. Instead he could be seen pacing up and down on the lawn. He was Dennis George Muldowney, the man who would one day murder Christine.[10]

Chapter 15.

Plots and Rumours of Plots

In mid-autumn 1943 Christine was told that any suspicion of her alleged treasonous behaviour had been lifted. She was reinstated as an SOE operative. There was more good news for Andrew whose leg had healed well enough for him to seek full and proper employment. Shortly after being cleared for a return to duty he was assigned to SOE's transport section where, Truszkowski observed, he had become a new man since taking on the job. He was said to be doing well despite a 'rather involved internal opposition.' This could well have been an oblique reference to those within SOE who still held lingering suspicions about his loyalties. He refused to become entangled in their internal politics and jauntily described his new post as 'minor activities in the M.T. Section.'

Andrew's satisfaction with his work however had a negative effect on his lover who was feeling useless. Lacking an assignment Christine began to devote more of her time to studying English which she never mastered, and seemed to have given up ever working for the Poles. Truszkowski commented, 'We are all racking our brains to find employment for her.'

Truszkowski was busily tracking developments within the Polish camp as well as shadowing her movements. In September he signaled Wilkinson that, in a reversal of previous positions, the Seizieme Bureau were becoming pro-Sikorski whereas the Deuxieme

Bureau, who had previously supported him, were losing interest.

Rumours of plots against Sikorski continued to incite rows between his supporters and General Anders' loyalists. SOE viewed the situation with alarm because Britain more now than ever needed a united Polish force in its fight against the Germans. Divided, the Poles could only hamper the war effort. A Seizieme Bureau operative, Captain Szymanski (cryptonym ECLIPSE), tried to stir up support for Sikorski by claiming that Poles in the home country were almost unanimous in their support for him. It was soon discovered that this was a ploy on Szymanski's part to bolster Sikorski's standing among Polish troops in Palestine.

Gradually, the tide of war began to turn in the Allies' favour. President Franklin D Roosevelt and Winston Churchill met in Casablanca in January 1943 to assess their efforts thus far, and to plan their next moves. The presence of these two statesmen in the Middle East gave rise to a flurry of rumours as to where the next Allied action would take place. Security in Casablanca was not tight enough to prevent speculation that Italy was next in line for a hammering as soon as North Africa had been cleared of Axis forces.

Once the veil of suspicion had been lifted from Christine, at least by the British, Patrick Howarth saw to it that she would have something worthwhile to do. He arranged for her to begin training as a wireless/telegraphy operator under the guidance of Sergeant Dick Mallaby. His only concern was that she would be the only female housed among some '300 thugs.' Fortunately she was able to find suitable living accommodation. After a slow start she progressed rapidly and by March 1944 was practicing transmitting between Baghdad and Cairo.

The loyal Guy Tamplin continued to work on Christine's behalf, still seeking to re-insert her into Europe. He proposed sending her to Yugoslavia where civil war was about to break out between supporters of the communist leader Tito and the nationalist/royalist Colonel Draza Mihailovic. While all Yugoslav political parties (except for the Croats) were united in their hatred of the Nazis, they were nevertheless quite prepared to fight one another in a deadly contest for domination in their post-war nation.1

SOE were backing Mihailovic primarily because they did not want the country to fall into the grip of Soviet-style communism. But it was also the case that SOE and Foreign Office policy generally favoured a return to the status quo, a Europe in which most of the deposed rulers would return to their respective countries. Nothing came of Tamplin's suggestion to send Christine to Yugoslavia.

Kate O'Malley, whose affection for Christine had never diminished, resumed contact with her by sending a letter in the British diplomatic pouch. Truszkowski thought it a good idea to encourage the correspondence and passed Kate's letter to Christine noting that, 'This arrangement is for the good of trade in general.' In other words, it might help in some small way to sustain good relations between the British and the Poles. Few of Kate's letters to Christine apparently survive. Either Christine destroyed them in the course of her transient existence or else Andrew Kennedy disposed of them after her death.

Kate went through a troubled time in her middle years. She married but began to drink heavily and 'became an alcoholic,' according to Lord Tweedsmuir who worked for Kate's husband. Tweedsmuir saw her at a party in the 1950s (he was uncertain about the exact date) where he noticed the change that had come over her. But when he met her again in the late 1970s she had stopped drinking altogether (Kate died in 1991.)

In early 1943, thanks to General Anders' intervention, Andrew secured a place on a para-military course which would qualify him as a weapons instructor. He was commissioned second lieutenant, HM Forces, General Orders. He would retain this rank until promoted to captain, General List, in 1945. Unlike his partner he had not been seduced by the sun and warm weather of Egypt and was anxious to get back to the war. Patrick Howarth observed that, 'Christine was certainly not pining for adventure during the years she spent in Cairo.'

Though she was back in SOE's good graces the Poles still viewed her with suspicion. Howarth reported to Wilkinson that a friend of hers in the Seizieme Bureau had seen a detailed report of her activities at the Gezira Club which warned that she was seen associating with 'dubious characters.' Howarth, for one, was amused by the notion that he had probably been included in this cast. Similar allegations dogged her throughout her years of service and afterwards in civilian life.

In addition to her training in radio telegraphy Christine had now begun to study Italian 'for the task which M/DH [Tamplin] has in mind for her.' He had shifted his focus from Yugoslavia to Italy, anticipating a posting for her once the Allies had established a foothold. But an alternative situation presented itself. Now that the Deuxieme

Bureau had dropped its objections to employing both Christine and her lover, Tamplin surmised, 'They would then enter purely Polish services; presumably the problem of what to do with her would be resolved,' or so he thought. But his optimism was not to be rewarded. The Deuxieme Bureau leadership abruptly decided not to employ her after all. Though a temporary setback this decision benefitted SOE in the long run for she was about to save lives in France after the Allies had secured the Normandy beachhead.

In the meantime Professor Kot continued to interfere in her life as well as in Andrew's. General Kopanski was about to employ him in East Africa but Kot overruled him and discounted Count Rozwadowski as well. There was an odd rumour that Kot himself was planning to employ Christine, according to Howarth. She however was warned off by a friend who 'begged her for her own sake not to accept it [his offer].' Howarth reckoned that this story 'gives a good picture of the state of security and the general intrigue going on among the I-landers [Poles] in the M.E.'

Major Wilkinson concurred. In a report to George Taylor he gave a warning to weed out Poles who did not support their government-in-exile. 'In view of the countless peripatetic Poles who offer their services to the British, this is not as easy as it sounds! For this reason, if you are thinking of employing Poles yourself, I would be very grateful if you would let M/DH [Guy Tamplin] check up on them before committing yourself.'

A new ingredient dropped into the stew of Polish affairs at this juncture. When the Red Army swept into Poland in 1939 millions of Poles, both civilian and military, had been arrested. Entire army units had been interned in camps in Siberia. General Anders, the heroic commander of the Novogrodek Cavalry Brigade, had also been captured and confined to the Lubyanka prison in Moscow.

As early as 1941 General Sikorski, anticipating a Soviet attack on German-occupied Poland, had begun to lobby Stalin for the release of Polish prisoners, in particular military personnel. Professor Kot, in his new capacity as ambassador to the Soviet Union, joined in the negotiations as did Anders upon his release from prison. Stalin was anxious to speak with the Poles and the Allies too as his forces were then (June 1941) under sustained attack from the German army.

Details of the meetings between Stalin, Molotov and the Polish leadership are too long and drawn-out to discuss here. In short, after numerous delays Stalin agreed to release upwards of 300,000 Polish officers and soldiers, provided they would establish their training camps on Soviet territory. The British had been anxiously watching these negotiations as they had hopes of incorporating Polish troops into their own 8th Army.

In order to obtain the release of the soldiers and civilians, Sikorski agreed to a series of compromises with Stalin that did not go down well with a large segment of the Polish community. Foremost among these compromises was an agreement that a second contingent of Polish personnel would be formed into a force to be integrated into the Red Army. Sikorski saw this as an opportunity to have Polish troops poised near the border for the anticipated invasion of their homeland.

Eventually more than a million-and-a-quarter Polish civilians and military were released. Virtually all of them sought refuge in the Middle East. Many of these men and women gave their loyalty to Anders who had shared their captivity, rather than to Sikorski. These divided loyalties caused even more friction within the Middle East community of Poles.

The Polish training camps in Iran were handicapped at the outset by a curious lack of officers. Stalin of course denied any knowledge of their whereabouts. Nevertheless, he and Sikorski agreed a military pact whose aim was to ensure that their forces would join in efforts to defeat Germany. Despite this agreement the Soviet government continually delayed the release of its Polish prisoners for much of 1942. Even after their release had begun the promised supplies to the re-organised Polish forces were delivered slowly and grudgingly. As for the missing officers, Stalin insisted they had all been released but when pressed could not say where they were.

In April 1943 the bodies of more than 25000 Polish officers were discovered in mass graves in the Katyn Forest on the banks of the Dnieper river, near the city of Smolensk.[2] This ghastly discovery put paid to any further cooperation between the Poles and Stalin as far as Sikorski was concerned. The Polish government asked the International Red Cross to conduct an enquiry, a move which infuriated Stalin. He quickly seized upon this request as a pretext for severing relations with the Poles. It did not go unnoticed that German forces were now in retreat and that Stalin was no longer so desperate for Allied help to clear the Soviet Union of his enemy.

Anders, his officers and men, now became fixtures in the mix of foreigners bivouacked in Egypt and in Palestine. His presence also set the stage for a power struggle between himself and Sikorski.

If Christine favoured either of the leadership contenders she certainly kept her own counsel. The only clue to a possible preference came in a remark she made about the Deuxieme Bureau, to the effect that 'their doom is impending' and that Anders would certainly fix them for all their intrigues against him. For a time the atmosphere was extremely tense and there could be no such thing as neutrality in this situation. One was expected to declare a favourite - Anders, Sikorski or the much older Sosnkowski, minister of war. No one was in doubt that he or she would return to a reborn Poland led by one of these men.

Each of the three leaders had acquired a devoted following. The rivalry among their respective loyalists became quite bitter and continued into the post-war years. Rumours of plots were rife within the Polish community, especially of an assassination attempt on Sikorski should he visit the Middle East. The rumour-mongers were certain that would-be assassins lurked in both the Anders and the Sikorski camps.

Though Christine's name was later mentioned in connection with Sikorski's death, she was never implicated in any plot to assassinate him and she never harboured a particularly strong antagonism towards him. But such was the distrust between her and the two Polish intelligence bureaux that her name was occasionally linked to attempts on the general's life. Furthermore, she was an easy target because among her numerous cousins and friends there were those who were either actively plotting or 'knew' someone who was.

Speculation about a plot to kill Sikorski was not without foundation. In March 1942 he had flown to Montreal, en route to America, where he was to meet with President Roosevelt. An incendiary device had been placed aboard the plane but was discovered by one of Sikorski's staff before it could explode. Wing Commander Bohdan Kleczynski carried the bomb into the toilet where he successfully dismantled it. It was a bizarre episode to say the least, for Kleczynski, who had 'accidentally' discovered the device, soon confessed to having brought it on board, describing it as a souvenir. Under interrogation he confessed to his addiction to morphine, the drug having been prescribed for him after an earlier plane crash.[3]

Ominously, Sikorski's last flight to America again via Montreal in October resulted in a forced landing. The plane, a twin-engined Lockheed Hudson, had climbed to just thirty thirty feet when both engines suddenly quit. Only quick action by the pilot brought the plane down without a resulting fire or a severe crash. The general and his staff were shaken but there were no serious injuries.

Alarmed by these two episodes the Americans thought it best if they provided transport for Sikorski. An American Liberator was sent to Montreal to collect him and bring him to Washington. Sikorski later quipped to one of his aides that it seemed to be his destiny to die in a plane crash.

Patrick Howarth took the threats on Sikorski's life seriously. He was quite concerned that the general's death would trigger a political explosion that would fragment the Poles even more, diverting their attention from the war against Germany to fighting among themselves. Major Wilkinson however assessed the reports coming out of the Middle East with equanimity and observed that 'the whole thing is nothing more than the usual Polish storm in a tea-cup.' He and Truszkowski agreed that the various conspiracy theories were not something to dwell upon.

Truszkowski continued to meet with Christine and reported either to Wilkinson or to Howarth the gist of their conversations. He reminded Howarth that 'she is a highly strung person and that much of what she says is highly coloured by its emotional context and by feelings of friendship towards the persons involved. One such person is her Colonel friend [unidentified] who arrived recently and who, according to the DAYS [Seizieme Bureau], is most highly dissatisfied with conditions in Z-land [Iraq], among Polish troops and is even said to have deserted from there, whereupon PLAGUE [Captain Klimkowski] was given command of his unit.'

Truszkowski went on to say that Christine had a tendency to report such conversations in good faith even though they may have contained half-truths at best. While Howarth was inclined to take her reports at face value, Truszkowski and Wilkinson were more sceptical.

Christine herself was not immune from the odd bit of SOE vigilance. In a signal to Howarth, Truszkowski mentioned off-handedly that any information on her and Andrew too, no matter how trivial, 'is always welcome.' He was nevertheless upbeat about the progress being made by the two of them in their respective training programs and said so to Howarth. 'I am so frightfully glad that FORCIBLE [Andrew] and WILLING are doing so well and that a brighter future is ahead of them.'[4]

Now and again there were signs of a thaw in the relationship between Christine and the Polish intelligence bureaux. In April, Colonel Tadeusz Kurcjusz suggested to Truszkowski that he might send her to Romania to gather intelligence, and possibly to work as a w/t operator for the Deuxieme Bureau. Truszkowski was surprised by the suggestion but was curious about Kurcjusz' motive. It was well-known that his ally, the influential

Professor Kot, would be very glad to have her out of the way given that General Anders, Klimkowski and other Poles talked to her about matters that the professor would have preferred to be kept secret. He suspected, with some foundation, that whatever was said to her usually found its way back to SOE HQ.

Christine's response to the Kurcjusz proposal surprised Truszkowski. She toyed with the idea of accepting the assignment then breaking contact with Kurcjusz once inside Romania, sending her reports to SOE rather than to the Deuxieme Bureau or to Kot. She had reason to be suspicious of those around Kurcjusz. Truszkowski noted that, 'WILLING ... volunteered some information about DWARF's [Kurcjusz] assistant mentioned in para A .. which if true, is fairly damaging although not altogether damning. The information was given her by a Poland (sic) *juge d'instruction*.'

Kurcjusz himself was already under suspicion from a number of quarters, primarily because as Polish vice-consul in Istanbul he had been accused of issuing passports to 'shady characters.' These were suspected enemy agents who had allegedly infiltrated ministries of the Turkish government. He was also suspect because of his relationship with a Mrs Buczynska *aka* Lucyna Rossie, his secretary, who was alleged to be a double agent.[5] Like Christine she was also the subject of a Polish intelligence ploy, this one designed to undermine the work of Kurcjusz. Colonel de Chastelain added the caution that Kurcjusz had once advised the Polish operative Majewski not to pass on messages to him from Gizycki in Budapest.

The more he considered it the more Truszkowski doubted that Christine would take up the offer from Kurcjusz. He knew that what she really wanted was to return to Poland

and report on conditions there but he was concerned that she might actually follow through on her threat to betray Kurcjusz. Truszkowski relayed his feelings to Howarth. 'This seems to me a slightly dangerous game.' He warned that SOE must do its utmost to avoid the suspicion that the Poles were being betrayed.

'I think WILLING would be very foolish if she started such a game... in any case, we could countenance no such procedure. Nor can I understand why she should want to go to I-land [Poland] in order to send us reports on the situation there as she is undoubtedly a very patriotic Pole and would surely not wish to do anything prejudicial to her own country, and the suggestion is that the reports we have been getting from our own agents are false.'[6]

As far as alliances were concerned the Poles had no alternative but to remain loyal, however grudgingly, to the British. Even if they were to be betrayed they would certainly not have switched their loyalties from the British to the enemy. They depended heavily on the British for arms, intelligence and not least what they considered to be temporary shelter on their island. They had to accept whatever situation was presented to them. Though many Poles thought an alliance with the Russians would be necessary to rid their country of the Germans (a suggestion that had its precedent in the eighteenth century), they were not about to espouse the Soviets' suffocating political agenda. Throwing their lot in with the Hitler regime did not even bear consideration. Their only option would have been to withdraw all military cooperation. This they would not have done, for it would have meant abandoning the Holy Grail of a return to an unoccupied country.

Though Truszkowski was satisfied that Andrew seemed to be getting on well at the weapons-training school, he was pessimistic about Christine. 'I do wish that WILLING could be equally well placed although the problem is obviously far more difficult.'

In addition to his report Truszkowski had forwarded a letter to be handed to Christine from an unidentified British officer 'who would be very glad to hear from her but assures her that even if she does not answer she may still rely absolutely on his unchanging friendship.' This was in all probability Lieutenant Colonel Henry Threlfall of whom Christine would write most favourably at a later date, one of the few times she would indiscreetly even mention an interest in a potential lover.* Her faithful paramour Andrew meanwhile excelled in his para-military course and it was anticipated that he would become a weapons instructor at the completion of the course. He was however to be bitterly disappointed when the chief of staff decided against employing him.

Rumours of General Anders' popularity and his soldiers' restlessness had now reached Sikorski in London. He knew he could not allow this situation to fester. Arrangements were made for him to visit Cairo and Palestine to review the troops and boost their morale. He would also have to confront Anders and end the damaging speculation over the issue of Polish leadership.

Because of the concessions he had made to Stalin feelings against Sikorski were running high. One of the more voluble of Sikorski's opponents was Captain Jerzy Klimkowski, Anders' ADC. He met Christine by chance in the street one afternoon and and invited her for drinks at the Continental Hotel. She agreed on condition that he would

---

*Threlfall had been head of X Section in Sweden 1942 and was selected to lead SOE's 'Torment' Mission in Italy in 1944.

not attempt to recruit her to his side. As she walked to the hotel a Deuxieme Bureau agent whom she described as 'fat, with a limp' followed her. He had the audacity to sit at an adjoining table where he clumsily tried to eavesdrop on her conversation with Klimkowski. No matter, for whatever was said to Christine was not enough to convince her to take sides against Sikorski. Another alleged plotter known only as Eclipse had a meeting with Howarth ostensibly to discuss policy matters. Among other items on his agenda he asked Howarth to arrange a meeting with Christine 'whom, of course, he visualises as a *femme fatale.*' Though this meeting was never arranged, the operative bragged that he knew her 'very well personally' and that an unidentified British captain had asked to be introduced to her. Eclipse was however was reluctant to make the introductions.

Captain Jerzy Szymanski was widely suspected of favouring a scheme to assassinate Sikorski and replace him with General Sosnkowski. He soon met the arch-conspirator Klimkowski. Though both wanted to see Sikorski removed from the leadership, Klimkowski's preference was for General Anders to become head of the Polish forces rather than Sosnkowski. The latter's candidacy had not rallied the Polish community primarily because of his association with Pilsudski's pre-war regime.

Klimkowski and Szymanski quickly fell out over this difference. The former warned Anders who contacted the Polish government in London and alerted them to the possibility of an attempt on Sikorski's life. In an almost comical display of hypocrisy, Szymanski was furious when he discovered Klimkowski's treachery and proceeded to blacken his name at every opportunity. Howarth commented: 'Sometimes in this job I feel as if I were paddling about on a very small plank in the middle of a seething maelstrom.'

Having been rejected as a weapons instructor, Andrew next decided on a more ambitious course, to become a PJI (parachute-jumping instructor). Obviously he would first have to pass the course himself. While realistic enough to know that he could not take part in combat, he believed he could be of more service as a PJI than stuck in the car pool.

In February 1943, to his delight, he was accepted for the parachute training course at RAF Station Ramat David, twelve miles southeast of Haifa. Howarth described it somewhat differently, writing that Andrew had been sent to Ramat David primarily to help construct the camp. However he arrived in Ramat David, he was responsible for making the decision to apply for training to become a 'straphanger', contemptuous of the obvious danger to his well-being.

Before he could begin training he developed an infection in the stump of his leg. He was fortunate enough to be treated by a talented Israeli doctor who expertly brought the infection under control. Afterwards he was fitted out with a new artificial limb. He quickly adjusted to the new prosthesis and departed for Ramat David.

A new phase in Christine's relationship with Andrew was about to develop for they were to be separated for the first time since meeting in Budapest where they had formed a relationship underpinned by the tensions of war. It was to be the first of several long periods of separation and the loosening of the bonds that had held them together. When she heard about this latest scheme, she was quite cross that he should be putting himself in harm's way. Howarth also felt her wrath for having encouraged him.

Andrew's friends were initially appalled, then inspired, by his desire to jump despite his disability. On the day of his first attempt the Red Cross had placed two ambulances and two lorries on stand-by at the training site where sixty men were about to complete the course. Andrew's maiden effort was successful and there were only a few minor casualties on the day, leaving the Red Cross ambulances idle. Andrew had proved himself and now there could be no opposition to his becoming a PJI.

Colonel Bickham Sweet-Escott, in training at the SOE camp** at nearby Mount Carmel, remembered him well. 'He used to accompany every party as they emplaned for their first jump, and Andrew would always be the first out of the aircraft. The theory seemed to be that if a Pole with a wooden leg could jump. so could you.'[7] After this display of courage he was posted to Benghazi to train as an instructor to await transfer to Italy, once it had been successfully invaded.

Plans for the invasion of Sicily were now well under way. An amphibious assault was launched by Allied forces in July 1943. Opposition was not as strong as had been feared and the island was secured by mid-August. A depressed Mussolini was dismissed by King Vittorio Emanuele III later that month, not only because he had dragged the country into a destructive war, but because of the military's dismal failures. He was replaced by Marshal Pietro Badoglio who immediately began negotiating with the Allies, through SOE, for surrender terms. An agreement was signed on September 3rd but was not formalised until early October.

As preparations for the invasion of Europe progressed, the Allied High Command established several bases outside the European mainland which would serve as 'listening posts' and jumping-off places for operatives being infiltrated into key areas of France and Italy. After the Germans had been driven out of North Africa and plans for the Italian campaign had been finalised, SOE with Eisenhower's blessing, established a base outside Algiers known by its cryptonym Massingham (Interservice Signals Unit 6). SOE had already begun preparing the ground for the base and probably would have gone ahead even without Eisenhower's approval. The Supreme Commander wasn't especially enamoured of SOE; he was more interested in encouraging cooperation between them and OSS (Office of Strategic Services), the American covert action and intelligence arm that would, post-war, mutate into the CIA.

Massingham's brief was to provide training facilities, communications and stores. It was also charged with the responsibility for conducting air operations by air and sea into enemy territory. Christine would to be launched into occupied France from this base and its staff were to play a major role in the most daring episode of her career.

**Known as Military Establishment 102, or M.E. 102.

Chapter 16.
Death and the Darkness of Night

Christine began to train as a radio operator in earnest in early 1943. When off duty she continued to socialise with Polish intelligence officers (mainly from the Seizieme Bureau) and influential Poles in Cairo, passing on their comments to either Wilkinson or to Howarth. But her PF does not contain a single memo, signal or letter for that year. Her name is often mentioned in other SOE dispatches dated 1943 so it cannot be that she was inactive during those twelve months.

Major Truszkowski wrote a lengthy note to Howarth in January acknowledging his source of intelligence on Polish affairs. 'I realised that the information in your [report] emanated from WILLING and naturally withheld all information as to the source.' [in his reports to other departments].1 Though Christine was still suspect in their eyes Poles of all political persuasions continued to speak with her, assuming that she would almost certainly be relaying their comments to the British. At times this was done deliberately by Polish operatives to confirm that she was in fact passing their remarks to the British, to see how they would bounce back.

Howarth found her 'indispensable during the present stress and strain,' a reference to the heated debate within the Polish community about the advisability of signing the Anglo-Soviet Treaty,2 a pact that called for a joint British-USSR attack on Germany.

Howarth's assessment of British officials on this subject was not very flattering. He had been unable to obtain a clear picture of his own government's position on the Treaty because of 'the astounding ignorance in British official quarters of I-land [Poland] affairs.'

The British government's attempts to persuade the Poles to sign the treaty took on the cloak of conspiracy when *The Literary News* (*Wiadomosci Literackie*) was forced to temporarily shut down. The London-based periodical had its paper supply withdrawn by the government and that led to an allegation by its last editor, Stefania Kossowska, that this was an act of revenge because of her magazine's anti-Soviet editorials. It did not resume publication until 1944. The government denied any discrimination against the Poles by pointing out that all British periodicals were subject to paper rationing.

Though Christine's main value to SOE at this time was her contact with the Polish community, she was also asked for her opinion on non-Polish matters. 'WILLING is now convinced that the correspondence from F-land [Hungary] is in code on account of the lists of telephone numbers in the F-land capital which are continually being included.' SOE had never given up hope of re-establishing a cell in Budapest and occasionally asked her advice on how that might be accomplished. Her input on Hungary was deemed important because of her experience there and her advice on the safest routes for delivering intelligence from mainland Europe to Cairo was still relevant. It is remarkable that, for someone who had been confined to the Middle East for two years, she seemed to be up to speed not only on the political manoeuvering within the Polish community at large but on intelligence matters in Europe. SOE never challenged her responses to their queries.

Christine's reputation had become so widespread, for her accomplishments as well as for her allure, that even after more than a year of virtual inactivity rumours about her continued to circulate but were frequently wide of the mark. 'WILLING claims that the "traveller" [Lieutentant Tadeusz Debicki] told a mutual friend that he had brought messages for her from the "engineer" but had not been allowed to deliver them as he had been told in Istanbul that she was in a concentration camp.' (Witkowski had sometimes used the cryptonym 'engineer' but had been killed in the autumn of 1942 so it could not have been him.) She was supposed to be suffering from tuberculosis when she was probably healthier than at any time in her adult life. She remained unfazed by the gossip. If the enmity of certain Poles annoyed her she seldom complained aloud about it. She remained incredibly focused on returning to Poland and to see it eventually restored to its pre-war status. Unfortunately she was not to experience either of those hopes.

Her life in Cairo continued to be relaxed, unhurried and perhaps even boring though she was not exactly living the life of a recluse. Andrew, finding himself with some free time, flew in from Italy and they managed several weeks together before he had to return. He recalled that their social life included invitations to soirees at the Polish Embassy and receptions at the homes of some of Cairo's upper-crust families.

Regardless of the brilliance of Christine's social life practical matters required attention. She needed to find suitable employment that would provide her with a satisfactory income. Marriage to one of her numerous suitors would have resolved that situation if she had wanted it and she could have retired from the war in comfort there and then. Among her alleged lovers was a Serb pilot George Michalov and the British Colonel Cookham. Vladimire Ledochowski also turned up in Cairo, on extended leave after having had his elbow shattered by an enemy shell during the battle for Tobruk.

Prior to taking up his post in Italy as a PJ instructor Andrew was posted to England to acquaint himself with the intricacies of other operational stations, the packing of air-dropped stores and to have adjustments made to his artificial limb. In London he became re-acquainted with a young woman he'd known earlier (almost certainly in Budapest but he wasn't specific in his recollection). Before long they allegedly became intimate. Owen O'Malley, who had provided Andrew with his new identity, found out about the affair. He made his feelings known in no uncertain terms, accusing Andrew of betraying Christine.

Though the woman has never been named she must have been especially well known to O'Malley for him to have taken such a personal interest. The most likely candidate was his youngest daughter Kate. Accounts of the few days that Christine and Kennedy spent at the British Consulate in Budapest make it quite clear that Kate had a terrible crush on him. The strength of her feelings is described in a fictitious account of the family's life in Budapest, written by her mother.*

Lord Tweedsmuir (son of the author John Buchan) had known the O'Malley family since the 1930s. He recalled Kate as 'a high-spirited girl' who had enjoyed her brief stay in the Hungarian capital. Tweedsmuir (1916 - 2008) occasionally saw a subdued Kate at her Chelsea home after the war and wrote of her, 'I never heard her speak of the war, or of her part in it.'** She developed personal problems after the war but managed to recover.

Andrew left England feeling contrite, so much so that he confessed his affair to Christine when they met later in Italy. She was furious but forgave him though she never

*Ibid.
**Letter to the author from Lord Tweedsmuir

forgot it. For a time she seems to have remained faithful to him except for the odd flirtation. Some of the international set in Cairo continued to spread gossip about alleged lovers but the hearsay remained just that. Even if she had not misbehaved in Cairo she certainly had not considered his feelings during her earlier affair with Ledochowski.

After completing his business in London, Andrew was designated a 'conducting officer' by SOE and was posted to the newly established Polish Special Operations base at Ostumi in Italy (cryptonym Impudent). Between the time of this posting in January 1944 and Christine's untimely death their meetings were sporadic. Though they were to remain close friends the initial passion of those exciting days in Budapest had run its course. He was to feel this loss more keenly whereas her restive personality would not tolerate the thought of settling down with him or with anyone else.

In June 1943 Generals Sikorski and Anders met in Cairo. Despite fears that the two men would clash the meeting turned out to be quite cordial. Sikorski emerged with his positions as prime minister and military leader intact. The anticipated confrontation had not taken place and Anders gave his unequivocal support to Sikorski. But the Polish leader had not long to live.

After this meeting [Howarth reported] Anders spoke to Christine and told her that as regards the ban against her working in Poland, 'his hands were tied by the K-land [Russia] situation.' Evidently she had asked him to intercede with Sikorski to have the ban lifted. That an officer of Anders' rank would confide in her is an example of how widely she was known and respected (except within the Deuxieme Bureau). She also attempted to arrange a meeting between Sikorski and Andrew but the Polish leader declined.

Just when it appeared that there would be no respite from her jobless predicament, there came a glimmer of hope. Lieutenant Colonel Douglas Dodds-Parker, Grenadier Guards, the then-head of Massingham, told her he was certain that he would be able to find something for her. But there was no follow-through. She and Dodds-Parker*** were to have a post-war falling out over another matter, perhaps sparked by this not-forgotten incident. Revenge may be a dish best consumed cold but Christine had an appetite for it nevertheless. Once Dodds-Parker had fallen out with her he was forever banished from her inner circle of friends.

The Americans offered her a position as liaison officer with the Polish government, pending approval by the Deuxieme Bureau. It almost goes without saying that the offer was stillborn. Upon hearing this Howarth commented, 'It is sometimes a little distressing to witness the persecution of brave and honest people by the sweepings of the European secret police.'

Though Christine began to train to become a radio-field operator in 1943 she did not complete the course until the spring of 1944. She found it difficult to master the technique necessary to become a good operator but eventually managed to acquire a basic skill. She also continued with her Italian language lessons, having been told that her next mission would be to Italy.

In addition to her surveillance and intelligence work for Howarth and for SOE Christine still received the occasional job offer. The wife of the new Polish minister to Greece (in-exile) turned out to be a woman she had known casually in Poland. She suggested that

***Dodds-Parker was knighted after the war and later became a Labour Euro MP.

perhaps Christine might work with her husband who would be coordinating intelligence work in Yugoslavia. She met with him but came away with the impression that he was too close to Professor Kot.

The summer dragged on without any resolution to the question of her permanent employment. It seemed that the war was passing her by. In July, Howarth wrote to Wilkinson saying that he had frequently urged her to write to Wilkinson's diplomatic friends concerning a permanent position. She always agreed to the suggestion but never followed through.

'WILLING, however, remains as she was, although we have asked A/M [Dodds-Parker] whether he has anything definite to offer her. When he was here he told her in my presence that he would certainly be able to find something for her at some time. No answer has yet been received, but if it is a negative one I think she should be sent back to England to examine possibilities there. If absolutely nothing can be found, then she should be returned to Cairo, although I can see nothing in view for her here. Both M/DH [Tamplin] and MX [Wilkinson] agreed with this idea when I put it before them.'

Though Christine seemed to glide through the hectic life of Cairo with equanimity, she was not worry-free. As Howarth noted, '... she is well in health but periodically depressed. The cricket season has a lowering effect on her, and she is in better shape when FORCIBLE [Andrew Kennedy] is about.'[3]

On the morning of July 5, 1943 the Polish community and its Allies were rocked by the news that General Sikorski had perished during the night in a plane crash off

Gibraltar. After completing his tour of Polish installations in the Middle East, Sikorski, his daughter Zosia and his aides had flown to Gibraltar on July 3 en route to England. General (later Sir) Noel Mason-Macfarlane, then Governor of The Rock, had made preparations to host a dinner for them that evening after which they were fly on to London.

Mason-Macfarlane's plans however were frustrated by a late-night message from the Russian ambassador, Ivan Maisky, announcing his imminent arrival at Gibraltar. Even on such short notice the governor was expected to provide the minimum hospitality now that the Soviets and Britain were allies. Sikorski and the Polish community worldwide were still seething over the discovery of the murdered officers in Katyn Forest. All fingers pointed in the direction of the Soviets though they protested their innocence and attempted to shift the blame to the Germans. In that heated atmosphere Sikorski would not have for a moment considered meeting with Maisky. Rather than make such an audacious suggestion, Mason-Macfarlane had to do some fast rescheduling of accommodation and flights.

First, he informed Maisky that, because of 'impending bad weather in Algeria,' his flight would have to leave Gibraltar by 11 a.m. on July 4. He then had to explain the situation to Sikorski and ask that he and his staff remain out of sight until after Maisky's plane had departed. (Their planes were parked next to each other on the tarmac.) Once Maisky had gone Sikorski was given a tour of Gibraltar and inspected Polish troops recently escaped from German captivity. A late-night dinner was served to the Polish leader and his entourage. Afterwards, Mason-Macfarlane and his aides accompanied him, his daughter and staff to their Liberator where the pilot had begun warming its engines.

When all were aboard the pilot, Flight Lieutenant Edward Prchal, a Czech in the RAF, positioned his aircraft for take-off and ran-up the engines just prior to departure. Most nearby field lights had been switched off to reduce glare and all seemed in order. Prchal was an experienced pilot and had flown from the Gibraltar airfield many times (Mason-Macfarlane had flown with him twice). Gibraltar's governor and his aide Anthony Quayle watched as the plane sped down the runway. They followed the trajectory of the Liberator's navigation lights, waiting until they were swallowed up by the darkness of the night. As he turned away he noticed that the plane's lights did not continue to rise into the air. He at first put this down to Prchal's take-off technique which was to dip slightly to gain speed before resuming the aircraft's ascent to altitude. But to his astonishment the Liberator flew straight into the water less than a mile from shore.

In that terrible instant Mason-Macfarlane realised that his high-speed launches were docked on the opposite side of the island and would take at least five to ten minutes to reach the crash site. Airfield personnel rushed for the only craft immediately available, a small dinghy. The launch crews were alerted and headed out to the site but the plane had disappeared below the water's surface by the time they arrived.

Mason-Macfarlane was uncertain of how long it took the launches to reach the wreckage and return to shore. When they did come in they had on board only three bodies - Sikorski's, his Chief-of-Staff Walter Klimecki and the pilot Prchal. The first two were dead, Prchal was unconscious. A sea-rescue mission was begun that night and continued for several days. Eighteen bodies were eventually recovered including that of Colonel Victor Cazalet, Sikorski's British Liaison.**** The bodies of Zosia Sikorska and four others were never found.[4]

Given the volatile state of affairs within the Polish exile community, both in London and in the Middle East, accusations immediately began to fly. There were more than enough suspects to sustain numerous conspiracy theories. Prominent on the list were the Russians. Stalin had been angered by Sikorski's refusal to sign the Anglo-Soviet Treaty and was already in the dock over the Katyn affair. With Sikorski out of the way, the Allies and the Soviets could conclude the treaty and get on with the business of opening a second front against the German army.

German intelligence agents were suspect too but they had not much to gain from Sikorski's death except for whatever propaganda value it might bring them. Whoever succeeded Sikorski would certainly not be German-friendly. Even the British government were implicated but with less certainty. It was no secret that Churchill and others in his cabinet were immensely frustrated by Sikorski's stubborn refusal to approve the treaty with the Russians. But no one on the Polish side seriously believed that Churchill would countenance such a despicable act.

Aside from these there were suspects among the Poles, ever on the alert for assassination plots. There had already been one attempt on Sikorski's life and there was was no shortage of rumours about another. Christine's name bobbed to the surface, first because of a casual remark she had made to the effect that there was a plot afoot to assassinate the Polish leader, something taken for granted among the fatalistic Poles. Secondly, because her childhood friend Count Rozwadowski was alleged to be the chief villain among

---

****Major Peter Wilkinson, who in 1941 had sacked Christine and Andrew, was scheduled to be a passenger on that flight. At the last minute his orders were changed and the unfortunate Cazalet replaced him.

those opposed to Sikorski's leadership.

This allegation was resurrected in 1993, fifty years after the tragedy. Mark Amory reviewed a biography of Ian Fleming, written by Donald McCormick in 1993, in which McCormick alleged that Christine 'was in some way connected with the death of General Sikorski . . . '5 Patrick Howarth sprang to her defense in a letter to *The Times*. He gave her credit for alerting him to a plot to murder the Polish leader, information which Howarth passed on to MI6.

Christine had met Sikorski but was not part of his inner circle and had had no political conflict with him. Those who knew her well were certain that she would not have involved herself in such treachery. Her report from Poland in 1940 had already expressed her fears about communist domination of Poland so she was hardly likely to connive with the Russians. There was absolutely no possibility that she would do anything to assist the Nazis who had already murdered her mother. Nevertheless, some Poles of the war generation remained sceptical into this century.6

As frequently happens in such tragedies there were unexplained occurrences. Much was made of the fact that the pilot Prchal did not ordinarily wear a mae west life jacket when flying, but on this particular night he was found floating in the water buoyed by the fully inflated garment.7 Because of the continuing rumours of threats against Sikorski's life his plane had been under continuous guard. The British had placed an NCO aboard the Liberator the night the Polish contingent arrived. He remained on board throughout the following day and evening. Yet the Gibraltar postal service insisted that it had placed two sacks of mail on the plane without being challenged.

Two separate Courts of Inquiry were held by the British government and both reached the same verdict: an accident, cause unknown. No evidence of sabotage was discovered despite an exhaustive investigation, thorough when one takes into consideration the war raging on mainland Europe and the fact that forensic science was still in its infancy. Captain Prchal survived and gave evidence that added nothing to the enquiry. As far as he was concerned the take-off had been normal but for some unknown reason the elevator controls would not respond to his efforts to gain altitude. He was not charged.

In Prchal's defense it should be pointed out that at least once before and once after this tragedy, Liberators had crashed for no apparent reason. It was thought that one of the mail sacks or some other object beneath the floor boards had been dislodged on take-off and had come to rest in such a way as to interfere with the elevator controls located beneath the pilot's seat. A Court of Enquiry however ruled that blockage of the mechanism 'could not possibly have occurred through badly packed baggage shifting.' Mason-Macfarlane, shocked by the incident, concluded that Prchal had suffered a temporary black-out or 'mental aberration.'8 The Polish government divided Sikorski's twin posts, naming minister of the interior Stanislaw Mikolajczyk as prime minister and General Kazimierz Sosnkowski as commander-in-chief of the armed forces.

Death and tragedy rolled in on Christine and Andrew like a bad weather front. The newspaper *Polska Gazeta*, published in Jerusalem, reported later in July that members of Andrew's family had been murdered in Zbydniow in the province of Galicia.+ A group of Gestapo officers had appeared at a wedding party where they found Andrew's mother, uncle and several cousins including an thirteen-year-old girl. They were all taken outside the building and shot. The report seemed to imply that the Gestapo had happened upon the wedding accidentally but there is some suspicion that the attack was planned by a German officer who wished to take possession of the family property.

Guy Tamplin was found dead at his desk in October, having suffered a massive heart attack. There were concerns about the nature of Tamplin's passing for on the day of his death another SOE officer had received a series of taunting telephone calls that had allegedly originated in the 'secret' Rustem Buildings. They were rumoured to have been instigated by one of SOE's most unpopular officers, Brigadier Mervyn 'Bolo' Keble. He was reputed to be a ruthless man, often in conflict with SOE administration but evidently quite efficient in his work. Tales of phone-tapping, poison-pen letters, anonymous phone calls and 'even suspicions of murder' were attributed to him. After Tamplin's death Keble, who had been experimenting with a new form of poison for use in the field, reportedly received a call 'congratulating him on his coup.'

In late 1943 SOE felt the need to re-organise Force 133, the cryptonym for its operatives in Greece and Czechoslovakia. The new mission would have a broader remit to include subversive activities in all the Balkans and in Hungary. The primary focus of activity would be to spread propaganda and to attempt the subversion of German troops. Officers trained in propaganda techniques, especially from the Political Warfare Executive (PWE), were to be recruited. Christine's name was submitted for the mission to Hungary

+The newspaper archive of the British Library has a complete set of *Gazeta Polska* except for the July issue which contains the news of the murder of Kennedy's family.

where SOE had had no operatives since 1942. Plans were drawn up for what came to be known as Operation Kris. Her duties would be to prepare the ground for SOE officers to enter the country and to begin a campaign of sabotage alongside a rather weak Hungarian opposition. Admiral Horthy was still in power but was under increasing pressure from the German government for closer cooperation, particularly in regard to the mass arrest of Jews for deportation to extermination camps.

In an atmosphere of uncertainty the planners of Operation Kris began to discuss the possibilities for the success of this mission, as well as the risks involved in sending someone to Budapest. Christine had emerged as the leading candidate because of her familiarity with the city and with the safest travel routes between the capital and the Slovak border. The papers of Lieutenant Colonel Julian Dolbey (*aka* Count Juliusz Dabrski), one of the leading proponents of Operation Kris, contain the exaggeration that she had crossed the Polish-Slovak frontier fifteen times.[9]

There is an intriguing notation in these same documents to the effect that 'she has a number of close personal friends in Hungary, mostly amongst the landed aristocracy.' But there were doubts about her friends' politics. A marginal note on one memorandum reads, 'right-wing friends will be pro-Nazi or at best anti-Soviet and therefore of little value.' Just to ensure that nothing had been left to chance the memo concludes, 'She also has, or had contacts of a more Left-wing nature.'

Christine's aims would be first, to establish contact with the Hungarian 'Left Opposition Group' and to arrange a reception for incoming British liaison officers. It would be their job to coordinate a campaign of sabotage and subversion in cooperation with the Left group. She was also asked to set up a wireless station.

In January, Captain Harold Perkins signaled Patrick Howarth that the decision to go ahead with this mission 'was final,' and that Christine should be sent to the London as soon as possible to be briefed. (Throughout the war British officers politely referred to her as 'Madame Gizycka'.) Still, a fragment of doubt over her role remained. Perkins closed his signal saying, 'Active work was envisaged for her either with the Hungarian Section or with Lt Col HAZELL's Section [Italy].'

Colonel Dolbey knew Christine well for they had travelled in the same social circles in Warsaw before the war. He had no doubts about her courage and her willingness to take on such a perilous assignment. He and the other planners were determined to infiltrate Hungary even though it would involve ' the greatest risks ... promising only a slight chance of success.' Despite such a gloomy assessment Christine would not have shrunk from the challenge.

Operation Kris was discussed quite thoroughly before a conclusion was reached. There are in SOE files four-and five-page memoranda listing the pros and cons of mounting this mission, the reasons for proceeding and suggestions for alternative missions. The scheme had to begin with the proposition that SOE had no Magyar-speaking operatives. It was pointed out that Christine couldn't speak the language either but she remained the preferred candidate on the basis of her familiarity with Budapest.

How to slip her, or anyone else, into Hungary posed an even greater problem. To parachute her blind into the countryside would be, as one officer suggested, nothing less than homicide. Dropping her into Slovakia and having her cross the border into Hungary would be only slightly less hazardous. Even though Slovakia contained a substantial number of anti-German partisans there could be no guarantee that the local population of wherever she landed would help her. It was agreed however, and with a straight-face, that her only possible disguise would be that of a Polish refugee. Other Force 133 military missions, code-named Flotsam, Geisha, Savannah and Sparrow were in progress on Hungary's borders. It was suggested that she might perhaps be infiltrated as part of one of these but that idea was discarded. A drop into southern Poland had to be considered even though that would require her to cross the Tatra mountains carrying a heavy radio set.

In April 1944, Cairo SOE requested a set of false documents for her in the name Maria Kaminska. The request noted that, 'This should be done without knowledge of Poles.' This alias was ultimately scrapped because it would necessitate an SOE obligation to the Seizieme Bureau, something SOE wished to avoid. Whether Polish intelligence would even consider working with Christine was still questionable. Dolbey and the others reluctantly concluded that sending her in via Slovakia seemed the only viable alternative even with its attendant risks. If Christine wanted action she would certainly be getting it if this mission were to proceed.

In preparation for Operation Kris she was sent to to Massingham HQ at Guyotville near Algiers in March as part of SPOC (Special Project Operations Centre), under the command of Lieutenant Commander (later Sir)Francis Brooks Richards, RNVR. Dolbey reported that by the end of the month she would have completed her wireless telegraphy training using a 'B' set (a wireless set with a range of about 1000 miles). In addition she would have finished the parachute training course at RAF Ramat David, a course in the use of 'elementary explosives', an SIS course and instructions on preparing a reception committee which would involve laying out Drop Zones and Landing Zones for airborne operations. She would also be required to take instruction in the creation of personal disguises. Though Christine had travelled in Europe under assumed names she had never received formal, or approved, instruction in the preferred methods of disguise.

Before embarking for Slovakia there would be additional training at SOE Bari in the use of S-phones (a microwave, line-of-sight, transceiver which enabled ground operatives to talk to another operator in an aircraft overhead up to a range of twenty miles). Elaborate preparations to be completed in a short space of time for a dangerous mission.

After all the guarded optimism attendant only a few weeks ago, Dolbey and other officers abruptly concluded that Operation Kris would be too hazardous, especially in view of Christine's lack of familiarity with Magyar. If they hadn't stopped it Bickham Sweet-Escott would have, for once he saw the plans he ordered that there should be no further progress on the matter. Once again, her hopes for a mission in Europe were dashed. Before signing off on this aborted plan, Dolbey recommended to London SOE that Christine should remain in Algiers and that she should continue to hone her w/t skills in the event that she might be needed in France. Sweet-Escott weighed in with a glowing recommendation, saying, 'She is a Polish lady of considerable beauty and great courage . . . as brave as a lion and as SOE-minded as the best of the Poles.'

Not everyone was as convinced as Dolbey had been that Christine was the right person for the job. Dodds-Parker thought she was 'too flamboyant and too valuable.' He proved to be right on both counts. But in a few months' time they would have a serious falling out. Julian Dolbey's prescient suggestion, for Christine to remain in Algiers in the event that she might be needed in France, was taken up by SOE Cairo. It had come to light that there were thousands of Polish men in France, some toiling away in labour camps while others had been drafted into the German army. Someone in central command must have realised that a Polish-speaking agent might be a valuable asset in France in the near future. A diary entry for 6-7 July 1944 submitted to the Jockey file in the *Bibliotheque nationale de France* states, 'Christine Granville (Pauline) from Algiers as a liaison officer to work with Cammaerts and to make contacts if possible with the foreigners [Poles] in the German army. Shortly thereafter working alone she came into contact with the polish [sic] soldiers incorporated in the German army and persuaded them to "lift" weapons from the base of Larche and to give themselves up carrying off the breeches of the heavy weapons. '

The decision to cancel Operation Kris did not sit well with Christine who had been primed and ready for action when the order came to stand down. That was followed by a lengthy period of waiting for her next assignment during which she continued her w/t training with Major Ben Cowburn. After the war Brooks Richards told of how she repeatedly clashed with the highly regard Cowburn's low-key approach to training. Brooks Richards, though a great admirer of Christine's, recalled that he had to intervene several times when she and Cowburn got into shouting matches. Brooks Richards referred to these occasions as Christine's 'diva' moments.

The frustrations encountered in the simple task of learning to ride a bicycle only aggravated her anxieties. A visit from the reliable Howarth finally helped calm her nerves.

Chapter 17.
Resistance in France

SOE and its predecessor, Section D, had been active in France since 1940. In the following years they inserted a number of operatives into the country in an attempt to create a resistance force to oppose the occupying Germans. But a combination of apathy and political divisions among the French, and the pervasive strength of the German forces made it difficult to establish a centrally controlled opposition. It was not until 1943 that the Allies were able to create and sustain combined British-French clandestine organisations that survived until the end of the war. In the early years of occupation the French had not presented a united front. Resistance took many forms and was provided by a variety of groups each with its own political agenda. As in Poland all eyes in France were on a post-war settlement. Though they had a common goal the resisters were not always eager to cooperate with one another.

Once the D-Day landings in Normandy had begun some cells rose against the Germans spontaneously. There was an assumption, tragically incorrect, that the Allies would reach their cities or their *departements* within a matter of days or weeks and that local resistance merely had to hold out until such a time. But plans for Operation Overlord did not include linking up with the *maquis** fighters. German forces throughout France reacted furiously to the invasion by conducting raids on suspected resistance cells, determined to root them out and crush them. Arrests, executions and even massacres took place.

Much of the success of covert operations achieved in France prior to D-Day was due to the work of operatives trained by F Section (SOE's French Section). Under the leadership of Major (later lieutenant colonel) Maurice Buckmaster the section was sub-divided into some forty circuits each with its own leader and each responsible for a particular geographic area. Buckmaster and another officer, Harry Ree, one of SOE's outstanding operatives, had conducted the initial interviews with the young Francis Charles Albert Cammaerts in 1942. Buckmaster was impressed with this rather tall Englishman except for what he thought was the candidate's limited French vocabulary that betrayed traces of an English accent. He also remarked that Cammaerts 'walked like an Englishman' and would probably stand out in any crowd. The trick would be to keep him out of situations where he might be readily noticed.

Christine's mission was finally given the green light in late June. Her destination was the Vercors, a high plateau rising out of the rugged French countryside south of Grenoble. It is a massive limestone structure covering almost half-a-million acres of land. Several towns and villages nestled atop this seemingly inhospitable plateau in the 1940s, offering refuge for thousands of Frenchmen fleeing German conscription and labour camps. The countryside surrounding the Vercors was covered with thick beech and pine forests and riven by deep gorges, providing excellent cover for hit-and-run operations against the enemy. But heavily armed German troops were not far away.

*The name generally applied to the French resistance.

This was also Francis Cammaerts' territory. The former British schoolmaster and his Jockey Circuit operated in a vast area that stretched from the French-Italian border west to Toulouse, north to Lyon and south to Marseille. This sector of France was of vital importance to the Germans because it guarded access to northern Italy as well as to the southern approach to the French interior.

Cammaerts was the son of a Belgian father, a poet, and an English mother in a multilingual home. By the time he came down from Cambridge University he was already fluent in French. Before the war he had registered as a conscientious objector but the death of his brother Pieter, an RAF pilot, made him re-examine his conscience. After completing the arduous training courses at SOE schools in England and in Scotland, Cammaerts received a lieutenant's commission in the General List of Infantry. Prior to departing on his first mission he was raised to the rank of captain. He was first flown to France on a Lysander in March 1943. His cover story described him as an English schoolmaster on holiday, recuperating from jaundice. This actually was an accurate description of Cammaerts' health as well as his profession.

Known among resistance fighters by the cryptonym 'Roger', he remained in France for approximately six months, traveling tirelessly across the countryside between Toulouse and Grenoble, making contacts with pockets of a French resistance that had not been united under a central command. He established headquarters at Seyne-les-Alpes in southeastern France, between the towns of Digne and Gap, but also set up secondary HQs in other towns to serve as fall-back positions.[1]

His work had its obvious hazards. He once narrowly escaped capture by the notorious

German army counter-intelligence operative known as Colonel Heinrich or 'Henri' (Sergeant Hugo Bleicher of the *Abwehr*). Henri's greatest success was the capture of the legendary Ensign Odette Sansom (cryptonym 'Lise') of the FANYs, and Captain Peter Churchill, Intelligence Corps of the Spindle circuit. Henri had managed to convince Sansom that he was an anti-Nazi who wanted to help bring down Hitler. Initially sceptical, Sansom agreed to proposals for cooperation put to her by Henri and then notified Cammaerts. He himself thought the German too good to be true and relayed his suspicions to her. Shortly afterwards Sansom and Churchill (her lover and future husband) were arrested by the Gestapo. Both were sent to concentration camps where she in particular suffered horrible torture but lived to tell the tale and was awarded the George Cross.

In June, Cammaerts was joined by two SOE operatives, Capitaine Pierre Reynaud ('Alain') and Section Officer Cecily Margot Lefort, WAAF ('Alice'). They had been in France for just three months when Alice was caught up in an SS raid on the town of Montelimar. But for the need for him to travel constantly Cammaerts would have been with her at the time. After interrogation in Lyon, 'Alice' was sent to Ravensbruck concentration camp where she was murdered in 1944.

The SS were now on the hunt for someone named 'Roger' and, what's more they had his photo. Cammaerts took refuge with the Turrel family in Seyne-les-Alpes and dispersed his team of operatives to avoid having them arrested together. Anxious to prevent Roger's capture, SOE sent a plane to pick him up and return him to London on the night of November 15/16. He remained there until the early spring of 1944 and spent much of his time laying plans for his return.**

Cammaerts returned to France in February but his journey was far from simple. He was a passenger in a Halifax aircraft that came under heavy ground fire from German batteries as it reached the south coast of France. The plane caught fire before reaching Lyons, forcing the crew to bail out before it crashed. Cammaerts landed some ninety miles from his designated drop-spot. Fortunately he was taken in by a friendly farmer and found that he was only about a few miles from a safe house in Beaurdpaire. Shaken but not seriously injured, he needed only a brief spell to recuperate before beginning the job of reactivating the resistance cells he had left behind. He took on the disguise of a road-surveyor, a perfect cover should anyone question his need to travel so frequently.

The Allied landings in Normandy were less than four months away and there was much to be done - roads and rail lines had to be sabotaged, factory assembly lines disrupted and German patrols ambushed. Less spectacular but still effective were the small avalanches Roger caused along the Route des Alpes. Cammaerts and his small army of resistors wreaked havoc upon the Germans' lines of communication. One rail line was sabotaged so often that the enemy finally ceased repairing it. The significance of these operations lay in the fact that the Germans were unable to rush reinforcements from Italy to Normandy, thus enabling Allied troops to gain a foothold on the Channel coast of France.

Reports of a second Allied landing (Operation Anvil) in the south of France had reached German intelligence by mid-summer. The German high command responded by flooding southern sectors of the country with troops, SS men and Gestapo agents. Some resistance cells were broken up, their leaders arrested. The date set for Operation Anvil

** See *A Pacifist at War, the life of Francis Cammaerts*, by Ray Jenkins (London: Hutchinson 2009).

(August 15) was less than six weeks away and, as a result of Cecily Lefort's arrest Cammaerts found himself in need of a deputy who could also manage his radio communications. He contacted Massingham, requesting that such an assistant be sent as soon as possible. He preferred a female, confident that a woman could move about in the local towns and villages less conspicuously than a male operative.

On the night of July 7/8, Christine Granville crouched in the second of four Halifax aircraft, 624 Squadron RAF, that overflew southeastern France as part of Operation Taile en route to 'Crayon', her designated drop-zone. Her papers described her as Pauline Armand, a French housewife but her camouflage outfit described another purpose. She was accompanied by a Free French officer-engineer, one Capitaine Tournissa (cryptonym 'Paquebot'), whose mission was to construct an airstrip atop the Vercors plateau. Weather conditions overhead the drop-zone were rough. Christine jumped into the wind and was immediately blown off course, landing a few miles from the intended site of her rendezvous near the town of Vassieux. She landed heavily, bruised her hip and smashed the butt of one of the two pistols that SOE parachutists carried. A second chute containing radio equipment and her personal belongings failed to open. Its contents were crushed as the chute hit the ground.

Unsure of her surroundings Christine hid herself as best she could, hoping that she would not be discovered by a German dog-patrol. In her report on this mission she wrote that she had narrowly avoided capture by hiding behind some dense shrubbery. The patrol's Alsatian dog passed the spot where she lay but before it could bark she petted it and whispered calmly, in Polish, and the dog returned to its masters.*** Local *maquisards* eventually found her and took her to their headquarters where she remained for several days until she was able to walk properly.

It was then that she was introduced to Francis Cammaerts. There was an instant rapport between them. Cammaerts saw before him a daring attractive woman who had just made a dangerous night-time leap into occupied territory. He was impressed by such courage and sensed then that Christine would have the strength to do whatever assignments he would set for her. He had requested a female w/t operator but by the end of that first meeting he suspected that she would make an excellent deputy as well as a courier, moving among the various cells of Jockey Circuit. Her obvious fluency in French was better than he could have hoped for.

Christine had been in France for only a week before she herself came under fire. On July 14, Bastille Day, French villagers and *maquisards* on the Vercors celebrated their national holiday by receiving a large daylight supply-drop from B-52s of the 3rd Bombardment Division, USAAF. This action, plus Capitaine Tournissa's*** arrival, had given them the false hope that Allied troops were not far behind.

German forces were not sitting idly by but were poised to strike on this most revered of French holidays. Bastille Day celebrations were brutally interrupted by the arrival of enemy aircraft bombing and strafing villages where *fetes* were in progress. The Luftwaffe turned their cannons and machine guns on unarmed men and women caught out in the open gathering in the hundreds of containers that had been dropped by the B-52s.

***Anecdote told to the author by Inka Nowotna-Lewicka OBE in December 2004.

Five days later German ground forces attacked in strength. An estimated 14000 troops arrived by gliders and by parachute. A bloody battle ensued as they began a determined effort to drive the French off the Vercors plateau. Opposing them were approximately 4000 lightly armed *maquisards* who had decided to stand and fight. Though they struggled valiantly they were no match for the well-trained German troops supported by artillery and air power. The battles fought here were witnessed (and later described) by two SOE officers, Major D. Lange and Captain John Houseman, who incidentally claimed to have met Christine once before, in London. The town of Vassieux was razed to the ground and nearby La Chapelle-en-Vercors was seriously damaged.

Cammaerts and Christine had not been caught up in the fighting but were in a small hotel in Vassieux when the attack began. In the early hours of the morning the building was set alight during the fighting and Cammaerts later described being awakened by the sound of heavy gunfire.[2] They had watched from a window as a German plane descended toward the hotel and released its pay-load. He saw the bomb fall and assured Christine that they would not be hit. The bomb caromed off the roof and struck a building behind the hotel but did not explode, leaving them free to walk away unharmed.

Because Cammaerts was held in great respect by those who knew him and even by those who knew him only by reputation, no one has ever publicly suggested that he and Christine had had an affair. His memoirs, recorded in 1985, form part of the SOE section at the Sound Archive of the Imperial War Museum. He made no mention then of an affair. Before Cammaerts finally acknowledged their brief liaison the hotel concierge had already

---

***Tournissa was killed in action on August 28, 1944.

given a strong hint of it some years before. Interviewed after the war for a book about the battle of Vercors, she naively began her account by saying that on the morning of July 14 she had taken breakfast up to 'their room.'

One of Christine's friends said with certainty that she was 'madly in love' with Cammaerts. He was the kind of man who would have been attractive to most women - soft-spoken but strong and courageous. In the fifty-odd years after her death he maintained a discreet silence about their relationship. If she was madly in love with him she never confessed it to anyone. For the two months they were together there were few opportunities for a dalliance. Both were dead-set on the task at hand and would not be diverted from their respective duties.

Cammaerts finally admitted to the affair three years before his death in 2006. He described being together with Christine in a small hotel in St Agnan the night before the Germans launched their fierce assault on the Vercors plateau. That night, amid all the chaos, he recalled, '. . . we simply went into each other's arms.'

Given the severity of the continuing attack Cammaerts understood that if they were to be captured or killed the Germans would have dealt a serious blow to resistance in southeastern France. With the agreement of the others, he, Christine and Colonel Henri Zeller**** gathered what equipment they could carry and took back roads to reach Jockey Circuit HQ at Seyne-les-Alpes. Local residents gave them the use of a 'farm vehicle' after they had walked a considerable distance down the mountain side. They then set out using what was probably a tractor and on foot to make the seventy-mile journey back to head-

---
****Head of French resistance for southeastern France

quarters without incident. Contrary to popular legend there is evidence that they did not walk the entire distance.

Christine's admiration for Cammaerts surpassed even his laudatory remarks about her abilities and her courage. On 27 July she signaled Commander Brooks Richards, RNVR, at Massingham in Algiers, pleading for more operatives and more overall assistance, much needed after the hammering the *maquis* had taken at Vercors. The language in her signal to Brooks Richards was both demanding and nearly hysterical.

She began by calmly stating that she was very well. High praise for Cammaerts followed before she descended into wild hyperbole, describing him as a magnificent person and that, 'the whole of the South of France depends on him.' This ignores the fact that the FFI (*Force Francaises de l'Interieur*) in particular, and other French fighters were actively engaged in sabotaging German targets. They would have continued to do so without him though their efforts perhaps may have been less well-organised.

The tone of Christine's text became progressively more insistent. One imagines that had she been in the same room with the commander she would have been shouting. 'You must support him and back up his prestige as much as you can.' She emphasised the trust the locals placed in him. She went on to demand more Jedburghs+ and missions, harrying the highly experienced operations officer by exhorting him not to wait until the war was over and insisting that nobody but Cammaerts 'could do any good at all.' She ended her harangue sarcastically: 'Of course if you think we have got another 2 or 3 years of war in front of us you can send new people and make them get contacts by themselves. 'Make up your mind.' She had turned a blast of her well-known *froideur* upon him, ignoring the fact that she was speaking to a senior officer. Surprisingly, Brooks Richards accepted her criticisms and demands without demur.

Turning to the subject of reinforcements she bluntly confirmed that the only important group were the Poles, adding as an aside that, 'there are Serbs, Checks (sic), some Ukrainians, Russian and Armenians who are allegedly always on the move and therefore not of much use.' She also insisted on knowing the reactions from the British and Polish governments and the British army in Italy. 'MOST IMPORTANT what about Poland and Russia.' She requested visas and travel documents, written in Polish, to be used by the defecting Poles, adding 'Do you realise that now that Poles are almost like the Ukranians.' The remark was not intended to be humorous but she was desperately searching for a way to express the plight of those Polish men.

Christine must have suspected that the British had no intention of confronting the Red Army on Polish soil, more or less ceding the country to the Soviet Union. She wrote: 'I do not want to tell them [the Poles] that the Polish Army is a foreign legion fighting as a mercenary army.' The truth is that, at their 1943 Teheran Conference, Churchill and Roosevelt, in separate late-night meetings with Stalin, left nothing to the imagination by implying that eastern Europe and especially Poland would remain within his sphere of influence in any post-war settlement.3 Thus the nation's fate had been decided even before the Yalta Conference of 1945 which formalised Soviet control of Poland.

As the war drew near to its conclusion it became more difficult for the British to

+Jedburghs: teams of three (leader, deputy and a w/t operator). Usually one American or British officer and one French. The radio operator could be any of those nationalities. Dropped behind enemy lines to advise local resistance and set up communications.

maintain their silence on the subject. There was now widespread feeling among certain elements of the Polish government that they were about to be betrayed. General Anders had already requested that the Polish II Corps be withdrawn from the British 8th Army. Morale among Polish pilots declined. They no longer saw any reason to sacrifice themselves for a lost cause unlike the Polish Parachute Brigade who were about to be sent to Arnhem, instead of to Poland, and were massacred. (In the *real-politik* atmosphere of post-war world, Prime Minister Clement Attlee added to the Polish humiliation by refusing to allow its servicemen to march in the Victory Parade in London [June 1946] for fear of annoying Stalin, the West's new friend.4 Attlee's government attempted to make up for this gaffe with a last-minute offer that would permit a small contingent of Polish men in civilian clothing to march at the rear of the parade.)

In her lengthy and rambling signal to Brooks Richards, Christine returned to the subject of Cammaerts, adding that his connections and influence could be felt everywhere. She noted that German morale was quite low and that, because of his leadership, one could now travel from the south coast of France to Lyon almost without hindrance. However, she added, in order to continue his work Cammaerts would need to have about ten days notice in advance of the forthcoming Allied landing on the southern coast of France (Operation Anvil).

Before closing this rambling two-page document Christine inserted some personal messages. She asked Brooks Richards to contact Howarth and ask what he intended to do with the mutinous Polish troops within the *Wehrmacht*. Andrew Kennedy had not been forgotten either and she implored Brooks Richards not to use him in Switzerland as conditions on the Swiss frontier were so difficult. She reminded him that there were no means of transport for him and every mission had to be carried out on foot. She suggested that if he had to send Andrew to Switzerland it should be only to deal with the Polish troops who had made their way into that country. She ended the communique by requesting that her old friend Havard Gunn, with whom she had trained at Massingham, be sent over. 'With Roger's [Cammaerts] contacts and advice he can produce miracles.'[5]

Gunn is one of the few of Christine's acquaintances to comment on her sharp sense of humour. While living at Le Club de Pins she frequently met the kilt-wearing Gunn for coffee and it was during those informal moments that she had expressed her frustration at having to wait to be summoned to duty in France. Gunn was also keenly aware of another, darker side of her personality. He recalled, 'She did not appear to have any roots . . . She lived entirely for the moment, and seemed to look upon the future with some trepidation.'

Cammaerts' biographer contends that Christine's primary mission was to 'mobilise her Polish compatriots in France, those who had been forced into ghastly labour camps or who had been dragooned into the German army.' Cammaerts' request for a female agent to replace Cecily Lefort now seems to have been a fortunate coincidence. The chronology of Christine's meetings with Poles who had been impressed into the Wehrmacht has been muddled after having been written about so often by so many. What is certain is that, prior to making contact with any Poles, she spent two weeks in early August 1944 acting as liaison between Jockey Circuit and bands of partisans operating in the *Hautes-Alpes* southeast of Grenoble. The goal of this mission, known as Operation Toplink and led by Major

LGMJ Hamilton, was to weld French and Italian partisans into a fighting force. (Hamilton, *aka* Leon Blanchaert, was a Belgian and one of six officers parachuted into the area.)

During the first week in August Cammaerts sent Christine up to Bramousse on the Durance river where Gilbert Galetti, the head of the Italian partisans, had his base. He was but a stone's throw from a small German garrison quartered in a seventeenth-century fortress that commanded a view of the 7000-foot high Col de Larche. Christine began the journey perched precariously on the motorbike of a local ski instructor, Gilbert Tavernier, who took her as high up the mountain as he could possibly go. She made the remainder of the journey on foot, a strenuous hike over the Larche pass. That took a day and a half of fighting her way through rough terrain. After a brief rest she resumed her uphill struggle even though her legs had been severely scratched.

Christine had always been a slender woman and has even been described as frail. Nevertheless, she was an indefatigable climber, a talent perhaps passed down from her earliest ancestors who were mountain people with the name *Skarbek z gory*, meaning 'from the mountain.'

She finally contacted a group of Italians led by a man known only as Marcellin. The arduous journey turned out to be a bust for Marcellin and his men were about to abandon their position after a bruising battle with German soldiers. Patrick O'Regan, one of Toplink's officers, recalled meeting Christine just after she had made met with Marcellin. 'She found the Italians who were gallantly trying to hold a valley for much too long [and] their forces in a bad way and she came back with an urgent message for us to hurry up and get there [to the valley].'[6]

Christine did not succeed in bringing news of the partisans to Cammaerts though, for as she descended the mountain Major Hamilton struck out in another direction. Despite this minor setback something good did come of her efforts. Cammaerts, Galetti and the heroic French leader Paul Herault have each been credited with alerting her to the presence of Polish soldiers within the German garrison. Regardless of the source, on or about August 8 Christine made contact with one of the Poles. He quickly gathered his companions (some had already deserted) out of sight of the Germans where Christine addressed them using a loudhailer. [7]

According to Cammaerts the Polish spokesman expressed his group's wish to join the resistance. Christine suggested that, to begin with, they should sabotage the Germans' heavy guns and bring their smaller weapons with them. More than sixty Poles are said to have followed her down the mountain. Afterwards, the FFI cratered the road over which the enemy would have travelled to attack the town of Larche.

Written comments by a Frenchman, A. Vincent Beaume, submitted to Cammaerts' file in the *Bibliotheque nationale* in Paris, support this version except for the use of the loudhailer. No one has explained how Christine could have spoken to the men using such an instrument without being overheard by the Germans who could not have been too far away. M Beaume gave yet another version of how Christine discovered the Poles. The source, he claims, was not one of the Toplink officers but a Polish soldier forced to serve in the 157th German division, captured by the French in a battle near Montelus in the Hautes-Alpes. He told his French captors that a number of his countrymen in his division wished to desert at the earliest opportunity.[8]

Cammaerts now seemed determined to use Christine's powers of persuasion to their fullest extent. She left Larche and made yet another trek into the Italian Alps, hoping to bring a group of dissident Italian soldiers on to the side of the resistance. But this mission did not go as successfully as the others. Christine stumbled into an enemy patrol before she could cross the French-Italian border and years later several versions of 'what happened next' emerged. Upon reaching the border she was challenged by German sentries who ordered her at gun-point to surrender. She responded by producing two grenades from her tunic and threatened to detonate them, killing herself and taking some of the soldiers with her. Uncertain of how to deal with this grenade-wielding woman, the patrol stood aside and allowed her to continue on her way. This tale was apparently told by Andrew to the author Madeleine Masson some years after Christine's death but there were no reliable witnesses to the actual event and there are no documents to support his story.[9]

Another version of this adventure has her holding the grenades but facing an Italian patrol, with the same result. There is still some confusion over what language was spoken and whether she was confronted by an enemy patrol or by a lone sentry. As she was returning from Italian territory it seems reasonable to assume that she would have encountered one or more Italians. But Hitler and his generals had long ago lost confidence in the ability and loyalty of the Italian soldier. German troops had taken over key positions in Italy allowing for the possibility that Christine might well have been challenged again by Germans. If so, then she could have readily responded for her Polish ID card, issued in 1928, lists German as one of her three languages. During the war she broadened her linguistic repertoire to include Italian while languishing in Cairo so all linguistic possibilities have been covered by those who have repeated this tale.

Over the years other versions have been produced, some of which have reached ludicrous heights. In 2010 another author, writing a brief sketch of Christine's adventures, wrote that she had approached a checkpoint with two grenades tucked beneath her armpits, having already pulled the pins.10 The creator of this tale doesn't explain why they hadn't exploded or what happened to the grenades once she had safely crossed the border. No author has ever bothered to describe whether the bombs were safely detonated or if they were of a type that could be de-activated. So many versions of this incident have been told that no one can say with certainty what actually happened at that border crossing. In fact, no one can say absolutely that this confrontation actually occurred. Christine seldom gave details of her exploits but Andrew, by contrast, had no such qualms.

The combined SOE-*maquis* force had lost a large number of its officers during the German assaults on the Vercors and on Montelimar. The most dramatic loss for Cammaerts and Christine was the death of their friend Paul Herault leader of the local FFI. Herault had left Gap on his way to meet with another resistance leader when he and his driver ran into a German convoy. Ordered to stop, Herault fled into a wooded area. The Germans shot his driver then pursued Herault into the forest. After destroying the papers he was carrying he broke cover and attempted to flee but was cut down in a hail of bullets.

Colonel Zeller had recently lost his deputy too and now officers of the FFI appeared on the scene. The question of who should take charge of the resistance in this quadrant of France, the military or the *marquisards*' own leaders, arose and had to be settled quickly.

Chapter 18.

Christine to the Rescue

On August 12 a meeting was convened by Colonel Jean Constans in the town of Lagarde to discuss the issue of command. Cammaerts was driven there in a Red Cross truck accompanied by a new addition to his team, Major Xan Fielding (cryptonym Cathedrale) and by Commandant Christian Sorensen (Chasuble). Their driver was Claude Renoir, son of the artist. Replacements for the dead officers were ultimately decided by Constans with little opposition and the meeting concluded late in the day. Cammaerts and his two officers decided to remain in Lagarde rather than risk traveling after dark.

In the morning they began their return journey to their headquarters in Seyne. Cammaerts had successfully navigated road-blocks on numerous occasions but remained cautious though he did not anticipate trouble on this trip. Control points were often manned by the local *gendarmerie*, sometimes with Gestapo officers lurking in the background. Secure in his command of the language, Cammaerts was confident that could talk his way around the police.

The trio's journey was interrupted by an Allied air raid, forcing them to take cover and wait until the all-clear signal was sounded before proceeding. At the control point they noticed that a *geheim Feld Polizei* unit was still in place, waiting to be relieved by the French. Still, Cammaerts was certain that he could bluff his way past whoever was in charge. The *Feld Polizei* studied the SOE officers' documents without comment and allowed them to pass. Everything would have gone smoothly but for a small item that Cammaerts had overlooked. As he and his colleagues pulled away from the control point the officer in charge had second thoughts and called for them to return for further questioning. In the course of searching the three men he had not seemed concerned about the large sums of money they carried but he did notice that the bank notes were not pinned and folded as was the custom in French banks before being gathered in sequentially numbered bundles in denominations of 50 and 100 francs. The serial numbers on the notes the men were carrying were also sequential, thus destroying Cammaerts' story that they were casual hitch-hikers, strangers to one another.[1]

Unfortunately, Xan Fielding, whose French had grown rusty after years of disuse, was the first to be questioned. When he responded awkwardly to routine questions the German officer suspected that something else was wrong. Fielding was asked where he was employed and he named the Electricity Works in Nime. His working papers however lacked a current stamp and the German officer ordered his arrest. Almost as an afterthought he also arrested Cammaerts and Sorenson. Renoir, playing the innocent, was allowed to go on his way. The three SOE men were taken to a dismal barracks in the city of Digne in the Basses-Alpes, between the Durance river and the Italian border, where they were sentenced to be shot without trial.

After two busy weeks in the Italian Alps, Christine returned to Seyne exhausted. Before she could have a proper rest the news of Cammaerts' arrest was brought by Captain

John Roper of Mission 'Confessional.' Major CB Hunter, a Canadian officer, was the first to learn that the operatives had been taken into custody, probably alerted by Cammaerts' driver Renoir, and he immediately sent Roper to Seyne-les-Alpes to inform Christine. As she was second-in-command to Cammaerts she immediately assumed control of the Circuit. Cammaerts had come to depend upon her and assumed that she would act appropriately without direct instructions from him. His instinct turned out to be spot-on.

Christine acted swiftly after conferring with Roper. On August 15 she summoned a team of Jedburghs plus Major Hunter, Captain Roper and five local maquisards to a meeting at a place known only to them as the Chalet. She broke the news that 'Roger' and his two companions had been arrested. She also declared that she would 'carry on his [Cammaerts] work as best she could.' None of the men present objected. She then arranged for trucks to take everyone and their kit to safety at Bramousse. Major Hunter noted in his report that, 'It is impossible to speak too highly of PAULINE's [Christine] conduct at this time. She was working under great difficulties and had had very little sleep.'

The maquisards' response to her dramatic news has been clouded by the passage of time. Some accounts claim that the French fighters clamoured to storm the prison in Digne but in her report dated the 1st of November 1944, Christine wrote that several FFI leaders 'declined to help on the ground that it was too dangerous.' While the first version emphasises the FFI's heroism, the second version is more realistic. They had after all just taken a terrific beating on the Vercors plateau and were in no position to mount an assault on anyone.

M. Beaume's comments in Cammaaerts' file in Paris describe Christine attempting to organise a 'free brigade' to attack the Germans in Digne. But she abruptly reversed gear and decided to carry out a rescue mission on her own. She next spoke to Dr Paul Jouve, Cammaerts' close friend, who agreed with her that an assault on the prison would be too dangerous. He suggested that she cycle to Digne, a distance of about twenty-five miles southwest of their location in Seyne, and find out exactly what the Gestapo intended to do with their captives. Her last-minute training in the art of cycling was now put to good use. Quite aware of the risk she was about to take she handed over to one of the Jeds, Major DEF Green, a list of her contacts in the event that she too were to be arrested. She acted calmly but decisively as if she had been trained for this very moment.

Christine arrived in Digne wearing the everyday dress appropriate for a local housewife. After a short while she found the shabby barracks where the SOE men were being held and was able to slip through the gates shielded by a crowd of visitors. Before leaving Seine-les-Alpes, Christine had been given the name of a gendarme, one Captain Albert Schenck, by Dr Jouve. Schenck had often acted as liaison between the French police and German troops, and tried to maintain friendly relations with both sides. Upon meeting him Christine impulsively discarded any claim to be a French woman and instead introduced herself as a British operative and Cammaerts' wife, perhaps a bit of wishful thinking. It was to be a repeat performance of her very persuasive action in Budapest when she claimed that Andrew was her spouse in order to help secure his release.

She attempted to enhance her *bona fides* by boasting that she was Field Marshal Montgomery's niece and for good measure hinted that Allied forces would be entering Digne very soon. The second D-Day landings in France had just taken place though Allied troops were still a considerable distance from the city. If he were to be taken prisoner, she warned, he surely would be handed over to the local maquis. Schenck was uncertain of what to make of these claims but he saw an opportunity to make provision for his life after the war. He agreed to act as intermediary between her and a Belgian working with the Gestapo named Max Waem. But for a price. Christine had obviously sown enough doubt in Schenck's mind so that he began to think of saving his own skin rather than informing the Gestapo of her presence in Digne.

Christine later wrote a detailed account of the negotiations with Schenck but her story has been 'improved upon' both by those who were involved in this adventure and by those who had only heard about it. Cammaerts recalled that she had walked around the perimeter of the barracks whistling the tune, 'Frankie and Johnny' in an effort to locate the room where he was being held. Cammaerts heard her and replied by loudly singing a few bars of the song thus assuring her that he was still alive.

The chronology of events thereafter is confusing because of the variations of this episode told by Christine's colleagues and the lack of detail in her own report. She wrote that she had returned to Digne two days after that first meeting and that Schenck had not yet contacted Max Waem. Fortunately for her Allied troops from Operation Anvil were now making their way north along the Rhone river and Digne had just been bombed. The sound of nearby explosions must have galvanised Schenck into action for he hastily contacted Waem and convinced him to meet Christine at the Schenck's flat. If her chronology is accurate and not purposely misleading then she appears to have made *two* round-trips by bicycle from Seyne to Digne, a total distance of about one hundred miles. This was a punishing endeavour, especially so since the route to Digne was uphill.

After her second meeting with Schenck Christine returned again to Digne, this time with a car and driver (the Turrels' son). She met Max Waem at the Schenck's flat at 16.00 hours (according to her) on August 17 and was told that Cammaerts and his two associates were to be shot at 21.00 hours that very evening. Obviously there was little time to waste.

A suspicious Waem, dressed in his Gestapo uniform, entered the flat and drew his pistol, covering Christine as they spoke. He holstered the weapon only after he assured himself that she was unarmed. He then poured two cups of coffee - real coffee, she emphasised, not a watery substitute - prepared by Mme Schenck. Christine reported* that she spent three hours trying to persuade Waem to release his prisoners. She put to him the same truths and half- truths that she had previously told to Schenck (he and his wife apparently remained out of sight), namely that the Allies were rapidly approaching. Once they had overrun the town, she asserted, Waem would be arrested and handed over to local French resistance fighters who would make short work of him.

Christine repeated the lie about her relationship to Field Marshal Montgomery, adding for good measure that she was also related to Sir Robert Vansittart. She inflated with some degree of truth Cammaerts' importance to the Allies' plans, again insisting he was her husband. If Waem would agree to release the men, she promised, she would immediately contact Montgomery and inform him that the prisoners had been freed and secure his safe-passage promise. As proof of her identity as a British operative Christine produced

---

*The historian Arthur Funk claimed that she spent ten hours with Waem. *See* his *Hidden Ally* (Westport, CT. Greenwood Press 1992.)

from her pocket several control crystals, components of her w/t set, and showed them to Waem (gambling that he would not realise they were in fact broken).

Waem took the bait hesitantly and agreed to release the men but first Christine would have to give her assent to three conditions on behalf of the British government. These were: that he would be shielded from the French mob, that he would be a free man and would never be imprisoned or sent to a camp, and the British would bring about his rehabilitation by notifying the Belgian and French governments that he had performed an important service to the Allies and was therefore not to be harmed.

With the tide turning decisively against the enemy, Waem was more concerned to restore his reputation and in saving his own life rather than in the final outcome of the war. He asked for the opportunity to speak to the French authorities in Digne, to assure them that he had never worked against them. He added an offer to work for the Allies, claiming he knew a lot about Germany's V1 and V2 rocket programs though how much he actually knew is questionable. Christine agreed to these conditions and once again, as she had done in Budapest, she assured Waem that she was speaking on behalf of the British government. Waem left the flat promising to contact her in an hour's time. Cammaerts recalled that when he saw the Gestapo man approach his cell he knew for certain that he was about to be stood up in front of a firing squad.

But Waem kept his word. One of his men went to the Schenck's flat and escorted Christine to a spot outside the prison. Waem arrived shortly afterwards. With him were the three astonished SOE officers, Cammaerts, Xan Fielding and Captain Sorensen, initially hesitant but more than grateful for their release and quite pleasantly startled to see a triumphant Christine and driver seated in a waiting car.

Their surprise was compounded when Waem piled into the auto with them. A short distance from the jail he asked for the car to be stopped and, accompanied by Fielding, climbed out and disappeared into a nearby woods. A few moments later he emerged wearing civilian clothes, having buried his uniform in the undergrowth. As previously agreed he was then dropped off en route to Seyne. The others hurried to the home of the Turrels where they had a joyful reunion with their friends.

The gendarme Schenck had agreed to help Christine not for altruistic reasons nor had he experienced a sudden conversion to democracy. He had instead an ulterior motive, a strong incentive to cooperate with Christine, something not mentioned in her account of this incident and which SOE never admitted to nor denied. What is missing from the official account is a million francs though others say the figure was two million. Because there is no official record of this transaction it is not clear whether she offered Schenck a bribe or if he asked for or demanded payment in return for an introduction to Waem. But Cammaerts' post-war account of this incident makes it abundantly clear that it was Schenck and his wife who received the cash rather than Max Waem.

When Christine returned to SOE HQ from her second trip Digne, and before her crucial meeting with Waem, she had contacted Brooks Richards in Algiers demanding he gather the money within twenty-four hours and have it dropped by parachute to a pre-designated spot. Brooks Richards collected the cash quickly though he never explained how he had managed it.

On the night of August 16-17, less than a day before Cammaerts' scheduled execution, the cash was packed tightly in the form of a large brick, bundled into a larger package and air-dropped near Seyne-les-Alpes. After it had been gathered up by the local maquis and handed over to Christine, she returned to Digne with the money but this time with a car and driver, so certain was she that Schenck would keep his word. Aside from this rather major omission most accounts of how she rescued Cammaerts and his colleagues from a firing squad are in agreement. Fielding's recollection differed only slightly. He recalled being taken from the barracks-prison across town to the Villa Rose, otherwise known as Gestapo headquarters, where he was interrogated just briefly. He also added that when the men got into the car with Waem Christine was not in it but was waiting to be picked up a few streets away from the prison.3.

Despite her promise to him of safe-conduct Waem was arrested by the British and taken to Nice. Some months later Christine happened to be there where she met with Colonel Dodds-Parker under whose authority Waem was being held. The French had already requested that he be turned over to them. She was furious when she learned that Dodds-Parker was about to accede to the French request. He recalled that after the war, whenever he had occasion to meet her, she curtly reminded him of this event. She never forgave him and would not entertain the possibility that they might become friends.

In a post-war interview** Cammaerts stated that when he returned to London, he and Christine met with SOE de-briefers. They raised the issue of Waem's imprisonment and demanded that he be released as promised. Cammaerts made the point that, in future, the good word of British officers would be suspect unless Waem was set free.

As it turned out Dodds-Parker did not release Waem to the French because a 'Higher Authority' intervened (not long after the London meeting). The ex-Gestapo man was freed and was permitted to travel to the Middle East. He eventually returned to Europe after the war and re-settled in Belgium. As for the bribe SOE did not want it generally known that they paid the Gestapo to have their operatives released. Their official policy was never to pay bribes but their archive reveals that there were a number of such 'exceptions'. As well as pricking SOE's pride, the idea that money had been paid to secure Cammaerts' freedom would also weaken the case for Christine's heroic persuasion.

Cammaerts added another dimension to the story by claiming that Madame Schenck was to be the beneficiary of her husband's chicanery. For some years after the war there were conflicting versions of what became of all the money. Less informed accounts claim that Waem had been paid to release the SOE operatives but he seems not to have known about the bribe for he never raised the issue with Cammaerts in their post-war correspondence. (Waem also sent condolences to Cammaerts upon hearing of Christine's death.) British authorities attempted to dilute the bribery story by boasting that the francs were all forgeries anyway, in keeping with the official policy of no negotiations with criminals.

Albert Schenck's scheming brought him no reward. Before the SOE group departed Cammaerts warned him to leave the area. Several days after Christine and her colleagues had left Digne his body was discovered in a wooded area outside the town. There was no sign of the money and no investigation was carried out into the circumstances of his death.

**Interview conducted by Slawka Wazacz for her documentary film, 'No Ordinary Countess.' 2004.

In a statement recorded after the war Cammaerts seemed to have resolved the issue of the missing francs. He had remained in France once the Germans surrendered and established permanent residence there. He was well placed to investigate the fates of those involved in his imprisonment and subsequent release. Albert Schenck, as he recalled, did pass the money to his wife who kept it until Charles de Gaulle and the 4th Republic were in place. Madame Schenck, perhaps thinking that it was now safe to make an exchange, attempted to cash in her husband's francs for the freshly minted notes of the new government. After being rebuffed by several banks she asked a British representative in Paris for help. The Foreign Office contacted Cammaerts. The bribe money turned out to be worthless but he arranged for her to get enough new francs to return to her family in Alsace.

As for SOE's stubborn refusal to admit to paying bribes, it has been reluctantly agreed that a large sum of money, counterfeit or not, did change hands. But that does not diminish in any way Christine's bold and defiant action. She had put her life on the line by going to Digne in the first instance to confront Max Waem. He could have had her arrested and shot alongside Cammaerts but his desire for self-preservation turned out to be stronger than his attachment to the Gestapo. For a few hours he had held in his hands the fate of the leaders of the Jockey Circuit and two of SOE's outstanding operatives. But Christine's vaunted persuasiveness won the day. Faced with the choice of saving himself or aiding the Germans Waem had chosen the safer option thus saving Christine's life as well as the lives of the three SOE officers. Fielding described this episode in his book *Hide and Seek* and confessed his melancholic love for Christine. But he also acknowledged that she probably preferred John Roper and wrote that he had graciously stood aside for his fellow officer.4 Not that it made any difference. Christine was in love with Cammaerts but he was unavailable to her and remained devoted to his family in his own fashion. Fielding and Roper may have been in love with her but they didn't stand a chance in comparison to Cammaerts. Ultimately however she selected a companion who would prove to be more destructive of her than the Gestapo.

Christine served in France for less than three months but this was undoubtedly her finest hour and she richly deserved the clutch of honours later awarded her. Unfortunately her post-war life was destined to be less than heroic, for both British and Polish governments treated her most shabbily in the last years of her life.

Chapter 19.
The End of a Perilous Journey

Christine's relationship with the Poles continued to be misunderstood by her SOE handlers even while in France. Colonel DJ Keswick complained to Major Ronnie Hazell, head of the country section for Poles outside Europe, that in addition to acting as Cammaerts' deputy '. . . it has turned out that like all Poles, she has congregated with other Poles, and anything that comes to hand from her in a Polish connection will of course, be passed on to you.'1

Keswick's charge is puzzling because during the brief time that Christine was in France she had not come in contact with any Poles other than the soldiers who had been persuaded to abandon the Wehrmacht. There were no Poles in Cammaerts' Jockey Circuit and there is no evidence that either of the Polish intelligence bureaux had placed operatives in southeastern France.

After making contact with the Polish men in German uniform Christine signaled London asking how to proceed. Her message was passed on to Special Projects Operations Center in Algiers (SPOC) because her contacts with these men were of interest to London as well as to Cammaerts. But to say that she 'congregated' with them is a bit of an exaggeration. She was merely following proper procedure.

Within days of the Allied landing on the shores of Provence, the American VI Corps commander General Lucian K Truscott, junior, decided to divide his forces and send a smaller, more mobile group north towards Montelimar on the Rhone river ninety miles south of Lyon. He appointed Brigadier General Frederic Butler to head an armoured and motorised column to be known as Task Force Butler. This force proceeded rapidly from the south coast as far north as the town of Sisteron on the Durance River where Butler established his command post. Upon hearing that the Americans had arrived Cammaerts and Christine drove over from Seyne to offer their services. Much to their chagrin their offer of support was thrown back in their faces by a hostile Butler without explanation. In his memoir the American general gave no reason for his rude response to Cammaerts' offer.

Butler had already made contact with the FFI and with Colonel Constans, and perhaps felt that they would provide adequate assistance. Nevertheless, there was no excuse for his boorish behaviour. There was no indication that either Cammaerts or Christine was aggressive towards him. Cammaerts was especially admired for his modesty and his soft-spoken style. As the senior officer he would have done the talking with Christine at his side. She would have been disciplined enough to maintain a dignified silence while he addressed Butler. Nevertheless, the American rejected Cammaerts' offer out of hand, saying that he had no interest in 'private armies.'

Christine was soon to suffer a second rebuff at the hands of the irritable general. In mid-August, Butler ordered Captain Thomas Piddington, in command of A Troop, to launch an assault on the wooded area of Puymaure, just outside Gap, where German forces had another large garrison. After being subjected to an artillery salvo which knocked out their radio tower the German commander sent word that he would be interested in talking terms. An exchange of emissaries took place after which the Germans agreed to surrender. Their commander and his troops gathered in the town square to hand over their weapons to the Americans. Piddington now had some 300 prisoners on his hands to add to a growing pool of more than a thousand including several hundred Poles. It was at this point that Cammaerts suggested having Christine address them and encourage them to join the Allies. At a stroke this would re-enforce Butler's troops while reducing the number of prisoners to be looked after.

After listening to Christine's rallying cry the Polish men allegedly ripped off their German tunics and offered to fight their former captors bare-chested. As is sometimes the case in Christine tales there is an alternative and more sobering version of the Poles' reaction. Citing the Geneva Convention, Christine reminded them that ex-prisoners were forbidden to fight against their erstwhile comrades while wearing the same uniforms. Christine suggested that the Poles would have to fight *torse-nu*, that is, naked from the waist up.[2]

These matters were conveyed to General Butler who would have none of it. Instead, he accused her and Cammaerts of interfering and threatened to have them arrested unless they left the area immediately. The two of them drove south to the American 7th Army headquarters to advance the argument for negotiating with the Poles. General Patch, in command, saw no merit in their case though he was not nearly as rude as Butler.

Christine and Cammaerts had now reached the end of their perilous journey. It had been a hectic summer during which they had accomplished much. With the enemy in retreat there was no longer any demand for couriers, for propaganda or for the need to stir up local resistance. SOE assigned Cammaerts to accompany the American Army B troop advancing up the west bank of the Rhone but there were no orders for Christine. There was nothing for her to do but return to London. There can be little doubt that she was very fond of Cammaerts and he apparently reciprocated her feelings. However, he had a wife and child in England anxiously awaiting his return. He would meet Christine again in London after the war but their relationship would never be the same as it had been during those dangerous but exhilarating days in France.

After bidding a melancholy good-bye to Cammaerts, Christine travelled to Avignon where SOE operatives had been summoned for their de-briefings. There she met Roper, eager to return to England and bored with waiting to be de-briefed. On impulse he, Christine and a fellow officer hitched a ride to Lyon from where they were able to catch a flight to London. She had no home to return to so Roper arranged for her to stay with his aunt, Mrs Ffrench. Roper also took a room in his aunt's house. Though he and Christine were close friends he was at pains to emphasise that they were not intimate, that he respected her and valued her as a friend.3

Christine returned briefly to France in late September. But before leaving London she had begun to make enquiries about the possibility of becoming a naturalised British subject, something she had secretly wished for since arriving in Britain in 1939. She received a reply from the Foreign Office Deputy permanent secretary informing her that an application would have to be submitted to the Home Office through the offices of a solicitor. Major Harold Perkins, head of SOE's Polish section and one of Christine's strongest supporters, thought this a careless response to someone who had worked so unselfishly in Britain's interest. He aired his feelings in a memorandum to his regional head, Colonel Keswick. At the bottom of the page he scrawled five questions: why had Christine returned to France, who sent her, what is she doing. number 4 is illegible, number 5, if we can help her, agree we should.

In the margins of the memo Keswick replied: 1. Went back with Rouget (*sic*) [Roger], 2. obtained permission from CD [Gubbins], 3. insuring R. does not get into trouble,4. Visit to France, 5. *[illegible]* with my knowledge and CD's permission. Christine obviously charmed both Keswick and Colin Gubbins who were mildly amused by her display of willfulness.4

That trip was uneventful and she returned to London in October to an uncertain future. She must have been depressed at the thought of life as a civilian in a country where she knew so few people. Andrew, her companion for the past five exciting years, was currently employed by the British military in Italy while many of her SOE colleagues were still fighting the war. A return to Poland was out of the question as she would have been arrested immediately by the NKVD. The Polish government-in-exile in London were still smoldering at her decision to become a British operative rather than join the Polish resistance. It was said that 'she sold her services to the British.' In short, she had no one to turn to and was in effect a person without a country.

Upon her return from France she submitted an account of her role in the Vercors battles. The report was classified 'confidential' and the details have not been made available to the public. She also continued to press the Home Office for naturalisation status. Cammaerts wrote a glowing reference for her, citing her courageous actions in France and added: 'I would like to insist again that the first and most important thing is to give her British nationality.' A copy of Cammaerts' report was submitted to Major Perkins who pencilled in the comment: 'good reading. I am going to make sure I keep on Christine's side in future.' His aide, Colonel Michael Pickles, added, 'So am I. She frightens me to death.'

In the run-up to D-Day, Andrew had been commissioned an Acting Captain (he was promoted to Temporary Captain three months later). He had seen no front-line duty in 1944 nor had he taken part in any covert activities. He was however selected to participate in a rather daring operation being planned in England. He, Patrick Leigh Fermor and thirty others were formed into a unit to be dropped in the vicinity of German prison camps once the D-Day landings had taken place, to prevent the slaughter of prisoners by their captors. Andrew and his small group were sent to the Sunningdale golf course in Berkshire, about twenty-five miles west of London, to prepare for the mission. But, like many other well-intentioned SOE schemes, this too was abandoned. Once the war had been concluded Kennedy, Leigh Fermor and the others were flown to Germany where, according to Leigh Fermor, 'we ended the war in Europe together by swanning into Hamburg, Flensburg and Kiel and then, deliriously into liberated Denmark.'[5]

In February 1944 Prime Minister Mikolajczyk wrote to Churchill and Roosevelt suggesting a British mission to Poland to establish contact with the AK and to assess political conditions in the country. For good measure he sent a copy of his letter to Lord Selborne* who in turn contacted Gubbins. They were both up for the proposal though their purposes differed slightly from those of the Poles. Mikolajczyk thought the mission should attempt

*Selborne was still Minister for Economic Warfare and head of SOE.

to determine the AK's need for weapons and officially sanction them as part of the Allied force on an equal footing with the Red Army. He also wanted Allied support in the event that the AK were to stage an uprising against the Germans. Lastly, he sought support for independent witnesses to corroborate the charge that the Soviets had committed atrocities upon Polish citizens.

SOE agreed to the first item but adhered to the FO line of maintaining good relations with the Soviet Union. By now even SOE had reluctantly concluded that there would be no struggle with the USSR for Polish independence. SOE also wanted to discourage a general uprising and preferred that the AK support the Red Army against the Germans rather than declare itself an equal partner.

Andrew had remained in London after his own mission to protect concentration camp prisoners had been aborted and was drawn into the discussions over Mikolajczyk's proposal. In early 1944 he invited the legendary courier from Warsaw, Jan Nowak, to meet with him at the Wellington Club.** The purpose, according to Nowak, was to solicit his opinion regarding the proposed mission. It was not readily apparent to the courier that Andrew was acting on behalf of SOE but it is unlikely that he would have discussed such a mission with Nowak unless authorised by senior Executive officers. Andrew acknowledged that he and the leadership shared the view that such a delegation would be of considerable value but 'were encountering opposition within the British government.'

Between February and September memoranda concerning Mikolajczyk's proposals were circulated within Whitehall and meetings held to iron out what were minor dis-

**See Nowak's memoir *Courier from Warsaw* (Detroit: Wayne State University Press 1982)

agreements between the government and SOE. In September Churchill finally authorised the mission which was assigned the cryptonym Freston. Additionally there were to be three sub-groups who would enter Poland as observers once the main group, led by Lieutenant Colonel DT (Bill) Hudson, had established a makeshift HQ. The sub-missions were each assigned cryptonyms beginning with the letter F. Once word leaked out that a team was being assembled for a mission to Poland, Christine and Andrew quickly volunteered their services. Each was assigned to a separate team of three operatives. She however was authorised to act independently and was given the cryptonym Folkestone. As a measure of how highly SOE valued her she was to have her own cyphers and would be treated as an entirely separate operation. She was to be Colonel Hudson's assistant and would be the designated courier, maintaining contact between the three other missions.

It was put to Hudson that she would be charged 'with the duty of snooping on your behalf.' That is to say, she was to report to Freston and the other sub-missions her observations on political conditions in Poland and what plans the AK had for such matters as cooperation with the Red Army. Once again she was treading a fine line between acting in the interests of Britain and those of her own country. In her defense it could be said that in the long run she would be doing what she and SOE thought would benefit Poland.

Perkins impressed upon Freston the importance of making the AK understand the British position, that is, why they were not willing to attempt to wrest control of Poland from the Soviet Union. 'It is realised that the Poles in Poland may be ill-informed on political conditions both in this country and also on the conditions ruling in world-wide politics to-day. All parties will therefore try to bring the Poles to an understanding of these conditions perhaps broader than they may have gathered from their own Governmental sources.'6

SOE placed the highest confidence in Christine and her knowledge of Polish politics. 'There is no question about it whatever that she is better informed on Polish political conditions in this country than almost any other single personality. . . . ' There can be little doubt that she convinced SOE of her insider's knowledge on the subject. But the fact is she had had little direct contact with Poland's ministers. Their government's intelligence bureaux, still unsure of where her loyalties lay, were unlikely to take her into their confidence. She undoubtedly had strong opinions about the London government and its plans for the future but perhaps SOE relied upon her opinions more than it should have.

The FO also depended on Christine's assessment because by its own admission '. . . we can no longer trust Polish Governmental sources in this country.' Given that the British had declined to confront Stalin on the issue of Polish independence, it is not surprising that the Poles were reluctant to confide in the Churchill government.

To facilitate her involvement in Operation Freston, Christine was promoted from Civilian Agent, MP Section, to Flight Officer in the WAAF (Women's Auxiliary Air Force), subject to vetting. In November 1944 the Air Ministry informed Christine of her Honorary Commission, adding that she was not to receive an 'outfit allowance' out of Air Force funds. She met with Prime Minister Mikolajczyk to discuss the mission and was then vetted, properly this time, at an SOE office in Bayswater. The operative there was told to ask what assurances she had given the Gestapo agent Max Waem. SOE were anxious to learn if she had put anything in writing, specifically, had she committed the government to look after him once the war was over. Her earlier, unauthorised commitment to the Musketeers were no doubt still fresh in their minds.

While waiting to be flown to Italy from where she would continue on to Poland, Christine took care of personal business. Acknowledging the hazardous nature of her mission, she left directions for the disposal of her personal effects and whatever money was due her in the event that she was to be taken prisoner, or worse. Her financial arrangements, and presumably those of the other teams, were to be looked after by Major Michael Pickles. An undefined sum was to be sent to her aunt, the Countess Helena Zaranska in France. She also made provision for her second husband, Jerzy Gizycki, requesting that money from her outstanding salary cheques should be sent to him, care of the Polish Consulate in Montreal. She left behind two diamonds with a declared value of £80.16.8.

Gizycki, who had acted so gallantly in occupied Europe, was now employed as superintendent of the Polish Home in Montreal, a shelter for Polish war refugees. He received his meals, lodging and a small monthly stipend for his services. His financial situation was adequate but not precarious. But there would be no return to the exciting days of the war.

Christine's personal business included submitting a claim to the Department of Finance for the personal belongings she'd lost when she had parachuted into France. The claim was rejected because it was 'out of all proportion to any claim for such losses which can be allowed on public funds inasmuch as the items included therein are on a luxury scale both as to quality and quantity.'[7] The official who handled her claim added the gratuitous comment that her annual tax-free salary was already on the high scale 'for a female agent.'

In her compensation claim she had asked to be reimbursed for her silk lingerie, lost when the parachute carrying her personal belongings failed to open over the Vercors, destroying everything when it hit the ground at speed. She was not a slavish follower of fashion and spent little time shopping but was nevertheless always well-dressed and well-groomed befitting her status as an officer and a member of the Polish gentry. The loss of her undergarments must have been quite upsetting. Years later the story of her claim for the lingerie reimbursement somehow found its way into the pages of *The Financial Times* (24-25/8/1996) in the midst of a longer piece about SOE.

While preparations for Operation Freston were ongoing Christine was recommended for one of Britain's highest honours, Officer of the Order of the British Empire (OBE). The recommendation had come from the office of Field Marshal Alexander and was made to the Under-Secretary of State, War Office. General Stawell, who had initiated the process, had actually recommended her for the George Cross.

The recommendation, made in December 1944, was accompanied by details of Christine's missions, in particular her work in France. Field Marshal Alexander's letter ended with this paean to her character: 'The nerve, coolness, and devotion to duty and high courage of this lady which inspired and brought to a successful conclusion an astonishing *coup de main* must certainly be considered as one of the most remarkable personal exploits of the war, and in the particular circumstances . . . '8 Colonel Buckmaster and other officers submitted letters of support.

Christine departed for SOE's Polish base at Bari together with her old chum Captain

Roper just after Christmas 1944, having been cleared for Operation Freston. There was of course a reunion with Andrew who was struck by how much thinner she had become. She was assigned a well-appointed room at the Imperial Hotel in nearby Monopoli while he and the other male officers had to endure life in a wind-swept barracks.

Freston's commander, Colonel Hudson, and his team who had been in Bari since October, had to put up with innumerable delays over a period of three months because of bad weather. Their frustrations occasionally boiled over and there were sharp exchanges with the officers looking after them. It was not until Christmas night that the cloud cover lifted enough for Freston to commence. The mission got off to an inauspicious start. The team were dropped too close to the ground in southwestern Poland and some of the men suffered minor injuries. But with a bit of luck they were able to establish contact with Polish partisans in the Czestochowa-Krakow area.

Things did not go as well as planned for Hudson and his team though they had not expected their mission to be trouble-free. At one point they exchanged gunfire with a group of German tanks and nearly got caught up in a firefight between German and Russian troops. Profoundly aware of their precarious position, Hudson wired General Kopanski in London suggesting that the sub-missions be held back but requesting that Christine and Andrew be sent in. Kopanski conferred with SOE and it was agreed that those two should remain in Italy for the time being.

It was a fortuitous decision, for shortly afterwards the Freston team encountered a Russian brigade. They were initially welcomed but within hours of their meeting the entire team was taken prisoner, accused of spying. After being held under house arrest they were moved around Poland, bivouacked in private homes commandeered by the NKVD. Conditions gradually began to deteriorate. Finally, Colonel Hudson demanded to be put in touch with senior Russian officials.

In February 1945 their hosts announced that the team would be released but instead they were flown to Lvov and from there to Moscow. Late one night they were visited by an official from the British Embassy and while arrangements were being made to get them out of Russia they were billeted in more comfortable surroundings. Finally, in April, nearly four months after they had left Italy they were flown to Cairo and then back to London.

Operation Freston had not accomplished what it had set out to do. But the team were able to gather a least some knowledge of the military - political situation in Poland. Most importantly they were able to confirm that Stalin had no intention of cooperating with the Armia Krajowa nor was he planning to surrender an inch of Polish soil.

This was to be Christine's last opportunity to re-enter her homeland and her final mission, aborted as it was, as an SOE operative. The next six years would be spent moving from place to place, from job to job. The truth of the matter is that without the chaos and excitement of war she was completely rudderless.

Despite her heroic efforts and the many lives she saved, Christine's name is largely missing from accounts of Poland's role in the Allied victory over Germany. Halik Kochanski's encyclopedic account (2012) of Poland's contribution to the Allied triumph makes no mention of her. The massive two-volume *Intelligence Co-operation between Poland and Great Britain during World War II* (2005) consists of more than a thousand pages of documents but only a few biographical paragraphs about Christine.

The Elusive Madame G

Andrew Kennedy in Munich c 1985 seated in his Mercedes Benz roadster.
Photo with permission of Jan Tyszkiewicz

The Elusive Madame G.

Dennis George Muldowney who murdered Christine in June 1952. He was hanged at Pentonville Prison in September 1952.
Photo with permission of The National Archives.

The Elusive Madame G

The Shellbourne Hotel in London, scene of Christine's murder. The hotel near to the Cromwell Road has since been re-named. In May 1957 Christine's friend Teresa Lubienska was stabbed to death in the nearby Gloucester Road Underground station.

The Elusive Madame G

Christine's grave, center, in St Mary's Catholic Cemetery, north London. Andrew Kennedy's remains are buried beneath the plaque in the foreground. The grave site has since been refurbished (2013) by the Polish Heritage Society and the Polish Embassy in London.

Part V. 1945 - 1952

Chapter 20. Surplus to Establishment

All the news coming out of Poland now was bad. Warsaw remained a ruin after the failed Uprising (August 1st - October 2nd 1944). Red Army patrols and NKVD agents were roaming the battered streets, killing members of the AK. Christine was bitterly disappointed at having been denied the opportunity to re-enter her homeland because of the failure of Operation Freston. Andrew thought it an appropriate time for them to have a brief holiday, to get some relief from the steady flow of news of tragedies. He also had it in mind to propose marriage once again.

He made arrangements for their trip, eagerly looking forward to springing a surprise on Christine. Before he could deliver the good news she pre-empted him by announcing matter-of-factly that she was leaving for Cairo almost immediately, having decided to take up an offer of a job with the Movements Section of GHQ. She gave no reason for this abrupt *volte-face* and he was unable to convince her to change her mind or even to postpone the trip.

Christine never confided to anyone the reason for her sudden decision but it was not merely because of his brief fling in London. With the end of the war only a few months away she must have realised that the exhilaration of the past few years would never be repeated, not for her. She was also painfully aware that she would not see Poland in the near future, if ever again. At that moment her own future must have looked very bleak indeed. There was nothing that the devoted Andrew could say or do to lift her spirits.

On January 6, 1945 Major Perkins put forward a proposal that Christine should be awarded the George Medal rather than the OBE because the former would emphasise her gallantry. He also suggested that perhaps she should be considered for the recently created Courage in the Cause of Freedom medal.

In that same month, by which time Christine was at work in Cairo, the Maryland mission* in Monopoli received a telegram addressed to her, breaking the news that her brother Andrzej had been discovered in a German POW camp and that he was well. His presence there has given credence to the assertion that he fought with the AK. Once the Uprising had begun to disintegrate many of Warsaw's civilians joined in the desperate battle and perhaps this is when Andrzej entered the conflict. But he is not listed as one of AK's regulars. It is remarkable that he survived at all, not simply because of the fierce fighting in the streets and sewers of Warsaw but because of his Jewish ancestry. That alone should have marked him out for death in the gas chambers. But in the chaotic aftermath of the failed Rising his religious background had apparently been overlooked.

When the smoke had finally cleared over the battered capital the vicious and methodical victors had tried to separate civilian prisoners from military personnel. Given the shambolic conditions resulting from the prolonged fighting some camps contained a mixture of both. Andrzej was discovered in one of these and eventually released only to die five years later. His life in Poland after the war could not have been very pleasant, for in

*Maryland was the code name for Massingham's advance HQ in Italy.

addition to his poor health he was also arrested and imprisoned by the new communist regime. He died in 1950 apparently from tuberculosis.

The news of Andrzej's survival was eventually forwarded to Christine but it took some time to reach her. In March, Perkins sent a note with the news about her brother and expressed his regrets at the collapse of the Freston mission. She replied in a lengthy, rambling letter thanking him for all the news and adding that she had sent her brother a parcel but added nothing further. There is no anecdotal evidence that she enjoyed a post-war reunion with him, certainly not in Poland.

In the same letter she conveyed to Perkins her gratitude for his continued support and for breaking the news, in a gentle way, about the collapse of the mission to Poland. This three-page melancholy letter, written in large but easy to read script, is one of the few surviving examples of Christine's handwriting. It also revealed the state of her mind at the time - anxious but hopeful, willing to do anything but uneasy about her future.

She had recently applied to join the RAF and in this letter asked Perkins to write them and say that she was 'an honest and clean polish (*sic*) girl.' She expressed the desire to parachute into Germany and help in the release of prisoners from camps and from prisons 'before they get shot.' She was emphatic about doing this: 'I should love to do it and I like to jump out of a plane even every day. Please, Perks, if it's not for your section - maybe somebody's else.' Apparently she had heard from Andrew that he was training for just such a mission. 'Please do look after Andrew and don't let him do anything too stupid.' She also asked if Perkins had heard from Gizycki to whom she was still married, and asked him to look after old lover.

In the middle of her letter she suddenly switched to a lighter tone, inserting the news that 'I have become very fond of Henry . . . We were getting along very well together.' This was a reference to Lieutenant Colonel Henry Threlfall, head of SOE's 'Torment' mission in Italy as well as chief of SOE's Polish Station at Monopoli. He was rumoured to be yet another of her exaggerated legion of lovers. She closed the letter by sending her regards to Gubbins and to all her friends in the Polish SOE section.

Christine's letter is *angst*-ridden, as if she feared her own death to be imminent. She asked about those closest to her as well as offering her support to Gardyne de Chastelain who had been ordered to appear before a court of enquiry in connection with his alleged mis-handling of Romanian affairs.1 She had already passed on to him a letter of support from one of his colleagues and insisted that it was the safest way of making the delivery.

Christine continued to pursue her application for naturalisation throughout 1945. Not everyone in government knew of her exploits and those who did know weren't always terribly impressed. One civil servant responded to a query by denying any knowledge of her application. He surmised that she had taken the name Granville in order to obtain a commission 'as they would not commission a Polish subject.' He closed on a note of indifference saying, 'I believe she was an agent in France before she took on her latest mission.'

For months civil servants and Christine's SOE friends continued to quibble over the merits of her case for naturalisation. In late January Major General JHF Lakin wrote a stiff note to the Air Ministry, saying that she was *not* in the process of becoming a British subject. He protested that there was no way that she could become naturalised, given that 'she is the wife of an alien.' This implied that her posting with the Movements Section could only be temporary. She must have been painfully aware of the transitory nature of her job, for the correspondence in her Personal File indicates that she had no career plans then, not even for the immediate future. There are some poignant remarks in her letters, indicating that with the war drawing to a close, she was sadly aware that her days of living dangerously would soon be over and she would be faced with the banality of civilian life.

 Christine began to tie up loose ends in preparation for the end of her intelligence career, something that she obviously did not relish. She wrote to Major Pickles in February asking if he would see to it that Major Xan Fielding, whom she had rescued from a German prison along with Cammaerts, be paid £150 from her account. This was repayment an earlier loan from him. She closed the letter with the plea, 'Please do remember me and find a good job for me as soon as possible.' This forlorn tone is also present in the long note (March 15) she wrote to Major Perkins: 'Please, please do not forget about me altogether.' A significant part of her life was now coming to a close and the thought must have frightened her.

 Perkins's reply (March 25) was frank and sympathetic. He told her in the very first paragraph that her prospects for inclusion in any operational matters, then or in the in the near future, were 'exceedingly bleak.' He repeated the bad news about Freston, writing that 'the operation in Italy had fallen through', and that all sub-missions including hers had been scrubbed. 'In view of the unhappy position of Poland there is obviously no possibility of an operational mission to that country.'

 Perkins added that it would not be possible to send female personnel either to

Germany or to the Far East, and that only British nationals were being considered for operations in Scandinavia. He sympathised with her dislike for office work and, obviously lacking any concrete suggestions, asked Christine to suggest something. She had been cleared to return to Britain but Perkins acknowledged that she would probably prefer to remain in Cairo. He assured her that her financial situation would be secure for at least three more months and that even afterwards she would receive some form of subsistence pay from the government. He passed on the news that Andrew was to return to London prior to being posted to West Germany where he would begin working with displaced persons, and perhaps assist with the interrogation of prisoners. Finally, he assured Christine that all efforts were being made to secure naturalisation for her and for Andrew but added that in all likelihood it would not be granted until after the conclusion of the war.

For the time being Christine remained an RAF Flight Officer with only general duties. Her friend Lieutenant Colonel Julian Dolbey, who had tried so hard to get Operation Kris off the ground, met her in Cairo in April. Afterwards he wrote to Colonel Keswick, assuring him that she had been informed that her services were no longer required, that it had been done in a tactful manner.

Dolbey's tact notwithstanding, she about to be cast adrift. Of course many thousands of military personnel were about to experience the same fate but she was a stranger in England as well as being unwelcome in the land of her birth. As far as the British bureaucracy were concerned she was just another alien. Some, like Xan Fielding whose life she had saved in France, complained bitterly that the government had treated her unfairly. Still, it was in no position financially to single out individuals for special treatment at a time when so many were so desperately poor.

Christine knew few people in London and many of her SOE colleagues were still in Europe. Those who had been de-mobbed had returned to their homes across Britain to restart their lives. Friends who met her in the years immediately following the war were convinced that she was depressed despite her cheerful demeanour. Upon returning to London she gravitated towards the borough of Kensington where a large number of Poles had settled and had established their clubs

Christine told Dolbey that 'the Poles' had approached her to work for them without specifying who 'they' might be. Dolbey admitted to Keswick that she was prone to exaggerate but he believed the offer to be genuine. The unnamed Poles supposedly wanted to make use of the knowledge she had accumulated during her years with SOE. If they did employ her, it would be something of a propaganda coup for them because they could claim her as 'a discarded British agent' who has been thrown away, 'having served its [SOE] purpose.'[2]

Despite Dolbey's assertion that Christine's discharge had been handled tactfully, documents in her PF contradict him. A note from the Air Ministry to the chairman of the Personnel Board reads in part, 'It now appears she [Christine] is no longer wanted and I have been asked to take the necessary action to transfer her to the Agents' Pool w.e.f [with effect from] . . . . Unless we have a job in the offing . . . it would be a simpler matter to arrange for her to resign her commission and to go back to that civilian life from whence she came.'

Action was finally taken a week later. Wing Commander JS Redding wrote to the secretary of state for Air, 'I have the honour to inform you that Flt./O C Granville, 9914 is no longer employed by us in a capacity where she requires officer's status. I shall be glad, therefore, if you will cancel her appointment to an honorary commission (w.e.f.)'. The language was probably standard for government bureaucracy of the day but it does seems unnecessarily harsh. The Air Ministry seemed in a bit of a rush to get rid of Christine as though having her in an WAAF uniform was somehow an embarrassment.

There were those too within SOE ranks who were happy to wash their hands of this troublesome woman. Colonel Terence Maxwell wrote to Dolbey, 'I have gone into the question very carefully and it does not seem to me that there can be any harm in her obtaining employment with her own people; in fact this would seem an admirable solution for her future.' Maxwell did not think the Poles would gain any propaganda value by employing Christine as a 'discarded' SOE agent.

Dolbey however would not be put off. He appealed to the Department of Finance, pointing out that she did not have a job and had no means of support. Furthermore, in order for her to find employment she would need identity papers which she lacked except for her WAAF card. He asked that something be done to 'regularise the situation.'

Once again Christine found herself being torn between remaining in Cairo or returning to London though her options now were distinctly limited. There were those who thought it wrong for her to 'be loose' in Cairo with WAAF identity documents, as her commission had been cancelled in May. Colonel EPF Boughey ordered Dolbey to withdraw from her those documents and replace them with civilian ones. He added that it would be unwise for her to return to London where she was still regarded with suspicion by many exiled Poles whereas she had friends in Cairo who might help her find employment. Boughey was perhaps unaware that the Egyptians wanted the British out of their country, that Christine would be thought of as one of them and therefore equally despised.

Her position seemed impossible. Boughey insisted that he had investigated the question of her naturalisation and 'that it is absolutely out of the question at present.' He did not elaborate and Christine was officially notified on June 21 that she must resign her WAAF commission. She was being tossed about like an unwanted bundle just as she had been after Major Wilkinson sacked her from SOE. No one would take responsibility for her and no one had any sensible solution to offer. After she had been de-commissioned Perkins received a note saying, '... She is therefore now surplus to Establishment. Would you please take the necessary action to transfer her to another Establishment.'

Efforts were being made by SOE and by War Office officials to detach Christine from their respective departments as if she were an embarrassing relative. In late June, Major Pickles reminded the Department of Finance that it had agreed to pay her for three more months and that period had now expired. He insisted that her position be clarified and that this should be explained to Andrew Kennedy 'who appears to operate in this country as her agent.' He had joined with the others to demand fair play for Christine, both in terms of her salary and her application for naturalisation. Without the latter obtaining permanent employment in Britain or in one of the colonies would be impossible.

Pickles also dealt with the rumour that unnamed Poles wanted to employ her for the express purpose of embarrassing the British government who had 'discarded a British agent.' He offered the opinion that ordinary Poles had the right to be looked after by their government but that she had forfeited that right by working for the British. They therefore were obliged to provide her with maintenance until she could get her life sorted out.

Pickles suggested to the DF that Christine be continued on half-pay until the end of the year and that the should arrangement cease after December 31, 1945. His suggestion was approved, leaving Christine about six months to obtain naturalisation papers and to find employment. Pickles wrote to her, care of the Gezira Sporting Club, informing her of this arrangement and offered his best wishes for success.

Unfortunately, this wasn't the end of the matter. In July Christine applied for a position with BOAC (British Overseas Air Corporation), predecessor to British Airways. The British Consul in Cairo notified London regarding her application, stating that as she had no passport she could not be considered for employment. BOAC questioned her nationality and warned that without a British passport and/or visas she could not remain in Cairo. Furthermore she could not reside in any British territory including Britain itself. As she could not return to Poland, she was truly a woman without a country. The sacrifices she had made for the British had brought her no reward except for the honours which in themselves did not guarantee her domicile in the UK. She grew increasingly angry at the bureaucracy and was minded to reject the George Cross and the OBE, for what good would they do her?

Julian Dolbey was told that her application for naturalisation could not possibly be dealt with until sometime in 1946. Moreover, if she were to lose her job with the Movements Section she would probably be obliged to leave Egypt with no guarantee of a job or living quarters elsewhere. It seems more than churlish that, for all the risks she had taken on behalf of Britain, its government were not even willing to lobby the Polish government-in-exile to provide her either with income or employment.

In November Dolbey heard that another attempt to secure favourable treatment from the Home Office would be made. But he was reminded that despite the honours Christine had been awarded she could not be moved to the head of the queue of refugees from across Europe anxious to be naturalised. Everyone who had ever met her was now being marshalled for an assault on the Home Office to hasten the approval of her application.

Still the bureaucrats continued to thwart her. One civil servant complained that she had not resided in Britain for the requisite five years, ignoring the obvious fact that residence had been rendered impossible by the nature of her duties as an SOE operative. This verdict was contradicted near the end of the month by the sensible news that 'residence and service qualifications are interchangeable . . . ' Therefore she qualified and was able to proceed with her application.

Upon receipt of a summary of her war-time exploits Dolbey wrote to several government departments, including the British embassy in Cairo, recommending that she be given whatever assistance required. Dolbey also added the frank reminder, 'You must also remember that her English is not perfect, that she cannot type, has no experience whatever of office work and altogether is not a very easy person to employ.'3

A movement was now under way to award Christine the George Cross.* The citation accompanying the recommendation states definitively that she attempted to cross into Poland four times, not the rumoured six or fifteen. It also clarified the details of her encounter with the Slovak border guards.

The same citation made clear that, from the very beginning of her employment by Section D, she had been asked to collect and transmit intelligence from Poland and not simply smuggle propaganda materials into the country. The list of witnesses to her achievements was lengthy and was drawn mainly from those with whom she had served in France. While SOE were preparing to recommend Christine for her heroism her friends had become concerned about her fate. But there appeared to be little they could do to help.

Though Dolbey proved to be a great friend to Christine he was also partly responsible for the rumour that the Polish government in London had declared her 'persona non grata.' That may have been the case but she had no difficulty in securing a meeting with Prime Minister Mikolajczyk while preparing for Operation Kris.

*The George Cross is the highest honour awarded to civilians for courage in extreme circumstances. The George Medal is awarded to military personnel for gallantry and distinguished conduct.

Chapter 21.
Missed Opportunities

Julian Dolbey once again took matters into his own hands in the quest to facilitate the processing of Christine's naturalisation application. He discovered quite by accident that a serving British officer could act as a commissioner of oaths. He therefore had Christine swear her oath of allegiance to the Crown in his presence. On the advice of a solicitor she signed the document 'Christine Granville', thus discarding forever her identity as Krystyna Skarbek. In 1946 her application was finally approved though it would take another year to acquire a passport. In the meantime she remained in Cairo. Andrew became a British subject the following year.

It was now suggested that, instead of the George Cross, Christine should be awarded the George Medal for her heroism in France. The recommendation was approved in June 1945 and two years later her nomination to receive the OBE was also approved

Unable to return to Poland to file for divorce from Jerzy Gizycki, she travelled with Andrew to West Berlin, as it was then, where her petition was granted in August 1946. Though she had previously turned down, or ignored, Andrew's suggestion that they marry, it wasn't until the 1st of August that she requested and received permission to contract a marriage to him. The application was made and approved by the Polish Military Mission,

Consular Department, and witnessed by Cammaerts who then held the rank of lieutenant colonel in the military's food and agricultural department.

Prior to that a married woman was 'debarred' from divorcing her husband unless she had proof of his death. Lacking that, Christine asserted in a notarised statement that Gizycki had abandoned her in 1942, that he gave her no financial support and that his whereabouts were presently unknown. Two of those three claims were false. He and Christine had been separated by their respective assignments, not by choice. For most of the war years she had been cohabiting with Andrew Kennedy and had carried on other affairs. Gizycki had lived alone as far as anyone knew and was intent on resuming their married life after the war. She was the one who had asked to terminate their relationship.

Secondly, when Christine signed that notarised statement she knew quite well Gizycki's whereabouts. In preparation for the aborted Operation Freston she had requested that any money due her should be sent to him at the Polish hostel for immigrants in Montreal where he was employed. The only true statement was that he had not provided her with financial support. Though her application for permission to marry Andrew had been approved they never wed in Berlin or in any other city.

In another of the many near-misses that dogged her career she was almost reunited with Patrick Howarth which would have vastly improved her morale. Her former Cairo section chief had been posted to the British Embassy in Warsaw. When Christine heard the news she immediately cabled him, asking if she could be of assistance in some way. Howarth spoke to the British ambassador, William Cavendish-Bentinck (9th Duke of

Portland 1897-1990), who seemed agreeable to have her come on staff but the Foreign Office threw a damper on her hopes, rejecting the ambassador's request without comment.

Howarth himself was to have a strange encounter in Warsaw with a character out of Christine's past. While crossing a congested street one afternoon he was struck by a Red Army lorry. His injuries were not life-threatening but he was temporarily hospitalised. One of his visitors was none other than Gustaf Getlich, Christine's first husband. He and Howarth had never met and it is unlikely that Getlich knew anything about him as he had not maintained a correspondence with Christine. Yet, either by coincidence or by design he visited the hospital where he met Howarth for the first and only time. They must have exchanged some interesting views on Christine but neither revealed what was said.1

With her new passport in hand Christine flew off to Geneva where she had secured a job interview. She was embarrassed to be told at the outset that, though she held a British passport, she was still considered a foreigner. She returned to Germany and enjoyed a brief visit with Andrew in Bonn where he was then employed by the Military Government's Food Office (21 Army Group) investigating black-market activities in West Germany.2 He announced then that he planned to settle there, an intention which did not go down well with her. Though she had repeatedly turned down his marriage proposals, she still felt the need to exert some control over his decisions and sulked when he remained determined to pursue his own goals.

From Bonn she travelled to the Haute Savoie in southern France where she stayed for a short time with her aunt Helena. She worked briefly in an estate agent's office, or so

Andrew has said, but found it not to her liking. Given her extraordinary powers of persuasion it would seem that she would have done remarkably well as a salesperson. She returned instead to London where a surprise of sorts awaited her. A source known only to Christine had bequeathed her a house in the city. True to her contrary nature she declined this generous gift without comment. Vladimir Ledochowski, her one-time lover, speculated in his memoir that the house had been left her by a married British colonel with whom she allegedly had an affair in Cairo. Though he did not name him, Vladimir was certain that he had died while on a mission to Yugoslavia. He surmised that she rejected the offer because the officer's family were certain to ask who she was and what she had done to deserve such generosity. Andrew too might be more than curious as to the source of her good fortune.[3]

Christine seemed unable to make a decision about her future. She had not given any serious thought to a career of any sort before the war despite her claim that she had been a journalist. Post-war, she did not adjust well to civilian life in a foreign country. Most of her friends were Poles in similar straits with whom she met frequently at the Marynka Cafe (234 Brompton Road), across from the Victoria and Albert Museum, or at *Ognisko Polskie* (Polish Hearth Club) a members' club and dining room in Princes' Gate.

The next three years were characterised by peripatetic movements that took her from London to Europe to North Africa and back to London again. She stubbornly refused to use her SOE connections, and her outstanding war record, to influence potential employers. Before beginning her travels she took on a series of menial jobs. She was first employed as a telephone operator at India House, an officers' club in Park Lane. However, a Polish friend, also employed at the club, thought that she had worked as a cleaner.

From India House she moved on to Harrod's who reportedly sacked her for being rude to a customer. Harrod's has always insisted that it had no employment record for anyone by the names of Christine Granville or Gizycki or Skarbek. From the world of retail she moved down the employment ladder to the position of seamstress at a Paddington hotel. Quite unexpectedly she received a letter in June 1947 from Michael Dunford whom she had known in Cairo. He had been a radar specialist and worked for the British Council after the war. They had first met at a crowded cocktail party in Shepheard's Hotel where he saw Christine surrounded by her many admirers. He was immediately captivated but lost her, a least for the evening, to a dashing Serb pilot with whom she left the party. Dunford suppressed his feelings for Christine but did not forget her.

Dunford, CMG, MC, told her that after his discharge from the Scots Guards he planned to settle in Kenya. Much to his surprise Christine, whose attempts to become a naturalised British resident were being frustrated by Home Office bureaucrats, impulsively replied that she would like to join him. Dunford has been described as one of her numerous lovers though he never made such a claim. But they frequently travelled together so the assumption has been made that they were in fact intimate. Virginia Cowles and Aidan Crawley saw them together occasionally and recalled that when in Kenya Christine stayed at the New Stanley Hotel in Nairobi while he remained in his home. From what little is known about their time together it seems she never gave herself wholeheartedly to him.

While grateful for Dunford's generosity she did not assume that he would support her for she was not about to surrender her cherished independence. She applied for a position with Kenyan Airlines but her application was rejected by the Colonial Office. Officials there suggested that since she carried a British passport, perhaps she should return to Britain.

Christine finally received her George Medal, OBE badge (Civilian Division) and the War Medal from the British consulate who had tracked her to Nairobi. The War Medal held four stars for service in Africa, France, Italy and Germany though she had not served in the last-named country. But her conflict with Kenyan Airlines had upset her to such a degree that she threatened to refuse all the honours. Only the intervention of the RAF commander in Kenya convinced her to change her mind. The governor of Kenya made the presentation at a low-key ceremony held at Government House in Nairobi. To assuage her feelings she was also given permission to remain in the country. Armed with that assurance she again applied for a position with the airline only to be rebuffed a second time. She alleged that the official who interviewed her had rudely asked why she hadn't bothered to return to her Poland. Insulted and infuriated Christine threatened to sue the airline.

Following this humiliating episode she flew back to London where she met Andrew who soothed her feelings of outrage and convinced her not to destroy her passport or medals. Together they approached Crawley whom they had last seen in Sofia. Thanks to his intercession she became one of that vast army of refugees known as 'Citizens of Great Britain and the Colonies,' thus protecting her from immediate deportation. In an interview years later Crawley re-enforced what most of her friends already knew, namely that Christine was 'very attractive to men but not so much interested in women.'

Throughout her brief relationship with Dunford Christine kept in touch with Andrew, seemingly oblivious to the strength of Dunford's feelings for her. She even invited him to join her in Kenya which must have rankled the hesitant Dunford. Andrew declined the invitation, preferring the unpredictable climate and cultural life of Europe. She was put off by his refusal but they were unexpectedly reunited when he was injured in an auto accident. She immediately flew to West Germany to be with him. He recovered quickly but they remained together for only a short while.

Francis Cammaerts contended that Christine had many job offers in the late 1940s. One such offer came from an agency run by a former naval officer whom Cammaerts did not name. One man who fits that description was Ian Fleming who was then foreign manager for Kelmsley Newspapers. Many of the stringers and freelance journalists he employed were former intelligence officers like Edward Howe who had allegedly suggested that Christine should apply to Fleming for a job.

Cammaerts did not describe these job offers and she apparently never seriously considered any of them. She had however decided not to return to Kenya and to Dunford. He had sensed that his guest was restless and never attempted to dissuade her from traveling. He was not possessive of Christine, not that she would have permitted it, and never interfered with her plans, such as they were. In retrospect he made the correct decision in not tying himself too closely to her.

A business opportunity, more for Andrew's benefit than for Christine's, arrived out of the blue. One of her numerous Cairo friends contacted her to announce that he and a partner in Australia had decided to open a string of automobile sales agencies. Those two men were the Serb pilot George Michalov, reputedly one of Christine's Cairo lovers, and an Australian pilot Norman Hamilton. She at once saw this as an opportunity for Andrew and a chance to repay him for the support he had given her over the years.

They immediately took steps to secure their own involvement in the fledgling business. Andrew knew a number of businessmen in Germany and began making contacts with an eye toward managing several such agencies in the western half of the country. During the next few months he occasionally met Christine in London where they began to develop a business plan of their own. For a time it looked as though they might possibly be reunited in way that he hadn't anticipated. Their application for a marriage license, made in West Berlin, seems to have been forgotten.

A letter in Andrew's PF describes a tentative offer of financial assistance in getting the business up and running. The letter-writer's name has been excised by government officials but there is one clue in the letter that points to Dolbey as the author. Commenting on Christine's success in obtaining a divorce from Gizycki, Dolbey (if it was him) told Andrew about a lunch meeting with Paul Harker, 'who incidentally brought me a letter from Christine'. Harker had been selected for the Operation Fernham team in 1944 along with Andrew, part of the larger Operation Freston. In 1947 they had worked together in the Military Government of the North Rhine Province, F[ood] & A[griculture] Office, in Bonn.

Dolbey remarked, 'I should now be able to press forward with her naturalisation.' He of course had been going all out to to assist her in this matter. He wrote of hearing that Andrew had a project in mind to be established near Nairobi, 'and that this project would be considerably assisted if certain finances were to be put at your disposal. I want you to write quite frankly how much will see you both clear, on your feet, and able to carry out your project? I do not promise to assist, but as you know, I feel a great moral obligation to both Christine and yourself and I will do what I can to assist.'

Things were definitely looking up for the couple for the first time in many months. While awaiting their prospective partners to arrive from Australia they took a holiday in France, arriving at the Vercors plateau in time to participate in a commemorative ceremony. Of course the survivors of that great battle fondly remembered 'Madame Pauline' and treated her as a local hero. They returned to Germany brimming with optimism only to have their hopes for a successful business dashed. The combination of a Europe-wide recession and a falling out between the two Australian partners put paid to their dreams.

Depressed, Christine returned once again to London. She spent the next few months rekindling relationships with Polish friends and occasionally met with Cammaerts, Howarth and Roper whenever they were in town. Friends later recalled that during this period she seemed distracted, uncertain of what to do with herself. Her sister-in-law Irena described Christine's letters as lacking in 'the optimism of earlier correspondence. The post-war correspondence is filled with bitterness, but also hope that the future would bring events which would change her life for the better.'[4]

Her lack of concentration nearly had severe consequences for while crossing Hyde Park Corner one summer day in 1951, she was hit by a taxi. Fortunately it had not been traveling at speed and she suffered no life-threatening injuries. However, she did sustain a head injury of some sort. When Polish student Teresa Myskow first met her Christine's hair had been cut very short and her head was swathed in bandages.

Myskow had won a scholarship to study at Battersea Polytechnic (now the University of Surrey, Guildford) and met Christine in London quite by chance. Myskow's Polish stepfather had once owned a restaurant in pre-war Lvov. After the war, and after his release from a Soviet gulag, he and several Polish officers opened a moderately priced establishment opposite Selfridge's in Oxford Street. Its menu consisted mainly of Polish dishes but the partners soon realised that concessions had to be made to non-Polish shoppers. Food more familiar to British customers was added to the bill of fare and the restaurant was renamed Lucullus. The staff were Poles, many of them previously unemployed. Among them were a number of majors and colonels unable or unwilling to return to Poland to join an army that propped up a Russian-imposed government.

Myskow's stepfather let it be known that any 'deserving' Pole, especially 'those in need' would be given a free meal at Lucullus. One of those deserving visitors was Christine and it was while seated at the same table that the two women met. Myskow described Christine as 'lovely but haggard, not too well-dressed and with her head shorn of hair and wrapped in white bandages. She was obviously embarrassed by her appearance and not too well in herself.'

Myskow recalled that as a young woman she had been 'awkward and shy' while Christine was withdrawn and probably still in pain as a result of her accident. Conversation at that first meeting was understandably desultory but when they met again some weeks later Christine spoke freely about the accident and said she had decided not to sue the taxi driver as she had somehow learned that he had a large family to support.

Meetings between Christine and her young friend thereafter were few and far between. They sometimes would see one another at a gathering hosted by one of the Polish social clubs in London. Their last meeting, Myskow recalled, took place on the upper deck of the number 74 Routemaster bus which ran along the Cromwell Road. It provided convenient transport for Christine, passing as it did near her hotel on Lexham Gardens and stopping close to the Polish clubs she frequented. Myskow and her mother were en route to the Brompton Oratory one Sunday morning to attend Mass after which they planned to lunch at Lucullus.

Christine left the bus near Exhibition Road for her own lunch date at Ognisko Polskie. Myskow recalled that Christine was better dressed on this occasion and described her as being in better spirits with a slight tan. The improvement in her appearance and in morale may have due to the fact that she had by then found suitable employment. She wore an embroidered white blouse and a full flowered skirt, according to Myskow, who commented that such a combination might had been considered fashionable attire in Warsaw in the summer of 1939 but seemed out of place on a warm Sunday morning in post-war London.[5]

Lady Deakin, who had once worked in the BBC's Romanian section, had returned to London from Cairo and occasionally saw Christine at the flat of a mutual friend where Julian Dolbey was one of the crowd. When Lady Deakin asked why she had never married Andrew, Christine ignored the question and announced instead that she no longer had any financial problems because she had at last found a job that might suit her.

Christine's cousin Hanka Nicoll, whom she had not seen since before the war, had suggested that she might enjoy the life of a stewardess aboard a trans-oceanic liner. Nicoll had been employed on a ship that regularly sailed from England to Argentina and had found it a very agreeable career indeed. She had returned to her old job after the war and encouraged her cousin to give it a try.

The idea appealed to Christine and she made application to join Shaw Savill Lines. She had no difficulty in securing a position with them and received her seaman's papers in May 1951. She was to be employed as a stewardess on ships sailing out of Southampton to Australia and to South Africa. It seemed a good choice as it would provide her with much-needed income and opportunities for travel. She especially looked forward to spending more time in the sunny climates she so loved. The photo on her identification card reveals a haggard-looking woman, not the beautiful creature so often seen at the Gezira Club. There was only one dark cloud in this silver lining. As Christine brought her belongings aboard the *MV Ruahine* for her maiden voyage, a bathroom porter named Dennis George Muldowney was observing her.

Inka Nowotna-Lachowicka, OBE, was a mutual friend of both Christine and Hanka Nicoll who often referred to themselves as 'cousins.' Hanka was the sister of the critic Tadeusz Breza who had introduced Christine to Gizycki in Zakopane. Inka recalled Christine saying, 'I cannot work in an office between 9 and 5, it would kill me of boredom.'6

Inka described the two attractive women frequently visiting the White Eagle Club (*Bialy Orzel*) at Albert Bridge road in Knightsbridge where Jan Marusarz, who had accompanied Christine on her first mission to Poland, was employed. In the crowded dining room, Inka said, Christine was not a social success. Some people recognised 'neither her beauty nor her intelligence, but others simply fell under her spell' like Jozef Kasparek, author of *The Carpathian Back Door (Przepust karpacki)*. He included his recollection of meeting with her at the club in his book. When Inka had to travel to Paris, Christine volunteered to look after her spaniel. In its owner's absence the dog became quite attached to her. When Inka returned Christine told her how, after parachuting into France, she had so charmed a German patrol's guard-dog that it did not bark and give away her hiding place. Inka was convinced that Christine knew no fear and therefore her body did not exude a scent that would have alarmed the dog.

Between assignments Christine made her home at the Shellbourne Hotel on Lexham Gardens just off the busy Cromwell Road in Kensington. The Polish family who owned the hotel treated her more as one of them rather than merely as a guest. Her cousin, the newly married Dr Andrzej Skarbek, soon to become the next Count Skarbek, lived on the square and Christine often visited him and his wife Shelagh. This was familiar territory for Christine as it was the same street in which she had met with Section D officers in 1940 at the home of Mrs Forbes Dennis. After so many years of wandering the circle of Christine's life was about to be closed.

Chapter 22.
End Game

Christine's new career lacked the excitement of struggling across the Tatras' wintry mountains or being under fire in France but at least it provided the illusion of endless travel. Now that she legitimately possessed a British passport there would be no more humiliating exchanges with civil servants keen to keep her out of Britain. Between voyages she kept in touch with Andrew who had remained in West Germany after his auto accident. The possibility of a permanent reunion between them seemed remote and for once Christine lacked a serious suitor. Michael Dunford had apparently been forgotten as were the men who had proposed marriage to her during her long enforced unemployment in Cairo.

Another of Christine's acquaintances, Halina Skrzynska, also found herself in postwar Germany, living in the British zone. She liked it so much that she wrote and invited her friend to visit. She quipped, 'I prefer you not to [travel by] parachute!'[1] The letter had been sent care of the artist Marek Zulawski who broadcast frequently on the BBC's Polish section. It was discovered among his papers after his death but apparently never reached Christine who was by then immersed in her new job. Zulawski had met her but seldom spoke about her, according to his wife Maryla. He seems to have been one of the few men who had not fallen victim to her charms.

Rumours about Christine's private life continued to circulate and were accepted as gospel truth. The importance of her work in Hungary and in France was frequently burnished by those who hadn't been there but who were anxious to lend their comments to her legend. But she steadfastly refused to speak about her exploits even with her closest friends. One of them commented, 'She told you only what she wanted you to know.'

One of the more unusual tales to emerge long after her death was one of an affair with the James Bond creator, Ian Fleming, told by the author Donald McCormick.[2] Christine's relatives and friends have dismissed this assertion for lack of solid proof and questions have been asked about why McCormick hadn't revealed his secret sooner. He had served with Fleming in Naval Intelligence (NI) and considered himself to be a close friend. Employing the pseudonym Richard Deacon as well as his real name, he wrote a number of books post-war though he was much less successful than his friend.

McCormick's supporting evidence for the alleged affair was thin on the ground, consisting of statements offered by just one person and a fragment of a letter. This was allegedly written by Fleming and sent to a man known both to him and to Christine. The journalist and SOE operative Edward Howe, MBE, had been one of her first contacts in Budapest and had become re-acquainted with her in Cairo after the war. He was also one of the few interviewed by McCormick for his biography of Fleming (1993). Howe reportedly told the author that he had run in to Christine in Cairo while working as a correspondent for Kemsley Newspapers, having been recruited by Fleming who enjoyed the post of 'foreign manager' (a title he had selected for himself) in the late 1940s.

Howe revealed that he himself had given Fleming's address to Christine, hoping that his friend would be fascinated by her and might find employment for her 'maybe as a correspondent somewhere or other.' Fleming initially arranged to meet Christine at the old Bertorelli's in Soho. McCormick remembered this, he wrote, because his friend had asked him to provide news stories about her and anyone who knew her, and report his findings to him at the restaurant.

McCormick offered only one hint for the date of this alleged liaison, citing bits of Fleming's letter to Howe, dated 1947, in which the former describes Christine. 'She literally shines with all the qualities and splendours of a fictitious character.' But a few pages later we read that the affair came to an end when Christine took up her duties with Shaw Savill Lines. She did not however make her maiden voyage until 1951 by which time Fleming was about to be married to the former Lady Anne Rothermere, the culmination of a long-standing and well-documented affair.

In his biography, published long after Fleming's death and shortly before his own demise, McCormick devoted an entire chapter to the assertion that, in addition to the affair, Christine had been in some respects the inspiration for the character Vesper Lynd, the *femme fatale* in Fleming's first novel *Casino Royale*. Questionable explanations have been offered by more than one person describing how Fleming came to choose this character's name.

In his own biography of Fleming (1995), Andrew Lycett gives the most convincing explanation for the source of the name Vesper, contradicting McCormick's claim, as well as Andrew's, that it had to do with the stormy weather raging in Warsaw on the evening of Christine's birth.[3] This version is completely without foundation whereas Lycett's explanation is based upon interviews with at least two witnesses.

The name Vesper was in fact a mocking reference to the church service of Evensong. Fleming's neighbour in Jamaica, a retired colonel, customarily had cocktails served to himself and to anyone who might be present at the hour during which less profane people were in attendance at a Church of England service. At the appointed time the colonel's butler would announce 'vespers' as he entered the drawing room with a tray of cocktails.

McCormick's only source for tales of Fleming's liaison with Christine was a woman named Olga Bialoguski who described herself as a friend of hers and who maintained that she had acted as a go-between, bearing messages from Christine to Fleming. She also claimed that the couple met in small discreet hotels either in London or on the Kent coast.

Queries by this author to individuals and organisations in the London Polish community asking for proof of Olga's true identity were met either with indifference or with negative responses. Several adverts in English and Polish periodicals brought no replies. Olga's name does not appear in any articles or books about Christine. A dozen or more former SOE operatives have written memoirs in which Christine is mentioned but Olga's name is curiously absent. Furthermore, there is no death certificate for any woman bearing that surname in the Family Records Archive in London though admittedly she could have expired anywhere outside the United Kingdom.

The existence of this source, if Olga indeed did exist, must be questioned particularly since she described herself to McCormick as one of Christine's closest friends when it was widely known that she had no female confidantes, preferring the company of men. Olga herself reportedly told McCormick that Christine was 'almost obsessively secretive,' confirming a characteristic of her personality well known to her family and colleagues.

That being the case, it seems out of character for Christine to have revealed the details of this affair to anyone including Olga.

From 1945 when she was de-mobbed in London until her death seven years later Christine travelled often. How she funded her many post-war trips has never been questioned or revealed. Fleming too led a peripatetic post-war life, spending a great deal of time in New York, Scotland and Jamaica in addition to taking skiing holidays in Europe. He frequently stayed at White Cliffs, Noel Coward's home near Dover. On those visits he was usually accompanied by Lady Rothermere who was still married to Lord Rothermere, proprietor of the Kemsley newspaper chain. If Christine and Fleming had had an intimate relationship it must have been brief and fleeting whereas Olga Bialoguski had given the opposite impression.

While researching his own book Lycett asked McCormick for some clue to Olga's identity but he declined to comment. My letter to him on the same subject went unanswered. It may well be that either the name was a pseudonym designed to protect his informant or else Olga was a figment of his imagination. In that regard it should be remembered that McCormick was well-versed in the shadowy world of intelligence-planning and wrote several books of fiction under his pseudonym. In light of the fact that he was once accused of perpetrating a literary hoax regarding the identity of Jack the Ripper - an accusation he neither admitted to nor denied- there is more reason to doubt his tale of an affair between the Bond author and the dashing former SOE operative.[4]

A new dimension to this story has been added with the disclosure, obtained via the Freedom of Information Act, that a female SOE agent well known to Christine occasionally used the cryptonym 'Olga.' That woman was Lady Livia Deakin. She probably knew Christine better than any of her female friends. Their friendship extended from their first meeting at the Gezira Club in 1942 to the evening of Christine's death thirteen years later. Several phrases that McCormick used in his Fleming biography had been previously used by Lady Deakin to describe Christine's personality, to wit, 'she was never a liar, not ever but *she just had to cover her tracks.*' [author's italics]. She was very much alive (d 2004) when McCormick's book was published. All the more reason for him to disguise Deakin's identity by giving her an alias. These are only circumstantial clues but for lack of more substantial evidence McCormick's tale of a romance between Christine and Ian Fleming remains highly suspect.

If McCormick's revelation of the Christine-Fleming relationship was part fantasy, part truth, the question must be asked why he would publish such a story and expose himself to public humiliation and possible legal action. As for his key source, Olga Bialoguski, McCormick steadfastly refused to identify her and never provided any secondary sources to support her allegations.

Christine's alleged dalliance with Fleming was overshadowed by the presence of her new friend, Dennis Muldowney. Christine had led a charmed life throughout the war, often sticking her head into the lion's mouth and emerging unscathed. She talked her way out of a Hungarian jail and bluffed her way into a German prison to secure the release of Francis Cammaerts. She had travelled in occupied Europe under assumed names with little attempt to disguise herself and had never been caught. Her judgment seemed infallible and her powers of persuasion irresistible. Her new friend however would prove to be less gullible and more persistent than the other men in her life had been.

Once aboard the *Rauhine,* Christine was met by Muldowney who introduced himself and then helped her to stow her belongings. He was handsome in a roguish sort of way with a headful of dark curly hair. At times he sported a thin mustache which made him look rather sinister. Word of her exploits had got around even before this first voyage to Australia. Some of the ship's staff reacted with envy and embarrassed her with their rude attitude towards her. To make matters worse Christine and other war veterans had been instructed to wear their honours' ribbons when on duty to impress the passengers. Muldowney, in his obsequious way, tried to make life easy for her. He explained the routines aboard ship and offered her moral support. He turned out to be as tenacious as Jozef Radzyminski had been in Budapest though he lacked the Pole's flair for the dramatic gesture.

True to her habit of picking up strays Christine befriended Muldowney who appeared to be a man with few companions. Between voyages she invited him to the Polish clubs she frequented in Kensington and introduced him to friends. For some months she appeared never to be without him. It was an unlikely romance for a handsome woman of such great courage, a woman who had survived every kind of danger and whose bed had been shared by men of action who had courted death. But not by ordinary bathroom porters.

Christine's colleagues took a dim view of Muldowney. Andrew Kennedy and Francis Cammaerts were particularly puzzled as to why she had befriended a man who was obviously ill-suited for her in every respect. Whenever invited to dine with them he seldom joined the conversation. At times he seemed almost morose.

Muldowney was painfully out of his depth amongst the cast of characters with whom Christine had served in SOE. Men like Cammaerts, Andrew and John Roper were genuine heroes who had risked their lives during the war. Virtually all of them were educated and bilingual, at ease with themselves. In such company Muldowney's insecurity was even more obvious.

Christine however was enjoying her new life - though she could never be described as 'happy' - and seemed unperturbed by queries about her companion. But gradually their relationship began to change. Even when not invited Muldowney would intrude upon a dinner party or appear at one of Christine's haunts. Unwittingly, she had opened the inner sanctum of her life to him. He knew her favourite restaurants, the route she took to and from her hotel to her Polish cafes. She made it easy for him to find her for she seldom ventured far from Kensington.

Muldowney had become Christine's predator and she had positioned herself to become his willing victim, seemingly incapable of breaking free of his grasp. Though she occasionally expressed annoyance at his behaviour she hesitated to terminate their relationship. On one occasion she invited him to accompany her and Andrew to the cinema. Prior to that she had told him that Andrew was a life-long friend. But during the course of the evening Muldowney got the impression that their relationship was more than that enjoyed by two friends. Envy began to eat away at him though he did not openly object to their friendship. Afterwards, as they returned to the Shellbourne Hotel, Muldowney lagged behind and was heard to make muttering noises. Kennedy later recalled that the porter had become highly agitated at his habit of clicking his fingers as they walked along.5

Christine finally had to admit that Muldowney had become more than just boring. He was obviously resentful of the company she kept and could no longer mask his envy. On several occasions he initiated rows in restaurants where she was dining with friends and he sometimes accosted her in the street. He began to appear at her hotel at all hours, demanding to see her.

Andrew wasn't the only one to notice Muldowney's odd behaviour. Diana Hall, Truszkowski's daughter, recalled that Andrew and Muldowney had accompanied Christine on a visit to the Truszkowski family home. But Muldowney refused to enter the house, preferring to remain outside while Christine remained inside having tea with Truszkowski. Diana remembered vividly, as a fourteen-year-old girl, bringing tea to her father's study only to find Christine seated on the floor with her head on her father's knee. Diana thought this was quite odd behaviour for a forty-year old woman. While Andrew was quite happy to chat with Diana and her younger sister, Christine ignored them altogether, making a bad first impression.6

Several nights after their unsettling trip to the cinema Muldowney was due to ship out on the *Dunotter Castle*. Christine accompanied him to the Albert Dock where she allegedly kissed him and promised to write often. She was also due to ship out soon, on the *New Australia*. Muldowney was certain that he had asked her to write to him, care of his ship, and was greatly disappointed when no letters arrived.7

Upon his return to England in mid-April 1952 he found a registered letter from Christine awaiting him, informing him that she would soon be going to Europe after which she intended to resign her position with Shaw Savill. Alarmed that he might never see her again Muldowney rushed to the Shellbourne and insisted on an explanation. Christine would say only that she was going away and wanted nothing further to do with him.

Undeterred, Muldowney returned to the hotel several nights later and found her in the company of an unnamed man. He demanded the return of the letters he had sent her. She refused, saying she had burnt them. She then slammed the door in his face, an action that finally sent him over the edge. Angered and humiliated, he decided then to kill her and commit suicide by swallowing poison.

In the days following that episode Muldowney bought a sheath knife and a bottle of powdered aspirin in order to make good his deadly plan. He resigned from the Merchant Navy and was given a reference saying that his work had been 'very good.' In May he was taken on as a porter at the Reform Club in Pall Mall where he was given accommodation in one of the rooms provided for staff. He did this, he confessed, so as to be closer to Christine. He attempted one last phone call to her but was rebuffed.[8]

Ludwik Popiel, who had shared Christine's adventures in Budapest, was then living in London working as a decorator. He recalled meeting Muldowney as he and Christine stood chatting outside her hotel. Muldowney asked to speak with her privately and when she refused he pressed on. Again, she refused and told him that she did not desire his company nor did she want him anywhere near the hotel.

In his statement to the police after the murder Muldowney admitted that he had fantasised about killing Christine for as long as six weeks before the event. With that thought in mind he had purchased the knife and added a home-made kosh for good measure, for as he told the police, he wasn't completely sure if he was going to kill her or merely injure her.9

By June 1952 Christine had come the to realisation that she would never have peace of mind as long as Muldowney was in London. Coincidentally, she had already found a comfortable bolt-hole in South Africa. The climate appealed to her, perhaps reminding her of the languid days she had spent in Cairo. Because of his busy schedule Andrew would be unable to see her off to her new home. Instead, they planned a brief holiday in Liege.

She expressed her apprehension about Muldowney in a letter to him. No one knows for certain exactly when she decided to break it off with the obstinate porter. But when her ship docked at the port of Southampton of Friday, June 13th, all the indications are that she had decided upon a course of action - to leave London - that would resolve her conflict with him. Before returning to her hotel she phoned Pussi Deakin. She recalled that Christine sounded upset and said, 'I am very tired. Can I stay with you tonight? I don't want food. I just want to sleep.'10 But she never arrived. There are conflicting versions here too. In the film 'No Ordinary Countess' Lady Deakin contradicted her earlier statement and said that Christine was to visit her on the 16th, not on the evening of Muldowney's fatal assault.

On Saturday Christine was notified that the plane she had booked for her flight had been taken out of service because of mechanical failure. At dinner with friends on Sunday the 15th she spoke of her intention to leave the country, at the same time confessing her fear of Muldowney. Afterwards, she returned to the Shellbourne.

Though Christine's movements for that day and early evening have been corroborated by witnesses, it was alleged years after her death that she had spent at least part of the afternoon in the flat of an English MP who remains unidentified. She was in the company of the Polish politician-writer Stanislaw (Cat) Mackiewicz, later post-war prime minister of the London Polish government. The source of this story* is emphatic that Mackiewicz volunteered the information. During the war Christine knew at least two men who subsequently became Members of Parliament. One was Aidan Crawley to whom she had passed on the news that the Germans were about to invade the USSR. The other man was Douglas Dodds-Parker with whom she had fallen out over the issue of the fate of the Gestapo agent Max Waem. Mackiewicz claimed that the MP, whoever he was, had given Christine the keys to his flat to use whenever she felt the need. He also claimed to have accompanied her to the Shellbourne on the night of her death but declined her invitation to come inside for coffee. Years later he expressed regret that he had not gone in and theatrically declared that he would have gladly been Muldowney's victim instead of Christine.

On Sunday, Christine began to sort through her belongings. She owned no furniture and, aside from her clothes, had few possessions. In the early evening she dined at the Polish Hearth Club. Afterwards she went to the Marynka Cafe in Brompton Road to meet Ludwik Popiel. The subject of Muldowney came up and she again confessed her apprehension. At the end of the evening Popiel offered to escort her to the Shellbourne but she politely declined. Though she must have been terribly fearful of a confrontation with Muldowney, she could not show fear in front of a friend. Popiel was one of two men to make

*Leszek Gondek, *Na tropach tajemnic III rzeszy* (WMON 1987 Warsaw). ('The search for the secrets of the 3rd Reich').

the lurid claim that they had spent time with Christine on that last day of her life and had walked her back to the Shellbourne.

Countess Tarnowska, who knew Popiel well, contradicted his account of that fateful evening. He had not accompanied Christine to the hotel, he allegedly told Tarnowska, because he had another engagement. He was said to have bitterly reproached himself later for not being there to protect his friend.[11] It hardly seems to matter now. Muldowney was intent on harming Christine and would have waited for as long as it took for the opportunity to present itself.

While Christine was making preparations for her holiday Muldowney had gone alone to the Carlton Cinema in Haymarket. Afterwards he met a man with whom he had worked on one of his ships. That unnamed person told Muldowney that, while working aboard the *Winchester Castle,* he had encountered a Polish stewardess who had mentioned Muldowney and alleged that he had been in trouble on the *Rauhine*. This acquaintance also said that the woman had flirted with the ship's officers though he did not mention Christine by name.

Fired by these allegations, Muldowney went directly to his rooms at the Reform Club where he collected the knife and the cosh. That evening, armed with his weapons he positioned himself on the Cromwell Road from where he had a clear view of Lexham Gardens and the Shellbourne. In his statement to the police he claimed that Christine arrived at the hotel just after 10:00 pm.

After greeting the hall porter Joseph Kojdecki, Christine went to her room to put her personal effects in order. Desperate to confront Christine, Muldowney approached the hotel in time to see her ascending the stairs. He entered and waited in the deserted lobby for a few moments, expecting to encounter her when she returned. Impatient for her to reappear he changed his mind and started up the stairs only to meet Christine on her way down, bearing an armful of uniforms to be stored in the hotel basement. Muldowney again asked for the return of his letters. Christine replied that she had destroyed them. In response to his question about her future plans, she repeated that she was going to Europe and would be gone for about two years and furthermore, wanted nothing more to do with him. Muldowney did not believe her and would not be bluffed. In her hour of desperate need Christine's famed powers of persuasion deserted her.

The row continued just briefly as they descended the stairs. By the time they reached the lobby Muldowney had reached the limits of his patience. He quickly removed the knife strapped to his hip and stabbed Christine in the chest. He struck just one blow but it proved fatal. It nicked her heart and almost severed her aorta. She fell on her back near a small table clutching in one hand a pen with a wooden barrel.

After stabbing Christine, Muldowney did not attempt to flee but stood there in the empty lobby of the shabby hotel, watching her life ebb away. As she lay dying he removed from his jacket a menu on the back of which he had printed in large letters the name, Christine Granville.[12] He then placed it on the table near where she lay.

Post-Mortem

Dennis Muldowney was arraigned in a central London court then remanded into custody at Brixton jail. The Polish community was rife with rumours that her murder had been politically motivated. Journalists sought out her former SOE colleagues for interviews, hoping to find the clue that had caused Muldowney to commit such a heinous crime.

The investigation into Christine's death continued throughout the summer. The tedious process of justice progressed over the course of three months as the Shellbourne staff gave their statements to the police. The porter Jozef Kojdecki testified that Christine returned to the hotel around 10:30 on the night June 15. He observed Muldowney, whom he'd seen before, enter shortly afterwards. Kojdecki left the front desk and made several trips to and from the lounge to the hotel's office. He observed Christine and Muldowney having a conversation on the stairs leading to the lounge but thought nothing of it. Suddenly, he heard a scream and rushed back to find the two of them standing 'quite close', as if locked in a macabre embrace. The porter grabbed Muldowney and pulled him away from Christine. She collapsed immediately and fell backwards.

A second porter, Michael Perlak, also heard the scream and ran to the lounge where he saw his colleague struggling with Muldowney. Perlak recalled him shouting that he 'wanted to see her' and 'I killed her because I loved her.' In the commotion neither of the porters noticed the knife handle protruding from Christine's chest.[1] Perlak at first thought that she had fainted and moved her, placing her body against a wall in a seated position but she slipped down. As she was lying close to the lounge doors Perlak's thought was to shift her again lest someone open the doors and slam into her. After moving the mortally wounded Christine a second time, he hurried to fetch a glass of water.

In the midst of the melee someone had telephoned for an ambulance and the police. The manager, Bronislaw Hryniewicz, who had rooms in the hotel, was called to the scene. Kojdecki was still holding Muldowney when he arrived. The manager, unlike his two porters, immediately noticed the knife handle and removed the weapon from Christine's chest, placing it alongside her body. That decision probably hastened her death as it quickened the pace of bleeding.

Statements from the police and medical examiners are straightforward about the time-sequence of that fateful evening. Inspector Leonard Pearcey testified that he had arrived at the Shellbourne at 10:40 which seems unlikely if the three hotel staff - and Muldowney - were accurate about the time, unless he was quite nearby. When he entered the lounge Pearcey observed the two porters grappling with Muldowney who was attempting to approach the dying Christine. He separated the three men and took Muldowney into a room off the lounge accompanied by two police constables. He left the room to examine Christine then returned and informed Muldowney that she was dead. He asked what had happened and Muldowney replied, 'That's the idea. I did kill her. She drove me to it. It is my knife.' Pearcey then cautioned him.[2]

Noel Henegan, a medical practitioner, examined Christine, observed the wound in her chest and formed the opinion that she had been dead for twenty to thirty minutes.[3]

Chief Inspector George Jennings turned up along with another detective at 12:15. He confronted Muldowney with what he had seen and the bathroom porter replied, 'I killed her. Let's get away from here and get it over with quickly.' Before leaving the hotel Jennings noticed a cardboard rectangle lying on a small table near to where Christine had fallen. It was the menu on which Muldowney had printed her name. 'I put it there,' Muldowney said. 'That is the cause of the trouble and I will tell you all about it at the police station.'

Percy Law, then chief inspector of the Photographic Department, was the last official to arrive, at 1:52. He photographed Christine's body and the crime scene. She had now been lying of the floor of the hotel lounge for almost three-and-a half hours. In a half-hearted suicide gesture Muldowney attempted to swallow the powdered aspirin he'd brought along. A uniformed policeman seized him and managed to extract most of it from his mouth. Even if he had swallowed the entire contents of the bottle it would not have been enough to kill him.

In his confession Muldowney did not offer the excuse that he had been blinded by rage or that he had lost control of himself. He gave no hint whatsoever as to what his emotional state had been at the moment he stabbed Christine. He did attempt to shunt some of the blame onto her, saying that she had dared him to kill her on three occasions and that she was responsible for putting the idea into his head. Some biographers and amateur psychologists have described Muldowney as schizophrenic but there is no clinical evidence that he was suffering from any mental illness. A police psychologist, perhaps not the most qualified of practitioners, examined and questioned Muldowney during that last summer of his life. He did not make a diagnosis of schizophrenia nor did he refer the prisoner to a psychiatrist. Muldowney claimed that he and Christine had had a sexual relationship. He bragged that his wife left him because of his constant sexual demands.

At his arraignment Muldowney was defiant and petulant but readily admitted to having committed murder and refused legal representation. At the sentencing hearing the judge had no alternative but to find him guilty as charged and pronounced the death sentence, concluding with the dreaded and familiar phrase, 'May God have mercy upon your soul.' To which Muldowney retorted, 'I am sure he will.' In prison, first in Brixton and then in Pentonville, Muldowney proved to be a difficult and uncooperative prisoner. He received no visitors and asked nothing of his warders who sometimes had to forcibly dress him in the morning. His divorced wife hurriedly changed her surname to shield their young son John from public embarrassment. On September 29, 1952, Muldowney was one of the last two prisoners ever to be hanged at Pentonville prison.*

Among Christine's personal belongings police found the telephone numbers for relatives living in the UK. Her uncle, Colonel Andrew Skarbek and his oldest son Jan were in Bedfordshire and so it fell to his youngest son Andrzej, still in medical school. to identify his cousin's body.4 He was summoned to the morgue in Kensington where he made the identification. John Roper, attached at the time to the Foreign Office, was also sent to the morgue for the same purpose. 'I remained in close contact with Scotland Yard until I saw her murderer plead guilty and receive the death sentence.'5

Teresa Szulczewska, Christine's niece in Poland, received no such cooperation from the government. 'I contacted the Foreign Office but received no reply from the ministry.

---

*The author's attempts to exam Muldowney's file at Pentonville were rebuffed by a prison official.

We do not know [at that time] in what state and where Krystyna's grave is. Lots of family matters remain unexplained to this day.'6 Colonel Skarbek and his son returned to London as soon as they could. Andrew Kennedy was notified of Christine's death at his home in West Germany but it took several days for him to arrange a flight to London.

The news of Christine's murder made the front pages of several of London's daily newspapers. Brigadier Colin Gubbins wrote an obituary for *The Times* and *Life* magazine in America published a two-page spread of photographs taken at her funeral. *The New York Times* announced the news of Christine's death and newspapers abroad published stories of the tragedy. In one way or another reports of this shocking event reached her SOE colleagues.

A funeral Mass was said in St Mary's Roman Catholic Church in Kensal Green on June 21st. Harrod's, Christine's alleged employer, had been engaged to provide the funeral arrangements. After the Mass a solemn and sorrowful procession of Christine's relatives, friends, high-ranking officials and the curious accompanied the coffin to its burial site. Mrs Dorothy Abramowicz was one of the latter. She had never met Christine but felt compelled to attend the funeral as a sign of respect for this courageous woman.7 Teresa Myskow, who had met Christine shortly after her hit-and-run accident, and who had shared a table with her at an Oxford Street restaurant, described the funeral ceremony as 'spectacular.'

Among the pall-bearers were Francis Cammaerts, Andrew Kennedy, Dr Andrzej Skarbek and his father. A dozen members of the FANYs formed a ceremonial guard around the grave. The Polish government-in-exile was represented by General Kopanski, the

British by Brigadier Gubbins. A group representing the survivors of the Vercors battle made the journey from France to honour 'Madame Pauline.' The white-and-red Polish flag was draped over Christine's coffin and a red pillow rested on the flag. Her Parachute badge and other military badges representing the French Resistance and the Polish Underground rested upon the pillow. The AK badge had been conferred upon her just before the funeral but there was no award from the Polish government-in-exile. Her medals - the OBE, George Medal, War Medal and Croix de guerre - were also placed atop the coffin as were a medallion portraying the Black Madonna of Czestochowa and Christine's signet ring.**

Andrew had brought with him a small quantity of Polish soil to sprinkle over Christine's grave and a metal cross was erected to temporarily mark her resting place. Shortly after it had been raised a strong gust of wind nearly dislodged it. The *Life* magazine photographer captured the dramatic moment when, as the cross tilted dangerously to one side, Andrew lunged forward to prevent it from collapsing. Nearly a decade after the funeral he ordered a cross sculpted from a Polish pine tree to replace the metal cross. It is still in place at the head of Christine's grave some fifty years after it was erected and can be clearly seen from the entrance to St Mary's chapel.

Having been appointed as executor of her estate the devastated Andrew carried out the melancholy task of disposing of her personal effects. After completing this final assignment he returned to Munich where he lived out a very long life. He was involved in a number of business ventures, most of them having to do with automobiles. He never married but enjoyed a long-lasting relationship with the married daughter of a well-known

**These awards and insignia are held at the Polish Museum and Sikorski Institute in London.

European businessman. His best friend, the composer and author Jan Tyszkiewicz, wrote of how the two of them had shared a week-end chalet in the Austrian Alps for several decades. Tyszkiewicz recalled with affection Andrew's love of skiing despite having only one leg. He recalled one memorable occasion when the two of them were flying downhill on a slope near Kitzbuehl when Tyszkiewicz lost control of his skis and crashed into his friend with such force that Andrew's artificial limb became detached. Undaunted, Andrew managed to reach the bottom of the slope by balancing on one leg. Or so it was said.8

Christine's presence continued to be felt long after her death. A number of her former colleagues and people who had only a nodding acquaintance with her named daughters after her though one of the girls was so distraught at the news of Christine's murder that she insisted on being addressed by her middle name. Francis Cammaerts named his daughter Christine to honour her memory but tragically, the girl was born with hydrocephalus and remained severely handicapped until she died age fourteen. Sofia Tarnowska also named one of her daughters after Christine.

In the early paragraphs of his letter to this author in 2001, Roper described how the Panel to protect Christine's reputation had been formed. He concluded by adding, 'It has been distressing to me to write this letter and I hope that you will spare me further correspondence.' He died the following year. Brigadier Henry Wilson, who knew about her only through reading her story, commented 'Poor Christine was an extraordinary character, so full of contradictions and I suspect deeply unhappy. There was an inevitability of tragedy about her.'

Andrew was not the only one of Christine's former lovers who attempted to shut down any investigation into her private life. In the documentary film of Christine's life Cammaerts claimed that the Panel had somehow prevented publication of two other attempts at biography. One of those was certainly Vladimir Ledochowski's unpublished manuscript, the other may have been Michael Dunford's. Vladimir's son Jan suggested that there was something suspicious about the efforts made by Andrew and Cammaerts to prevent others from writing about Christine. In that regard Jan wrote, 'The death of heroes is not usually followed by Panels to protect their memories and stop books about them.'

Cammaerts always spoke of Christine with great admiration but never admitted to having been intimate with her until shortly before his death in 2006. Mrs Masson complained that 'he [Cammaerts] resisted all my efforts to ask his help in writing my book. He like many of Christine's devoted male friends and colleagues had formed a kind of blockade to keep out anyone wanting to delve into the life of their heroine, their very own pure and spotless Joan of Arc.'[9] Masson also contacted Major Wilkinson. Before replying to her Wilkinson wrote to Brigadier Gubbins, alerting him to Masson's request for information about 'Polish SOE' and Christine. In his letter Wilkinson wrote 'I do not want to meet her [Masson] and I hardly knew Christine at all.' In a parenthetical comment he wrote that he believed her to be a victim of 'Polish political *Schweinerei* [a mess] but this is no place to say so and the policy of putting all our money on the Home Army [rather than on independent organisations] was obviously right.'

Vladimir Ledochowski wrote two books or rather, one book and one manuscript. The latter was an autobiography revealing intimate details of his affair with Christine. As he considered Andrew to be his good friend despite their rivalry, he asked him to read a copy of his manuscript. That was followed by a frank discussion during which Andrew cajoled Vladimir into canceling his plans to publish. *The Diary Abandoned in Ankara* published posthumously in Poland, was an account of Vladimir's war-time adventures and contained a long section about his relationship with Christine. Dunford, her long-suffering suitor, was supposed to be writing a biography too but no manuscript has ever been found.

There was no shortage of anecdotes and commentary told by those whose lives had been touched in some way by Christine. At least three people recalled that they had dined with her on that last day. Mrs Lewanska-Szyc, who had once crossed the Hungarian-Slovak border with her and whose husband had been a Musketeer courier, gave an interview to a Warsaw newspaper, describing her late friend as 'a great conspirator and a gifted story-teller.'[10] Christine added to the welter of tales of her adventures, perhaps because she had at last tired of hearing exaggerated stories of her accomplishments. She is alleged to have bragged about using her SOE-issue stiletto 'on many occasions.' In fact, she had few encounters with enemy soldiers. She had always been accompanied by a guide on her attempts to enter Poland who would have witnessed such actions. No one, not even Andrew Kennedy, Vladimir or the men who worked with her in the French and Italian Alps, and who later recounted their adventures, passed on any anecdotes of what surely would have been bloody episodes

Unanswered questions still remain about some of the details of Christine's life and the characters who crossed her path. No documents or witnesses have been found to support the claim that she had been involved with a pre-war intelligence cell in central Europe. The pseudonymous Fryday of Section D who spoke so admiringly of her in the autumn of 1939 has never been identified. If Christine ever enjoyed what Lady Deakin called her 'Paris years,' no one recollected them. Her coy hint that she had once been a journalist remains just that, and the benefactor who bequeathed his London house to her has never been named though Colonel Cookham seems the most likely candidate. As for Christine's affair with Ian Fleming, that has been debunked by several writers but remains an interesting subject for speculation.

There is unfinished business too. Presenter James Gleason broadcast a series on the BBC titled 'Now It Can Be Told,' which included a segment about the FANYs and was to include a bit about Christine. But no such material was appended to that segment. The journalist Florian Sokolov left this note for a program to be broadcast in 1955: 'Mr Sokolov knew Christine Granville before the war & wrote and delivered an eight-minute script about her work and character.' That program was never produced. Now and then talk of a feature film based on Christine's life surfaces, only to fade away. The film 'No Ordinary Countess' remains the only cinematic account of Christine's story.

Despite her heroic efforts she did not live to see Poland freed from the grip of occupation, first by the Germans and then by the Soviet Union. Indeed, she never saw her beloved homeland after 1940. Her poignant entreaty to Major Perkins, 'Please, Perks, don't forget me', has been answered to some degree by a spate of articles, three biographies and at least three books written in Polish which have not been translated into English.

Andrew Kennedy died of cancer in Munich in 1988.[11] In his will he asked that his ashes be buried at the foot of Christine's grave, a request granted by the Skarbek family. His cross remains upright above her resting place. Over the succeeding years the grave fell into a state of neglect but was rescued in 2013 through the combined efforts of the Polish Heritage Society and the Polish Embassy in London. In May a ceremony complete with a Polish military presence, British and Polish officials and those who still remembered Christine was held at the cemetery's chapel. Afterwards a small but solemn procession gathered round her grave to observe as the Polish flag was removed to reveal a newly polished stone still bearing the bogus 1915 birth date.

Major Wilkinson may have unintentionally summed up Christine's legacy in his letter to Mrs Masson in 1973. 'So far as I remember, but I may be wrong about this, she was not particularly in sympathy with the Polish government in London, nevertheless she was an extremely dedicated patriot, and she was obviously bitterly disappointed that all her efforts had been for nothing. But war is like this, and she accepted it quite realistically. I mention this because there is a tendency (increasingly fashionable) to romanticise World War II, and special operations in particular. To do so gives quite a false picture; not least of Christine herself.'

FIN

Notes

Introduction

1. W Stanley (Billy Moss) served in the Coldstream Guards and SOE. After the war he enjoyed a long career as a journalist, writer and broadcaster. His book *Ill Met by Moonlight* was made into a film of the same name.

Chapter 1. A Country Idyll

1. Fearful of a possible powerful democracy on its western border Russia and her allies, Austria and Prussia, launched a series of wars against Poland beginning in 1764. These resulted in three partitions of the country in 1772, 1793 and 1795. After the final partition the Polish king, Stanislaw Agustus Poniatowski, was sent into exile and Poland disappeared from the maps of Europe. Poland did not regain its independence until the conclusion of the first world war.
2. The information concerning the Goldfeder dowry and the Skarbeks' marriage was provided in correspondence with the Polish genealogist Tomasz Lenczewski.
3. While Russia dominated Poland throughout the 19th century Poles who wanted to claim an ancient aristocratic title had to apply to the tsar for permission to use it. The two Skarbek clans each laid claim to the title of 'count' but Tsar Nicolas I approved only the petition submitted by the Galicia branch. There was no reply to the claim submitted by Christine's grandfather.
4. Exactly how and when Stefania Skarbek died is not known. Many Poles died in Pawiak during the war. Jewish prisoners in particular were removed from the prison in large numbers and taken to isolated wooded areas near the village of Palmiry, on the edge of the Kampinoski National Forest northwest of the city center, where they were executed and buried.
5. The Convent of the Sisters of the Immaculate Conception is located in the city of Jazlowiec in southeastern Poland. The convent contains a white statue of the Blessed Virgin. A regiment of Polish soldiers repelled an attack by Russian troops here in 1919 after which the statue became known as Our Miraculous Lady of Jazlowiec.
6. Stanislaw Witkiewicz (1885-1939) was universally known as Witkacy (*Veetkatzee*). He had a successful career as an artist and portrait painter before taking up writing. He wrote novels, short stories, plays and philosophical tracts. He committed suicide in 1939 upon hearing news of the Russian invasion of Poland.
7. Tadeusz Boy-Zelenski, author and critic, was arrested by German police near Lvov in the late autumn of 1939. He died while in their custody.
8. Zofia Nalkowska's best known work is *Boundary Lines* (*Granica*). She continued to write throughout the war and afterwards published Medallion (*Medaliony* 1946), a collection of stories about the Nazi genocide. She also served on the Commission for the Investigation of German War Crimes.

9. Marshal Jozef Pilsudski commanded a division of Polish troops as part of the Austrian army during the first world war. At the time Poland had not yet regained its independence. After refusing to take part in a German army awards ceremony, he and his aide Kazimierz Sosnkowski were imprisoned but released shortly before the Armistice of 1918.
10. In the final days of the Austro-Hungarian empire Senator Skarbek was once arrested because of his affiliation with Austrian aristocrats. For some years he was kept under surveillance by the Viennese police.
11. The Black Madonna is the title of a depiction in oils on wood of the Blessed Virgin Mary holding the Christ child. It has been a fixture at the Paulite monastery of Jasna Gora (mountain of light) since the 14th century. There is no reliable date of origin but it was apparently re-painted in 1434. The monastery was once assaulted by a large contingent of vandals during which the painting was damaged. The monks repelled that assault and another by a Swedish army in 1655. Since then the power of miracles has been attributed to the painting.
12. Witold Gombrowicz (1904-1969), novelist and short-story writer, is best outside Poland known for the novels *Ferdyduke* and *Cosmos*. He was awarded the *Prix Formentor* in 1967 for the latter novel. He left Poland in June 1939 and never returned.

Chapter 2. Secrets and Lies

1. The Munich Accords of 1938 ceded the Sudetenland to Germany on Hitler's demand, thus averting war, if only temporarily.
2. Jerzy Gizycki wrote several books in Polish including *The Whites and the Blacks*, a study of race relations in South Africa and *A History of Chess*. He occasionally wrote articles for *Wiadomosci Literackie* (*The Literary News*), a Polish literary periodical no longer published.

Chapter 3. 'Notes on Madame G.'

1. At the conclusion of the second world war Prime Minister Winston Churchill ordered the destruction of SOE's files in 1945 to avoid the possibility of documents falling into enemy hands. The task was never completed. A mysterious fire in 1946 at SOE HQ in Baker Street destroyed more files, especially those of the Middle East and Polish sections. Many files survived however and are housed at The National Archives at Kew.
2. Fryday's identity has never been revealed. Key features of her interview with Madame Gizycka, not yet Christine Granville, can be read in the file HS4/109 at The National Archives.
3. Claude Dansey's biography is *Colonel Z, the life and times of a master of spies*. (London: Hoddard and Stoughton 1984)
4. The complete papers of Mrs Forbes Dennis, *aka* Phyllis Bottome, are held in the Humanities Room, number 2, at the British Library.
5. This and other information about Gizycki is contained in his unpublished memoir, *The Winding Trail*. How the memoir was discovered and by whom is not known. The document has not been authenticated by anyone.

6. See HS 9/109
7. See Gizycki op.cit.

Chapter 4. An Obstreperous Pupil

1. Admiral Miklos Horthy served in the navy of the Austro-Hungarian empire and was appointed Regent of Hungary in 1920. He ruled the country during the interwar years and for much of the second world war.
2. See HS4/184 at The National Archives (TNA).
3. More of Sir Owen O'Malley's report to the American government can be seen in his autobiography *Phantom Caravan* (London: John Murray 1954). An Irish woman claims to have many of the O'Malley family's private papers including some of Christine's letters to Kate.
4. O'Malley's report to American authorities. *op. cit.*
5. See *Intelligence Cooperation between Poland and Great Britain during WW II*. p 446 (2005).
6. In Andrew Kennedy's PF at The National Archives. HS9/830/3

Chapter 5. To Poland and the Musketeers

1. See Andrew Kennedy's remarks to Madeleine Masson in *Christine, a search for Christine Granville* (London: Hamish Hamilton 1975, Virago 2005).
2. Roman Buczek's book on the Musketeers, *Muszkieterze* (Toronto: Century Publishing Co Ltd 1985), has not been translated into English.
3. Vidkun Quisling was a Norwegian former soldier and politician. Between the wars he founded his own newspaper and political party, and eventually espoused the Nazi philosophy. He readily agreed to collaborate with the Germans when they invaded Norway and betrayed many of his fellow Norwegians who were summarily executed. Thereafter, his name became synonymous with 'traitor.'
4. See K S Rudnicki's book, *The Last of the War Horses* (London: Bachman & Turner 1974).
5. See *The Report of the Anglo-Polish Historical Committee vol 1 (London: Vallentine Mitchell 2005)*
6. A full account of the courier's assassination appeared in a three-part series in *Polska Newsweek* (March 2004).
7. For this account of Witkowski's death see *Polska-Brytyjska Wspolpraca Wywiadowcza Podczas II Wojny Swiatowej (Intelligence Cooperation between Poland and Great Britain During World War II*. Bi-lingual edition. (Warszawa: The Head Office of State Archives 2005).
8. This account of Christine's journey across the Tatras was told to Madeleine Masson by Andrew Kennedy and appeared in full in Masson's book *Christine, a search for Christine Granville* (London: Hamish Hamilton 1975, Virago Press 2005)

Chapter 6. The Woman in the Tyrolean Hat

1. Ledochowski gives a lengthy account of his conversation with Jasinska in his book *Pamietnik pozostawiony w Ankarze (A diary abandoned in Ankara)*, published in Warsaw. Not available in English.
2. op. cit.
3. The text of Gizycki's correspondence with X.3 can be found in HS4/198.
4. op.cit.

Chapter 7. Lost among the Magyars

1. Christine's report on her initial mission to Poland is contained in her Personal File (HS 9/109) at TNA.
2. A Polish intelligence source suggested to the British the concealment of 'delayed action bombs in every second boat (the barges - made of wood - are moored more or less *en masse*) so as to ensure a proper conflagration.' *Intelligence Cooperation between Poland and Great Britain during World War II* (Warszawa: The Head of State Archives 2005).
3. This author was in touch with an Irish writer who claimed to have access to the O'Malley family private papers and was considering a biography of the family. I provided answers to questions she asked about Jerzy Gizycki but questions to her about Christine went unanswered and the writer never contacted me again. Kennedy may have destroyed or taken any letters from Kate to Christine he found in Christine's room after her death. Quotes from Christine's letters to Kate eventually appeared in another biography.

Chapter 8. The Fall of Paris and a Narrow Escape

1. This version of Christine's escape from the Slovak border guards was told to Mrs Masson by Andrew Kennedy. There is no documentation in SOE files to support his story.
2. The German pocket battleship *Graf Spee* was sunk by the British Royal Navy off the coast of Uruguay in 1940.
3. From Gizycki's report op.cit.
4. This description of Paris appears in *Sylvia Beach and the Lost Generation, a history of Paris in the Twenties & Thirties*, by Noel Riley Fitch (New York: W.W. Norton & Company 1983).
5. From Lees' oral contribution to the Sound Archives at London's Imperial War Museum.
6. Vansittart's papers are held in the Churchill Archives Center, Cambridge University.

Chapter 9. Last Mission to Poland

1. Roman Buczek, *Muszkieterowie* (Toronto:Century Publishing Company Ltd 1985).
2. Alfons Filar, *Palace: Katowania Podhale* (Warszawa: Wydawnictwo Ministerwa Obrony Narodowej. ed III. 1976)
3. See Christine's Personal File HS9/109.

4. From correspondence between Gizycki and X.3 contained in HS4/198 at TNA.
5. Howarth made this remark to the author during an interview at his home in Sherbourne 2002.
6. Andrew Kennedy's version of his escape from the Budapest prison with Christine is contained in HS 9/109.
7. Cammaerts' comments were first recorded at the Sound Archive of the Imperial War Museum in 1985.
8. The tactic of simulating a consumptive haemorraghe is described in detail in an SOE propaganda document titled 'First Aid' (HS7/210). The document is unsigned and undated. Its intended audience were German munition factory workers seeking to avoid being caught up in RAF bombing raids on their places of work. It has been suggested that the propaganda expert Defton Selmer was the author.
9. Ibid.
10. Kennedy's version of how he and Christine fled to the British Embassy was told to Madeleine Masson. op.cit.

Chapter 10. Breakout from Budapest

1. O'Malley's account of this episode is contained in HS 4/193 at The National Archives.
2. op. cit.
3. op. cit.
4. See *Lunch with a Stranger* by David E Walker (New York: W. W. Norton & Company Inc. 1957)
5. The Wilkinson-Gubbins correspondence is included in HS4/198.
6. The Tripartite Agreement was a defensive pact agreed between Germany, Italy and Japan. Other Balkan and eastern European countries joined during the course of the war.
7. Kennedy told this anecdote to Madeleine Masson in preparation for her biography of Christine. There is no other anecdotal evidence regarding Christine's musical preferences.
8. *See* Aidan Crawley's comments in the HS 4 series at TNA.
9. Richard Sorge was born in Germany but spied for the Soviet Union in Germany and in Japan. He was arrested by the Japanese in 1944 and hanged though the Japanese denied this and insisted they had turned him over to Soviet authorities.
10. Szymanska's husband had been military attache to the Polish embassy in Berlin before the war. There she met Canaris who offered her assistance should she ever need it. Trapped in Poland with two young daughters in 1939, she contacted him and he provided her with safe-conduct passes to Berne. She told her story to Polish and British authorities who encouraged her to maintain contact with Canaris. He wanted to conclude a peace treaty using her as intermediary with the Allies but CIA chief Allen Dulles did not think the offer was genuine and refused to negotiate. After the war Szymanska and her daughters emigrated to Britain.
11. David Walker op. cit.
12. As told to Madeleine Masson by Andrew Kennedy for her book. op.cit.

Part III. 1941-43
Chapter 11. The Flight into Egypt

1. Bickham Sweet-Escott's memoir is titled *Baker Street Irregular* (London: Methuen & Co Ltd 1965).
2. Col Gardyne de Chastelain and two colleagues were dropped into Romania in 1943. His mission was to encourage sabotage in the oil fields supplying fuel to Germany. While in custody de Chastelain attempted to negotiate a peace deal between the Allies and Romanian rebels. Negotiations were never completed and after his release he was flown to Cairo.
3. Dansey's comments appear in his biography *Colonel Z*. op.cit.
4. The Pera Palace Hotel was almost destroyed by a bomb planted in the lobby by Nazi sympathisers in March 1941. Six people were killed including two British women employed at the embassy.
5. Before the war the head of Interpol had the title' president'. Interpol members held the office in rotation for periods of two years. At the death of the pro-Nazi Austrian Interpol president in 1939, Heinrich Himmler appointed Reinhard Heydrich to succeed him. After Heydrich's assassination Himmler took control of Interpol and moved its headquarters to Wannsee.

Chapter 12. Honourable People

1. Lt Col Jozef Matecki had served with distinction in the first world war.
2. Major Wilkinson's comments can be found in HS 9/109.
3. *See* Wilkinson's book op.cit.
4. HS 9/109
5. op.cit.
6. op.cit.
7. Brigadier Gubbins' remarks are in HS4/198.

Chapter 13. Breaking Hearts at the Gezira Club

1. See *Cairo in the war, 1939-1945* by Artemis Cooper (London: Penguin Books 1995).
2. op.cit.
3. Lady Deakin's comment was made to Slawka Wazacz in the documentary film 'No Ordinary Countess.' 2004.
4. *See* HS 169/3949 for the 8th Army's War Diary at TNA.
5. See *The Secret History of SOE, Special Operations Executive 1940-45, by William Mackenzie* (London: St Ermin's Press 2000).
6. Excerpted from Gizycki's unpublished memoir *The Winding Trail*.
7. Letter from Lord Tweedsmuir (*aka* William Buchan) to the author. May 2001.
8. Excerpt from O'Malley's report on Hungarian matters to the American government. 1941

9. This and the following comments are from Gizycki op. cit.
10. See HS 4/286 for the letter recommending termination of Gizycki's service to SOE.
11. Major Wilkinson's comments are contained in HS 4/198.
12. Upon being notified that her husband was missing in action in the Middle East, Lady Ranfurly set out to find him, accompanied by her butler Whitaker. See her autobiographical *To War with Whitaker* (London: Wm Heineman 1994, Arrow Books 1995).
13. Tamplin's comments are contained in HS 4/193
14. General Wladyslaw Anders commanded the II Polish Corps composed of men who had been held prisoner by the Russians after the invasion of Poland in 1939. Anders led his troops in the bloody battle of Monte Cassino which was captured at great loss of life for the Poles.
15. Tamplin op.cit.
16 op.cit.

Chapter 14. Mixed Doubles

1. Truszkowski's comments about Christine are in HS 9/109.
2. Wilkinson's note is in HS 4/193.
3. Interview with Howarth at his home in 2002.
4. The villa known as Tara is described by Artemis Cooper *ibid*.
5. Interview with Countess Sophie Tarnowska in London 2002.
6. Operation Torch was the code-name for the invasion of northwest Africa by a combined American-British force in November 1942. Once German and Italian forces had been overcome the Allies controlled much of the shipping in the Mediterranean and were thus able to mount a successful invasion of Sicily and then the Italian mainland.
7. Christine's remarks about Rozwadowski are in her Personal File HS 9/109.
8. Truszkowski op.cit.
9. op.cit.
10. Interview with Diana Truszkowski Hall at TNA in 2005.

Chapter 15. Plots and Rumours of Plots

1. Initially, SOE supported Mihailovic but later made the disastrous decision to switch its support to Tito who became dictator of a communist state.
2. See *Katyn 1940* by Eugenia Maresch (The History Book Club 2011) for details of the massacre of some 25000 Polish officers by the Russian NKVD and Russian troops.
3. Guy Liddell, in his *Diaries (vol 1: 1939-1942)* noted that SIS were sceptical of Kleczynski's confession which included the statement that the explosive 'was given to him in the course of a visit to an SOE establishment.' Sharkovitch [probably Szarkowicz] of the Deuxieme Bureau was by no means satisfied with this explanation.'
4. Truszkowski op.cit.

5. Buczynska's stepfather had been arrested on suspicion of being a double agent. She also had connections in Bulgaria which heightened suspicions. No charges were proved against her. She was subsequently employed at the Polish consulate in Jerusalem.
6. Truszkowski op.cit.
7. *See* Bickham Sweet Escott op.cit.

Chapter 16. Death and the Darkness of Night

1. Truszkowski's revelation that Christine was the source for his information garnered from Polish intelligent agents can be found in HS 9/109.
2. The Anglo-Soviet Agreement guaranteed that Britain and the Soviet Union would cooperate in their efforts to defeat the Hitler regime. It was assumed that Polish forces would fight alongside the British but Sikorski refused to sign the document after the discovery of the massacred bodies of Polish officers in the forest of Katyn.
3. Howarth's comments on Christine and Andrew are in HS 9/109.
4. This version of events is taken from the papers of Sir Noel Mason-Macfarlane, collected and stored at Churchill College, Cambridge University. SOE documents also contain commentary on this tragedy
5. Mark Amory's review of Donald McCormick's *The Life of Ian Fleming* contains a number of errors including the allegation that Christine was murdered in 'mysterious circumstances' and the mis-spelling of her surname In his book McCormick alleged that Christine was killed because 'she knew too much about General Sikorski's probable assassination.'
6. In 2002 the author was part of a group touring barracks and radar sites outside of London used by the Poles during the war when Christine's name came up. A Polish member of the group said, 'Ah, yes,'Skarbek - wasn't she involved in the plot to kill Sikorski?'
7. Mason-Macfarlane op.cit.
8. op.cit.
9. Dolbey's papers are held at the library of King's College London, in the Liddell Hart Collection.

Chapter 17. Resistance in France

1. See *Hidden Ally*, by Arthur Funk for a detailed description of the run-up to the battle of the Vercors plateau and its aftermath.
2. Cammaerts' comments on events surrounding the struggle for the Vercors are on record at the Sound Archive of the Imperial War Museum. Recorded in 1985.
3. At the Teheran Conference in 1943 Churchill, Roosevelt and Stalin met to plan an assault on Germany. The fate of eastern Europe was also discussed during which the two western leaders 'implied' that they would not contest Russia for domination of Poland. See Norman Davies' *God's Playground, a history of Poland vol ii*. See also *The Report of the Anglo-Polish Historical Committee vol 1* (Middlesex: Vallentine Mitchell 2005).

4. The letter inviting a group of Polish veterans to appear at the rear of the parade is on file at TNA.
5. Havard Gunn met Christine at the SOE facility in Juan-les-Pins where they became close friends but not lovers.
6. See Cammaerts biography by Ray Jenkins. op.cit.
7. There are several versions of how many Polish men actually defected from the ranks of the German regiments in southeastern France. The best researched account is by Arthur Layton Funk in *Hidden Ally*. He gives the figure 53 Polish soldiers. Masson's account in her biography of Christine is not authenticated and was based on Andrew Kennedy's second-hand account. Christine used the figure 250 in her letter to Brooks Richards but there is no official source for that number. SOE accounts give varying numbers.
8. The file held in the *Bibliotheque Nationale* in Paris is SOE. A.8.555.
9. See Madeleine Masson's biography of Christine. op.cit.
10. See Beryl Escott's book, *The Heroines of SOE:F Section: Britain's Secret Women in France* (The History Book Club 2010). This book contains a number of errors in the author's description of Christine's life and career.

Chapter 18. Christine to the Rescue

1. Cammaerts' description of his arrest can be heard at the Sound Archives of the Imperial War Museum. Recorded in 1985. See also *A Patriot at War, the life of Francis Cammaerts*, by Ray Jenkins (London: Hutchinson 2009).
2. This account appears in the Virago edition (2005) of Masson's revised biography, *Christine, SOE Agent & Churchill's Favourite Spy*.
3. In his memoir *Hide and Seek* Fielding wrote 'we should feel as guilty of Christine's murder as the man who hanged for it.' A sentiment not shared by all. He also dedicated his book to the memory of Christine.
4. Ibid.

Chapter 19. The End of a Perilous Journey

1. The letter written by Col DJ Keswick is contained in HS 9/109 at TNA. His comments are puzzling because, aside from the one group of Poles whom Christine encouraged to defect from the German side in the Italian Alps, there is no record of her contact with other Poles who might have been be in the area. Nor is there any evidence that Polish intelligence personnel were operating nearby.
2. See Ray Jenkins *A Pacifist at War, the life of Francis Cammaerts* (London: Hutchinson 2009 p 206).
3. Roper's letter to the author regarding his relationship with Christine. 2002.
4. Keswick op.cit.
5. Patrick Leigh Fermor's comments were made upon hearing of the death of Andrew Kennedy. See *The Spectator* magazine January 1st, 1989.

6. Major Perkins' remarks are contained in HS 9/109.
7. For this response to Christine's claim for lost clothing see HS 9/109.
8. Field Marshal Alexander's letter of support for awarding Christine the OBE is contained in HS9/109.

Chapter 20. Surplus to Establishment

1. Gardayne de Chastelain had been accused of mis-handling affairs in Romania. *See* Chapt 11, note 2.
2. *See* Julian Dolbey's papers in the Liddell Hart collection in the library of King's College, London.
3. op. cit.

Chapter 21. Missed Opportunities

1. Interview with Patrick Howarth in Sherbourne 2002.
2. MilGov, North Rhine Province, F[ood] & A[griculture] Office, Bonn, BAOR.
3. Ledochowski would say only that Christine's benefactor was a British colonel killed during the fighting in Yugoslavia.
4. From the interview given by Teresa Szulczewska to *Kurier Polska* in 1975.
5. This and other comments by Teresa Myskow are excerpted from her correspondence with the author, 2011-2012.
6. The account of how Christine came to be employed as a stewardess was described in a letter to the author by Inka Nowotna-Lachowicka OBE in 2004.

Chapter 22. End Game

1. Letter found among the papers of the artist Marek Zulawski and quoted from with the permission of his widow Maryla.
2. Donald McCormick served in Naval Intelligence during the war where he met Ian Fleming. He later worked for Fleming as a stringer for the Kelmsley newspaper chain. McCormick wrote novels under various *noms de plume* and wrote on a variety of subjects under his real name including books on Jack the Ripper and Lord Kitchener.
3. In the 1975 biography of Christine, her father Count Jerzy Skarbek is alleged to have said that his daughter was born on a stormy night. He then gave her the nickname 'Vesperale' or 'evening star.' No source has been found for this anecdote.
4. Jeremy Duns, an English novelist living in Sweden, has written widely on the life of Ian Fleming. He gives a lengthy and authoritative account of this affair on his website jeremyduns@yahoo.com.
5. This anecdote, told to Madeleine Masson by Andrew Kennedy, lacks confirmation.
6. Interview with Diana Hall at TNA.
7. From the statement given to the police by the murderer Dennis Muldowney, contained in CRIM 1/2252.

8. op. cit.
9. op. cit.
10. Interview with Lady Deakin for the documentary 'No ordinary countess' 2004.
11. Interview with the Countess Sophie Tarnowska in London 2002.
12. From the report filed by detectives at the crime scene in June 1952. *See* CRIM 1/2252.

Post-mortem

1. Statements from the Polish porters at the Shellbourne Hotel are all contained in CRIM 1/2252.
2. From the testimony of Inspector Leonard Pearcey July 1952. In CRIM 1/2252.
3. Testimony of Noel Henegan CRIM 1/2252.
4. Dr Skarbek described his visit to the morgue in a conversation with the author May 2001.
5. Roper was appointed ambassador to Luxembourg for the years 1970-75. This comment is from his letter to the author August 2002.
6. *See* Szulczewska's interview in *Kurier Polska* 1975.
7. Letter to the author from Mrs Abramowicz.
8. Letter to the author from Jan Tyszkiewicz March 2002.
9. *See* Madeleine Masson's internet article on Selwyn Jepson. www.pharo.com/intelligence/selwyn_jepson/articles/ifsj_00_introduction.asp.
10. From Lewanska-Szyc interview in *Kurier Polska* 1975.
11. Andrew Kennedy had no children. His niece who died in 2004 was apparently the executor of his estate and may have had letters, photos or other private effects belonging to Christine.

Acknowledgments

This book could not have been written without the assistance and critical comments of many people. The late Madeleine Masson deserves full credit for first bringing Christine's story to wider public attention. She generously shared her knowledge of Christine's life with me both at her home in West Bosham and during numerous phone conversations. Christine's cousins, the brothers Jan and Count Andrzej Skarbek patiently answered my frequent queries about the Skarbek family history.

The 'regulars' at The National Archives at Kew provided valuable assistance - Diana Truszkowski Hall, John Gallehawk, Eugenia Maresch and David List. Danuta Lasik and her son Janusz gave generously of their time to provide translations from Polish texts, as did Adam Zulawski. Maryla Zulawska first suggested that I should write about Christine and provided much-appreciated shelter at The Studio in Maida Vale. Slawka Wazacz shared the results of her research in Poland and photos from her film 'No Ordinary Countess.'

Jarek Garlinski encouraged me and introduced me to the publisher Stefan Mucha in Guildford who volunteered valuable assistance in helping me to understand the mysteries of online publishing. Lisa Howard applied her editing skills to the text at a very late stage of production. Rebecca Cohen provided much-needed last-minute technical assistance with the photographs. Kerry Johnson at Book Tower Publishing gave technical advice on the design and the photographs. Maika Decker in Warsaw guided me around the city and was a most indulgent hostess. Teresa Myskow in Luxembourg shared her recollections of meeting Christine just after her hit-and-run accident at Hyde Park Corner. Inka Nowotna-Lewicka, OBE, told a number of anecdotes about Christine's appearance at the White Eagle Club in London, of her love of dogs and how she came to be employed as a stewardess after the war. Julia Delille-Gomory spent many hours at the *Bibliotheque National de France* in Paris searching for Christine's by-lines in old French newspapers.

The author and composer Jan Tyszkiewicz sent photos and anecdotes about his good friend Andrzej Kowerski (Andrew Kennedy). From within the London Polish community Dr Andrzej Suchcitz at the Polish Museum and Sikorski Institute, Krzysztof Stolinski at *Studium Polski Podziemnej w Londynie* (Polish Underground Movement 1939 - 1945) and the librarians at POSK in Hammersmith all provided assistance and rapid responses to my questions.

The late Patrick Howarth, former SOE officer, shared with me his memories of Christine though very ill when we met, and confessed to being very fond of her. Vera Long, first secretary to the Polish section of SOE, shared her memories of meeting Christine and Andrew in Italy. Vera's friend Margaret (Julia) Cope Widgery, formerly of the FANYs, began the war as a tea-lady during the Blitz and finished as secretary to Brooks Richards in Algiers and in Italy. Duncan Stewart, post-war keeper of the SOE flame, gave much-appreciated help and encouragement in the early days of my research.

The Elusive Madame G

The author Andrew Lycett discovered the source of the name Vesper while writing about Ian Fleming and introduced me to the story of Phyllis Bottome and her circle of friends in Lexham Gardens. Jeffrey Bines provided the details for *Operation Freston* and helped with the research at TNA. Peter Skinner in New York and Marcia Danik Salvatore in York, Pennsylvania, were unstinting with their editorial advice.

For an insight into the family of Sir Owen O'Malley I am indebted to Lord Tweedsmuir (William Buchan) who also provided the photo of Kate O' Malley. The O'Malley family doctor, Dr Neville Young, shared his recollections of the family over tea at *Daquise*. Tomasz Lenczewski, researcher *par excellence* in Warsaw, discovered vital documents that helped fill in the gaps in Christine's early life story. The Countess Sophia Tarnowska regaled me with tales of life in Cairo during the war and described how Andrew Kennedy and Vladimir Ledochowski competed to write Christine's biography. Vladimir's son Jan shared many recollections of life with his father and on other matters Polish.

The staff at The National Archives answered my sometimes demanding queries with great patience. The reading room personnel at the British Library, the Churchill Library, Cambridge University and at Kings College, London were extremely responsive to my many queries. The staffs at the Imperial War Museum and Sound Archive in south London and at the British Newspaper Library formerly in Colindale were more than generous with their time as were the librarians at the London Library in St James's Square.

I am eternally grateful to the Geek Squad for solving my unsolvable computer problems on more than one occasion. This book was produced by CreateSpace, an Amazon publishing program, who deserve my humble thanks for their assistance and their technical advice. And as always, Diana Liu gave her quiet support throughout the many months required to complete this project.

Bibliography

Christopher Andrew, *Her Majesty's Secret Service, The Making of the British Intelligence Community* (New York: Viking Penguin 1986)

John Bierman, *The Secret Life of Laszlo Almasy, The Real English Patient* (London: The Penguin Group, Viking, 2004)

Fenton Bresler, *Interpol* (London: Sinclair-Stevenson 1992)

Ann Bridge, *A Place to Stand* (novel) (New York: The Macmillan Company 1953)

Peter Calvocoressi et al, *The Penguin History of the Second World War* (London: Penguin Books 1972, 1989)

EH Cookridge, *They Came From the Sky* (London: Heinemann 1965)

Artemis Cooper, *Cairo in the War 1939-1945* (London: Hamish Hamilton 1989, Penguin Books 1995)

Benjamin Cowburn, *No Cloak, No Dagger* (London: The Adventurers Club 1960)

Cyril Cunningham, *Beaulieu: the Finishing School for Secret Agents* (London: Leo Cooper 1998)

Hugh Dalton, *The Fateful Years (London: Muller 1957)*

Norman Davies, *Rising '44* (London: Macmillan 2003)

Norman Davies, *God's Playground, A History of Poland, vols I and II* (New York: Columbia University Press 1982)

Douglas Dodds-Parker, *Setting Europe Ablaze* (Windlesham: Springwood Books 1983)

Xan Fielding, *Hide and Seek* (London: Secker and Warburg 1954)

MRD Foot, *SOE in France* (London:HMSO 1968)

MRD Foot, *SOE: an Outline History 1940-1946, 4th edn* (London: Pimlico 1999)

Arthur Layton Funk, *Hidden Ally* (Westport, CT: Greenwood Press 1992)

Jozef Garlinski, *Poland, SOE and the Allies* (London: Allen & Unwin 1969)

The Guy Liddell Diaries, vol. I: 1939 - 1942, edited by Nigel West (London: Routledge 2005)

Jerzy Gizycki, Unpublished memoir *The Winding Trail*, date unknown

Harry Hinsley, *British Intelligence in the Second World War* (London: HMSO 1979)

Patrick Howarth, *Undercover: The Men and Women of the SOE* (London: A Phoenix Press paperback 2000)

Grace Humphreys, *Come with me through Budapest* (Budapest: Dr George Vajna & Co. Publishers 1933)

Ray Jenkins, *A Pacifist at War, the life of Francis Cammaerts* (London: Hutchinson 2009)

Phillip Knightley, *The Second Oldest Profession, Spies and Spying in the Twentieth Century* (New York: W.W. Norton & Co. Inc. 1987)

Halik Kochanski, *The Eagle Unbowed, Poland and the Poles in the Second World War* (London: Allen Lane, proof copy, publ date Nov 2012)

Karolina Lanckoronska, Countess, *Those Who Trespass Against Us, One Woman's War Against the Nazis*, preface by Norman Davies (London: Pimlico 2005)

Vladimir Ledochowski, *Christine*, unpublished memoir (South Africa: c 1973)

WJM Mackenzie, *The Secret History of SOE: the Special Operations Executive 1940-1945* (London: St. Ermin's Press 2000)

Leo Marks, *Between Silk and Cyanide: A Codemaker's Story* (London: Harper Collins Publishers 1998)

Madeleine Masson, *Christine: A Search for Christine Granville* (London: Hamish Hamilton 1975, reprinted and revised by Virago 2005)

Donald McCormick, *17F, The Life of Ian Fleming* (London: Dufour Editions 1993)

Stanislas Meyer, *My City, Reminiscences* (Newtown, Mont. 1947)

Clare Mulley, *The Spy Who Loved, the secrets and lives of Christine Granville* (London: Pan Macmillan 2012)

Ron Nowicki, *Warsaw, the Cabaret Years* (San Francisco: Mercury House 1992)

Stanislaw Okecki, ed., *Polish Resistance Movement in Poland and Abroad 1939- 1945* (Warsaw: PWN - Polish Scientific Publishers 1987)

Owen O'Malley, *The Phantom Caravan* (London: John Murray 1954)

Margaret Pawley, *In Obedience to Instructions: FANY with the SOE in the Mediterranean* (Barnsley: Leo Cooper 1999).

Michael Pearson, *Tears of Glory: The Heroes of Vercors 1944* (New York: Doubleday & Company, Inc 1978))

Aude Yung-De Prevaux, *Jacques and Lotka, A Resistance Story* (London: Bloomsbury Publishing 2000)

The Countess of Ranfurly, *To War with Whitaker* (London: Arrow Books 1995, William Heinemann 1994)

Anthony Read and David Fisher, *Colonel Z, The Life and Times of a Master of Spies* (London: Hodder and Stoughton 1984)

General KS Rudnicki, DSO, *The Last of the War Horses* (London: Bachman & Turner 1974)

David Stafford, *Secret Agent, Britain's Wartime Secret Service* (London: BBC 2000)

Tessa Stirling et al, *The Report of the Anglo-Polish Historical Committee, vol I* (London: Vallentine Mitchell 2005)

Bickham Sweet-Escott, *Baker Street Irregular* (London: Methuen & Co. Ltd 1965)

Douglas Sutherland, *The Great Betrayal: the definitive story of Blunt, Philby, Burgess and MacLean* (New York: Times Books 1980)

Michael Tillotson, editor, *SOE and the resistance* (London: The Continuum International Publishing Group 2011)

David Walker, *Lunch with a Stranger* (London: Allen Wingate 1957)

Nigel West, *MI6, British Secret Intelligence Service Operations 1909 - 1945* (New York: Random House 1983)

Nigel West, *Secret War, The Story of SOE, Britain's Wartime Sabotage Organisation* (London: A John Curtis Book, Hodder & Stoughton 1992)

Peter Wilkinson, *Foreign Fields: The Story of an SOE Operative* (London: IB Tauris 1997)

Peter Wilkinson and Joan Bright Astley, *Gubbins & SOE* (London: Leo Cooper 1993)

Elizabeth Wiskemann, *The Europe I Saw* (New York: St Martin's Press 1968)

Adam Zamoyski, *Chopin* (Garden City, New York: Doubleday & Company Inc. 1980)

In Polish

Roman Buczek, *Muszkieterowie (The Musketeers)* (Toronto: Century Publishing Company Ltd 1985)

Alfons Filar, Michal Leyko, *Palace: Katowania Podhala* (Warszawa: Wydawnicstwo Ministerwa Obrony Narodowej, ed. III 1976.

Witold Gombrowicz, *Wspomienia Polskie, Wedrowki po Argentyne* (Paris: Instytut Literacki 1977)

Leonidas Kliszewicz, *Baza w Budapeszecie* [A base in Budapest] (Warsaw-London: Polish Library, POSK 1998)

Leonidas Kliszewicz, *Baza w Kairze [A base in Cairo]* (Warsaw-London: Polish Library, POSK 2000)

Jan Larecki, *Krystyna Skarbek, Agenta o wielu twarzach [Agent with many faces]* (Warszawa: Ksiazka i Wiedza 2008)

Wlodzimierz Ledochowski, *Pamietnik pozostawiony w Ankarze [The Diary Abandoned in Ankara]* (Warszawa: Wydawnictwo Ministerstwa Obrony Narodowej 1990)

Kazimierz Leski, *Zycie niewlasciwie urozmaicone (Panstwowe Wydawnictwo Naukowe Warszawa 1989)*

Stanislaw Marusarz, *Na skoczniach Polski i swiata* (Warszawa: Wydanie 2 uzupelnione i poprawione 1974)

Maria Nurowska, *Milosnica* (Warsaw: Wydawnicstwa Twob Wydanie II 2001)

Genealogie rodow utytulowanych w Polsce (The titled family in Poland), vol 1 (Ofi-Oficyna Wydawnicza "Adiutor" Warszawa 1997). Tomasz Lenczewski, editor

Polsko-Brytyska wspolpraca wywiadowcza podczas II wojna swiatowej, tom II (Intelligence co-operation between Poland and Great Britain during world war II) vol II bi-lingual edition, ed by Jan Stanislaw Ciechanowski [2005] *Polski slownik biograficzny, vol 38* (Warszawa: Polska Akademia Nauk 1997).

In French

Mankowska, Clementine, *Espionage malgre moi* (Monaco: Editions du Rocher 1994)

Newspapers and Magazines

Victor Azam, 'Shyest secret agent', *(London: News Chronicle, May 23 1947)*

Daniel Farson, 'Riddle of the woman pimpernel' (London: *Observer Magazine* 20 October 1974.)

Elizabeth Jacobi, 'Rainbow Hues from Hungary,' (*The National Geographic Magazine*, Washington, DC: National Geographic Society. June 1932)

Christopher Kasparek, 'Krystyna Skarbek: Re-viewing Britain's Legendary Polish Agent' (New York: *The Polish Review vol 49 no. 3 2004)*

Special correspondent, 'Woman opened escape route from Germany,' (*London: Daily Telegraph and Morning Post, May 23, 1947)*

Patrick Leigh Fermor, *The Spectator* magazine (London: January 1, 1989).

Life Magazine, July 7, 1952 'Who Was Christine Granville?' *(New York: July 7, 1952)*

Christian Tyler, 'The guardian of the truth, Christian Tyler investigates the secretive world of the Special Operations Executive' *(London: Financial Times. August 2004)*.

Dariusz Baliszewski, 'Tajemnica doktora Z' (Warsaw: *Newsweek Polska* 2004) 3-part series.

Jan Larecki, 'Mucha Jej Krolewskiej Mosci' *(Warsaw: Pomocnik Historyczny,*

27 Dec 2007)

Rafal Przedmojski, 'Polscy Bondowie' *[The Polish Bond]. Historia. (Warszawa: 21-28 grudnia [December 2008.])*

Anna Szulc, 'Krystyna, corka wojny' [*Daughter of War*)]. *Przekroj. (Warszawa: 27 kwietnia [April] 2010.*

Documentary Film

Slawka Wazacz, producer, *No Ordinary Countess* (Warsaw: TV Polonia 2005)

The Secret War: Christine Granville, Polish Spy (Yesterday Channel 2011)

Recordings

Sound Archives of the Imperial War Museum, London. SOE memoirs recorded in 1985.

Web page

bletchleyparkresearch.co.uk/authors-researchers/ron-nowicki/

Interviews

Tomasz Getlich

Diana Truszkowski Hall

Patrick Howarth

Jan Ledochowski

Vera Long

Andrew Lycett

Madeleine Masson

Anna Mencwel

Piotr Muszkowski

Izabela Muszkowska

Teresa Myskow

Inka Novotna-Lewicka

Count Andrzej Skarbek

Jan Skarbek

Sofia Tarnowska

Lord Tweedsmuir

Jan Tyszkiewicz

Margaret Cope Widgery

Dr Neville Young

A Selective Index

Abramowicz, Dorothy Mrs 334
Aleje Nalewki 28
Alexander, Field Marshal 288
Amery, Julian 139
Amory, Mark 241
Anders, Wladyslaw Gen 117, 191, 196, 215, 217, 219, - 21, 224, 226, 235, 260 225-226, 259
Anglo-Soviet Treaty 240
Armia Krajowa (AK. Home Army) xvii-xviii, 3, 75-76 80, 82, 87, 89, 103, 111, 120, 128-29, 204
Atkins, Vera 67, 191
Attlee, Clement 260
Azam, Victor vi

BBC 38
Beaume, A Vincent 263, 268
Beck, Jozef Col 23
Beczkowice xii, 9
Bialoguski, Olga 319-21
Bond, James 316
Bottome, Phyllis (*see* Mrs Forbes Dennis)
Boughey, EPF Col 297
Brooks Richards, Francis Lt Com 246, 258, 260-61, 273
Buchan, William (*see* Lord Tweedsmuir)
Buckmaster, Maurice Lt Col 67*ftn*, 250, 288
Burgess, Guy 37
Butler, Frederic Gen 278-79

Cairo in the war 1939-45 176
Cammaerts, Francis Lt Col xiv, 251-54, 255-58, 265, 272-282, 309, 321, 334, 336-37
Chamberlain, Neville v *ftn*, 101
Channon, Chips 140
Chopin, Fryderyk 6, 80
Churchill, Peter 252
Churchill, Winston v *ftn*, 33, 116, 215
Command of the Union of Armed Struggle (ZWZ) 75
Constans, Jean Col 271, 285
Continental Action 56, 120
Cookham, Capt 233
Cooper, Artemis 176
Coward, Noel 320
Crawley, Aidan 143-46, 307-08, 327
Croix de guerre viii
Cromwell Road 328
Czestochowa 17

Dalton, Hugh Dr 192
Dansey, Claude 39, 63
Deakin, Livia Lady xi, 13, 24, 172, 313, 321, 326 339
Deakin, William Sir 13ftn
Deuxieme Bureau 49, 55, 76, 80, 78, 86, 104, 109, 206 213, 216-219, 222-23
de Chastelaine Gardyne 152, 208
de Gaulle, Charles Gen 112, 276
Dictionary of Polish Journalists 47, 131
Dimitrov, Georgi 145-46
Dmowski, Roman 16
Dodds-Parker, Douglas Col 236, 237, 247, 274-75
Dolbey Julian Lt Col (*ne* Count Juliusz Dabrski) 244-48, 296-98, 300-03, 310, 313
Dunford, Michael 306-08, 316, 337-38

Eden, Anthony Sir 192
Eisenhower, Dwight D Gen 229
El Effendi Durani 172
Electra House
Emisarski, Jan Lt Col 144, 169

FANY vii-viii *ftn* 252, 334, 339
Farson, Daniel
F-section 257
Fermor, Patrick Leigh ix, 61, 203*ftn*, 204, 283
Fielding, Xan 204, 266-267, 272-74, 276-77, 295-96
Fleming, Ian 42, 65, 241, 309, 317-21, 339
Foot, MRD 153
Forbes Dennis, AE Capt 42
Mrs Forbes Dennis, Phyllis 42-43, 65, 315
Foreign Office (FO) 29, 33, 56, 117-19, 138, 141, 153, 216 281, 305, 333
Forsythe, Frederick 361
Fryday 35, 36-38, 46-47, 337

Gambier-Parry, Richard 95-96
General List vi, 251
George Cross 252, 288, 300-03
George Medal 292, 302-03, 308, 335
Getlich, Gustaf 10, 12- 13, 15, 20, 36, 305
  Anna Mencwel 14
  Tomasz 13-14, 18
Gezira Sporting Club 175-77, 201-02, 211, 217, 300, 314, 321
Gibraltar 238-39, 241
Gizycki, Jerzy (George) xiii-xiv, 21, 24-31, 32-

Gizycki (cont) 33 45, 92-95, 96, 142 Paris 148, 181, 208, 303-304
Gleeson, James 336
Glenconner, Lord 194-95
Goldfeder, Adolf 1, 2
 bankruptcy 18
 Roza 2
 Stefania 1-4, 6-7, 9 (see also Skarbek)
Gombrowicz, Witold 17
Gondek, Leszek ftn 334
Goodwill, Archie 56, 95-96
Gradowski, Leon (Michael Lis) 104-05, 202
Grand, Lawrence Lt Col 44, 162
Granville, Christine aka Krystyna Skarbek, Mme Gizycka ix-xx. Early life in Poland 1-11, education 7-8, Miss Polonia 12, marriage to Getlich 9-12, illness, Zakopane, divorce 13, Marriage to Gizycki, honeymoon in Africa (1928-29) p 28.
London 1939: (p 32) recruited to Section D, leaves for Hungary as Mme Marchand, 33- 69; Budapest (p 51). Meets Owen O'Malley, begins affair with Andrew Kennedy 138- 50. SOE and Poland as 'X', affair with Ledochowski, escape from Slovak patrol 73-137; as Willing meets with Musketeers, arrested by Hungarian police, escape with Andrew.
Cairo: (p 161) sacked by SOE 151-237; Gezira Club, unemployed 1941-1943, recruited to go to France 1944, training in Algiers. **France:** (253) as Madame Pauline (254) parachutes into France, meets Francis Cammaerts, mission in Italian Alps; affair with Cammaerts, rescues him from firing squad, returns to London alone (306)
Post-war: (p 291) travels frequently, stay in Kenya, medals awarded, with Andrew in Munich, as stewardess with Shaw Savill Lines, meets Dennis Muldowney 1951, his obsession with her. Christine murdered in Shellbourne Hotel June 15, 1952. (326.) Funeral (334).
Green, DEF, Major 268
Grenadier Guards 243
Grenoble 257-58
Grunwald, Battle of 5

Gubbins, Colin Brig 144, 163, 169/281-82, 188-89, as M (76, 196), 224, 293, 333
Gunn, Havard 261

Hall, Diana 45 ftn, 213, 324
Hankey, Lord 6
Happy Valley Set 31
Harker, Paul 310
Harrison, Hubert 46-49, 65, 69, 75, 90, 91, 95, 98, 100 115, 120, 123, 127-28, 130
Hazell, Ronnie Maj 58-59, 245, 278
Heczka 161, 166, 178
Hemel 161
Herault, Paul 263, 265
Hitler 22-23, 43, 46, 51, 58, 69-70, 92-93, 102, 133, 149 169, 174, 225, 252, 264
Horko, Tadeusz 22, 23
Horthy, Nicolaus Admiral 46, 52-54, 59, 100-01, 103 133, 135, 148-49, 244
Howarth, Patrick 24, 45, 58, 78, 108, 211, 215, 217-18, 222-23, 224, 227-28, 231, 235-37, 241, 245, 248, 260, 304-05, 311
Howe, Edward (Ted) 65, 311
Hudson, DT (Bill) Lt Col 222, 285, 289-90

Jakub Alek 206
Jasinska, Pani 81-82, 83
Jazlowiec 7-8
Jepson, Selwyn 35
Jouve, Paul Dr 269

Kasparek, Jozef 315
Keble, Mervyn (Bolo) Brig 243
Kelmsley Newspapers 309
Kennedy, Andrew (also Kowerski) vi, x, xiii, xvi, 31, 48, 59-61, 66, 69, 82, 86, 88-90, 104, 112, 120, 131, 136-37 142, 147, 155, 160, 162, 165, 175, 191, 216, 226, 235 242, 260, 264, 269. 282-83, 299, 303, 318, 322-23 326, 335, 340
Kerensky Alexander 115
Keswick, DJ Col 278, 282, 296-97
Khedive, Terefil 176

King George 109
Kleczynski, Bohdan Wing Commander 221-22
Klimecki, Walter, 239
Klimkowski 223-24, 226-27
Kojdecki, Joseph 328, 330-31
Konopka, Adam Baron 62, 82
Kopanski, Stanislaw, Colonel 60, 112
    168-69, 195, 211, 222-23, 289, 334
Kossowska, Stefania 232
Kot, Stanislaw Professor 61, 158, 164-65, 195, 212, 218
    289, 334
Kreipe, Major General 203
Kristalnacht 27
Krzesiolowska 18
Kurcjusz 223-25

Lajos, 101
Lakin, JFF Maj Gen 294
Larecki, Jan 12
Laski, Father 104, 123
Leake, Phillip 128 *ftn*
Ledochowski, Jan 337
Ledochowski, Wlodzimierz (Vladimir) ix,10, 11, 82, 83-
    84, 88, 98, 183, 233, 235, 306, 337
Lees, Gwendoline 116
Lefort, Cecily ('Alice') 254, 261
Lewanska-Szyc 125-26, 338
Lis, Michael (*also* Lisowski) 104, 202-03
Lubienska, Teresa 75-77
Lubomirski, Marcin 105
Lycett, Andrew 317, 320

Mackiewicz, Stanislaw (Cat) 327
Maczynski, Richard 189 -90
Maisky, Ivan 272
maquis vi, 249, 255-56, 258, 265, 268, 270, 274
Manchester Guardian 33, 35
Mankowska, Klementina 185
Marcellini, 261
Marchand, Madame 47
Marusarz, Jan 70-71, 73
    Helena 72
    Stanislaw 70, 73
Maryland mission 292
Marynka cafe 306, 327
Massingham 236, 243, 254, 261, 265
    268, 314
Mason-Macfarlane, Noel Sir 238-39, 242

Masson, Madeleine ix-x, svii, 13, 107, 137, 264, 340
Masterson, Tom 139
Matecki, Jozef Col (*aka* Jakub Alek) 158, 159-160, 165-66
    167-68, 206
Maxwell, Terence Col 188,194, 298
McCormick, Donald (*aka* Richard Deacon) 241, 317-21
Mercik, Walerian 168, 206
Mihailovic, Draza Col 216
Mikolajczyk, Stanislaw 242, 283-84, 286, 302
Miss Polonia 11
Mitford, Bruce Capt 175
Molotov, Vyacheslav 219
Montgomery, Bernard Field Marshal Sir 204, 269, 271
Moscicki, Ignacy President 29, 121, 149
Moss, William (Billy) vi, ix, 203
Movements Section 291, 295, 300
Muldowney, Dennis George ix, 213, 314, 321 - 333
    333, 338
Musketeers xiv, xv, xvi, 29, 49, 57, 68-69, 75-77, 79 81
    92, 104-05, 117, 121, 124-29, 140, 143, 145, 153-54
    157, 159-60, 162, 164, 166, 174, 180, 182, 185-86, 200-
    02, 204-05
Mussolini, Benito 169-70, 229
Myskow, Teresa 311-13, 334

Nalkowska, Zosia 11
National Democrats (ND, Endeks) 16
Nelson, Frank Sir 187, 195
New World Avenue (*Nowy Swiat*) 20, 74
Nicoll, Hanka 313-14
NKVD (KGB) 193, 228, 290-91
No Ordinary Countess 275, 326, 339
Nowak, Jan 284
Nowogrodek Cavalry Brigade 219
Nowotna-Lewicka, Inka 255
Nowy Sacz, 73, 75, 88

Ognisko Polskie 306, 313
O'Hallaron Eileen 95, 111
O'Malley, Kate 106, 136, 149, 195, 216, 234
O'Malley, Ann Lady 106 119, 179, 181
O'Malley, Owen Sir 53, 55-57, 110, 116-120, 130, 135-39
    141, 148-49, 152, 155-56, 179-81, 195
Operation Anvil 253, 260, 270
Operation Barbarossa xi, 144
Operation Fernham 310
Operation Freston 286, 288-91, 304, 310

Operation Kris 200, 244-48, 296, 302
Operation Overlord 249
Operation Taile Crayon 254
Operation Toplink 261
Ordonowna, Hanka 19
O'Regan, Philip 262
OSS 230

Paderewski, Ignacy 19
Palmer, Roundell Cecil 195
 (3rd Earl of Selborne)
Panel to Preserve Christine's reputation viii
Partridge, Col 53
Pawley, Margaret viii-ix
Perkins, Harold Maj 56, 59, 128-29, 172, 245, 281, 283 285, 292-93, 295-96, 299
Perlak, Michael 330-31
Philby, Kim 25, 36
Pickles, Michael Col 283, 287, 295, 299-300
Piddington, Thomas Gen 279-280
Pilsudski Jozef Marshal 15, 16, 34, 56-57, 72, 158, 227
Popiel, Ludwig 104, 325, 327-28
Potocka, Clara 45
Prince Paul 140, 142, 153
Polish pronunciation ii
Prchal, Edward Fl Lieut 238-39, 241-42

Quayle, Anthony 239

Radzyminski, Jozef 47-48 ftn 64-65, 69, 88, 99-100 112-115, 131, 322
Ranfurly, Lady (Hermione Llewellyn) 187
*Red Courier (Kurier Czzerwony)*11
Redding, JS Wing Com 296
Ree, Harry 249
Renoir, Claude 265
Reynaud, Pierre Capt 252
Romek 59, 87
Rommel, Erwin Marshal 170, 174, 194, 204
Roosevelt, FD Pres 92, 215, 221, 259, 283
Roper, John vii-viii, xi, 268, 276-77, 281, 289, 311, 323 333, 336
Rothermere, Anne Lady 318, 320
Rothermere, Lord 320
Rozwadowski, Wiktor 189, 2-6, 218, 240
Rudnicki, KS Gen DSO

Sacre Coeur 7, 8
Sansom, Odette Ensign 252

Sapieha, Andrzej 282 ftn
Schenck, Albert Capt 269-70, 272-76,
Schenck, Mme 276
Section D v ftn xiii, 20-22, 26, 29, 33-34, 39-41, 43-47, 49 51, 55-56, 58, 65, 70, 76 78, 90-91, 93-96, 98-99, 101 103-04, 110-113, 115-117, 120, 122, 127, 130, 136, 140 164, 199, 211, 241, 302, 315, 339
Seizieme Bureau 49, 55, 58, 76, , 121, 154, 158,161,166 171, 178, 197, 200, 214-15, 217, 231, 246
Selborne, Lord 192, 195-96, 206, 283
Sikorski, Wladyslaw, Gen 27, 46, 56-57, 75-77, 78, 82 84, 109-110, 114, 117, 120-21, 142, 145, 149, 152-53 160, 166, 205-07, 214-215, 235, 237, 242, 336
Sikorski, Zosia 27, 238-39
SIS (Secret Intelligence Service, MI6) vii, xv, 20-21, 28- 29, 31, 34-36, 38-40, 42-43, 63, 104, 121, 125, 140 152, 157, 159-61, 164, 175, 192-93, 199, 247
Skarbek, Jerzy Count xvii, 1-2, 6, 8, 12, 16-18, 213
 Alex, Senator 16
 Andrzej 3, 6-7, 80, 292-93
 Andrzej Dr & Count 332, 334
 Andrzej, Col 332-33
 Fryderyk Florian 5, 80
 Helena (Zaranska) 286, 305
 Irena 6, 310
 Jan xvii, 17, 334
 Stefania, Countess 3-7, 9, 16-17, 18, 79-81
Smigly-Rydz, Marshal 62
Sobieski, Jan III King 5
Sokolov, Florian 34, 339
Solidarity xii
Sorensen, Christopher 266, 272
Sorge, Richard 144
Sosnkowski, Kazimierz Gen 73, 117, 158, 221, 227, 242
Special Operations Executive (SOE) v ftn vi-viii, x-xi xiv, 13, 22-24, 26, 33-34, 41, 44-45, 47ftn, 49-50, 67- 68, 75, 78, 90, 96,98, 102, 107, 115-16, 119-122, 128- 29, 130, 133, 134-35, 137ftn, 138-140, 142-43, 146 148, 150-53, 157-167, 171-73, 175, 179-184, 86-87, 192-99, 209, 212-18, 223-26, 229-33, 35-36, 243- 245, 252, 254, 256, 265, 267-70, 278, 281-86, 288- 290, 294, 297-99, 301-02, 306, 317, 319-320, 323 330, 332, 334, 337-38, 340
Sporborg, HN Col 196
Stalin, Joseph 92, 144,174, 219-20, 226, 240, 259- 60,286, 290
Stamper, Evelyn 40, 42

365

Sweet-Escott, Bickham 98-99, 176, 229, 247
Szulczewska, Teresa 34, 333-334
Szymanski, Jerzy Captain 215, 227
Szymanska, Halina 144
Szymanowski, Karol 11, 19

Tamplin, Guy 159, 168, 171, 175-76, 184-85, 189-91 195-96, 198, 201, 216, 217-18, 237, 243
Tarnowska, Sophie Countess 89, 145, 176, 203-04, 328 336
Tarnowski, Andrew 145, 205
Tavernier, Gilbert 262
Taylor, George xiii, 35-39, 41-42, 43, 44, 46, 47, 48, 49 57, 64-65, 79, 95-96, 98-99, 139, 141-42, 148, 155 161, 165, 176, 196, 212, 218
The National Archives (TNA) vii, 34, 59 *ftn* 201, 255, 314
Threlfall, Henry Lt Col 45, 226 *ftn*, 294
Tito 216
Tournissa, Gilbert Capt 254-255, 256*ftn*
Tripartite Agreement 142
Truszkowski, Richard Capt xv,197*ftn*, 197-99, 204-214 216, 222-26, 231, 324
Trzepnica xii, 5, 9, 18
Turrel family 252
Tweedsmuir, Lord (*aka* William Buchan) 181, 217, 234

Tyszkiewicz, Jan 336

Vansittart, Robert Sir xiii, 33, 35, 39, 41-44, 118 162, 271
Varsovians 74
Vercors 250, 254-58, 265, 311, 335
Vesper Lynd 318
Virtuti Militari 10ftn, 61, 104, 201
Vittorio Emanuele III, King 220
Voigt, FA (Freddy) xiii, 21, 33-41, 40-45, 47
von Arndt, Irena (*aka* Skarbek) 3

Waem, Max 270-276, 286, 327
Walker, David 146
Wavel, General 170, 192
Wazacz, Slawka xvi, 275
Wiadomosci Literackie 232

Wilkinson, Peter Major 78, 141-42, 158, 159-66, 171-175, 177-178, 182-83, 185-86, 188-89, 191, 193, 197, 198-99, 200, 212-14, 217-18, 222-223, 231, 237, 240 *ftn*, 299, 337, 340
Wilson, Henry Brig 336
Witkacy (Stanislaw Witkiewicz) 11
Witkowski, Stefan 28-29, 69, 75-79, 124-126, 143, 153-54, 159-60, 185, 200, 205
XY 59, 184
XYZ trio 59
X.3 94, 97, 112, 120, 128, 131

Zakopane xiv, 11-12, 14, 17, 19-21, 25-26, 28, 60, 70-71 73, 82, 123, 126, 155, 314
Zamek (Royal Castle) 4
Zaranska, Helena (*aka* Skarbek) 24, 287
Zazulinski, Col 171
Zelazowa Wola 6
Zelenski ,Tadeusz Boy 11
Zeller, Henri Col 257, 265
Z-Network 39
Zulawski, Marek 316
Maryla 316
ZWZ 73, 204-05

Made in United States
Troutdale, OR
05/12/2024